Getting Started with
UNIX™ and X™

Getting Started with
UNIX™ and X™

Torbjörn Andréasson

Konsulthuset AB

Jan Skansholm

Chalmers University of Technology, Gothenberg

ADDISON-WESLEY PUBLISHING COMPANY

WOKINGHAM, ENGLAND • READING, MASSACHUSETTS • MENLO PARK, CALIFORNIA • NEW YORK
DON MILLS, ONTARIO • AMSTERDAM • BONN • SYDNEY • SINGAPORE
TOKYO • MADRID • SAN JUAN • MILAN • PARIS • MEXICO CITY • SEOUL • TAIPEI

Translated by Logotechnics Ltd (Sheffield-Zurich)
Cover designed by Design & Partners, Oxford
and printed by The Ethedo Press, High Wycombe, Bucks.
Typeset by Logotechnics Ltd (Sheffield-Zurich).
Printed and bound in Great Britain by T.J. Press (Padstow) Ltd, Cornwall.

First printed 1992. Reprinted 1994.

British Library Cataloguing in Publication Data
A catalogue record for this book is available from the British Library.

Library of Congress Cataloging in Publication Data is available

ISBN 0-201-63170-9

Trademark Notice
UNIX is a trademark of UNIX System Laboratories, Inc.
X Window System is a trademark of Massachusetts Institute of Technology.
Motif, OSF/1 are trademarks of the Open Software Foundation.
PDP-7, Ultrix are trademarks of Digital Equipment Corporation.
Xenix is a trademark of Microsoft Corporation.
SunOS, Solaris, Open Windows are trademarks of Sun Microsystems, Inc.
AIX is a trademark of International Business Machines Corporation.
POSIX is a trademark of the IEEE.
Interleaf is a trademark of Interleaf Corporation.
HP/UX is a trademark of Hewlett Packard.

Preface

This book is intended for anyone who wishes to learn how to use the UNIX operating system. The book could be useful, for example, for computer courses which involve running programs on a UNIX system; but it is also ideal for home study. No previous special knowledge is needed.

Working with UNIX is exciting! It is easy for an inexperienced user to get started, and for the more advanced UNIX user, new and interesting possibilities open up all the time. There is always something more to learn. We hope, therefore, that the reader will find it just as fascinating to work with UNIX as we ourselves have done.

It is becoming more and more common to use the X Window system when running UNIX; so, besides a detailed description of UNIX, the book also includes an introduction to X. This covers the principles of how X works and how to start up the X system. As well as this, a number of practical X programs are described, which can be useful in the user's day-to-day work. All the sections of the book concerned with X are clearly marked in the margin, and anyone who does not happen to be interested in X can quite simply skip over them.

Exactly how things will look on the screen when X is being run will depend on which *user interface* is being used. The two most frequently encountered user interfaces at present are *OpenLook* and *Motif*. Both of these are dealt with in the book. In addition, a fairly exhaustive description of the *OpenWindows* X system is included, covering the most important areas. OpenWindows is a widely used windows system based on OpenLook; it offers the ordinary user an integrated, user-friendly environment with a number of practical application programs and other facilities.

A few words should be said about the arrangement of the book. Overall, the book could be said to cover three levels: an elementary level, an intermediate level and an advanced level.

The elementary level comprises chapters 1, 2 and 3 and sections 4.1 and 4.2 of the following chapter. Much of the content of these chapters is information every UNIX user should know in order to make effective use of the UNIX system. They describe, for example, how to log on and off and what UNIX commands look like. The way the file system is set up and the basics of the command interpreter 'shell' are also explained here.

The intermediate level comprises the rest of chapter 4 along with chapters 5 and 6. At this level the reader can learn the finer points of using the shell—for example, how to handle parallel processes and how to use environment variables and shell variables to set up his or her own customized UNIX environment. A number of fascinating communications programs are also described at this level: for example, you can see how to run programs on other computers, how to read and send electronic mail and how to read news on the 'network'. Finally, the intermediate level explains how you can edit your own text files using text editors.

The advanced level takes up the remainder of the book, that is, chapters 7, 8 and 9. Here, we describe how you can write your own 'shell scripts'—files containing commands for the shell. Shell scripts can be regarded as a type of program executed by the shell. At this level we also describe the various factors involved in writing your own application programs in standard programming languages. In the examples, the 'C' programming language is used. The final chapter contains a number of practical tips for those responsible for the administration of the UNIX system. Examples of areas covered are starting up the system, registering new users and taking security copies (backups).

The vast majority of what is described in the book is common to all the different UNIX variants and shells. To make it clear where something is different in one or the other, the book uses a system of symbols in the margin. The various symbols used are as follows:

 A section marked in this way deals with constructions which apply to the Bourne shell.

 This symbol indicates that the section covers something applying to the Korn shell.

 This symbol indicates that the constructions dealt with are relevant to the C shell.

 Sections describing something specific to the TC shell are marked in this way.

 Sections marked in this way deal with unique characteristics of UNIX System V.

 This symbol indicates that what follows describes something which exists only in Berkeley UNIX BSD and the Open Software Foundation's UNIX OSF/1 system.

 This marks a section concerned with the X Window system, and which will only be of interest to someone using or thinking of using X.

 This symbol indicates that the following section deals specifically with the *OpenLook* user interface and the *OpenWindows* X system.

Sections dealing specifically with the *Motif* user interface are marked in this way.

This symbol is used to indicate something which could cause problems or which you need to be on your guard against. The symbol is also used occasionally to draw attention to useful tips.

With the exception of the last of these markers, these sections can always be skipped over if they are not of interest. The book has been written so that there is no risk of losing the thread or missing any general information if you do so. For example, if you are only thinking of using the Bourne shell you can skip over all the sections dealing with the C shell—and vice versa. In the same way, anyone running UNIX System V can quite safely skip sections concerned with BSD or OSF.

The UNIX commands given in the book have been test-run on a number of different, independent UNIX systems. We hope, therefore, that they will all be correct and that not too many errors have crept in.

Finally, we would like to offer heartfelt thanks to our colleagues Per Lundgren and Sven Westin of the Department of Computer Science at Chalmers University of Technology in Göteborg, as well as to Lars Jerrestrand at Sun Microsystems, Göteborg and Mats Forser at Digital Equipment, Göteborg, who gave us the benefit of their valuable ideas on the content of the book.

The authors
Göteborg,
1992

Contents

One
An Introduction to UNIX and X

Hundreds of computer manufacturers are now marketing UNIX-based computer systems. Most public authorities and large companies throughout the world use UNIX or are including it in their future plans. UNIX has come to be the industry standard in the same way that COBOL and FORTRAN became the industry standard for programming languages in the '60s and '70s.

Why has UNIX become so popular? There are many reasons, but perhaps the most important is that UNIX is simple and convenient to use and that it is not tailored to any particular type of computer, but can run on most machines, large as well as small.

This chapter provides a short historical survey of the development of UNIX. The different UNIX variants now existing are discussed, and a summary of the characteristics and structure of UNIX is also provided.

The system which can now be considered the industry standard in the field of graphical user interfaces (GUIs) for workstations is the *X Window* System. The system is operating system independent but is often used together with UNIX. An introduction to X is given at the end of this chapter.

1.1 History

In the mid-'60s, Bell Telephone Laboratories, General Electric and a group from the Massachusetts Institute of Technology set up a project to develop an operating system, called Multics, which would allow several users to make use of a computer at the same time. However, the project was closed down after a time because it was not living up to expectations.

A number of the Bell Labs researchers who had taken part in the Multics project continued working on the development of an operating system in their own time. This small group of researchers included Ken Thompson, Dennis Ritchie and Brian Kernighan. The development work had its origin when Ken Thompson came upon an abandoned minicomputer (a PDP-7) on which he planned to implement a game called 'Space Travel'. The game simulated the movement of celestial bodies and involved landing spaceships on them. In due course (1969), the result of his efforts amounted to not only a working version of the coveted game, but also an operating system and a number of programming tools. The operating system was initially called Unics but was later re-named UNIX.

The first UNIX prototype was developed in a programming language specific to the PDP-7 minicomputer. An important milestone in its development was reached in 1973, when UNIX was implemented in the C programming language. C is a high-level language, similar to Pascal, developed by Dennis Ritchie. The new language meant that the programming work took very little time and that UNIX could easily be ported to any computer, provided it had a C compiler.

In 1975 the first version of UNIX was distributed outside the walls of Bell Labs, *UNIX Version 6*. It was primarily colleges, universities and other non-commercial organizations that made use of the system. At the University of California at Berkeley they were not satisfied simply to use the UNIX system, but developed it further. A large number of changes and additions were made, and this UNIX family, *Berkeley UNIX*, has gained a good deal of popularity, especially at universities and colleges. The latest version is called BSD 4.3.

The first commercial UNIX system was *UNIX Version 7*. The system was introduced in 1977 after improvements based on feedback from the university's Version 6. In 1981, Bell Labs introduced *UNIX System III* and 1983 saw the arrival of *UNIX System V*, which began to be actively marketed by AT&T. The system was priced to suit a broad computer market and has been distributed in large quantities over the last few years.

Nowadays there are a number of UNIX variants—System V, Berkeley, Xenix, Ultrix, SunOS, AIX and others. There is an urgent need to combine the different variants and create a common standard. This will require co-operation among the different computer manufacturers; but unfortunately two independent and competing consortia of suppliers have formed, OSF and UI.

OSF (the Open Software Foundation) was formed in 1988 by IBM, DEC, HP and others with the aim of producing an operating system which is independent of licenses under AT&T's System V, and has over a hundred members. This aim has been achieved by integrating a number of existing UNIX variants which are independent of System V.

The other consortium, UI (UNIX International), was formed in 1988 by those suppliers who chose to use AT&T's System V as a basis and develop it further. Some of the founder companies are AT&T, Sun, ICL, NCR and Unisys; today there are around 175 members. (Many suppliers are members of both OSF and UI.) In 1989, UI introduced System V.4, which has integrated System V.3, Xenix, BSD 4.3 and SunOS. UI has also drawn up a 'road map', a five-year plan for further development of System V.

At this point, it's worth mentioning a few names which are sometimes encountered in a UNIX context. *X/Open* is an organization which aims to make programs more easily 'portable' between different computer systems. (X/Open has no direct connection with the X Window system.) The organization publishes the *X/Open Portability Guide*, which describes how different interfaces are to be standardized. First and foremost, this concerns the interface between the application program and the operating system. Most of the larger computer suppliers are members of X/Open and therefore follow its recommendations in their UNIX systems.

POSIX (Portable Operating System Interface) is a set of standards for the interface by which users and application programs communicate with the operating system. POSIX is a product of the American standards organization IEEE. One of the POSIX standards (POSIX.1) concerns UNIX, and is included as a section in the X/Open Portability Guide.

For the 'ordinary' user, fortunately, the differences between the UNIX variants described are small; and what above all decides how the user communicates with the UNIX system is the *command interpreter* or '*shell*' that is used. The shell is a special program which reads the user's commands and arranges for them to be carried out by the system. The two most common command interpreters, the *Bourne shell* and the *C shell*, are both available in most UNIX variants, and both will be described in this book, along with the *Korn shell* and the *TC shell*, which are expanded and more advanced forms of the Bourne shell and the C shell respectively.

1.2 UNIX characteristics for the user

UNIX is a multi-user system, that is, it allows a number of users access to the computer at the same time. The system is of an interactive type known as a 'time-sharing' system, which means that several people can sit at their own terminals and give commands to the system independently of each other. As long as the computer is not too heavily loaded, each of the users can have the impression that only he or she is using the computer.

UNIX was designed from the start to be a tool for program developers, but the characteristics of the system make it equally suited for end-users, that is, those using ready-made programs. There are many programs in a UNIX system, and they can be used in a consistent manner. Different programs can often be easily combined with each other. As well as all the programs supplied together with the system itself, there is a good deal of software which has been developed to run under UNIX and which can be bought or sometimes even obtained free of charge.

UNIX has a well thought-out hierarchical file system which makes it easy for the user to keep files in order. The ordinary user need not know anything about the physical configuration of the files or what disk memory is available etc., but will work with the logical filenames at all times. The same applies to external units such as printers and terminals.

If the computer you are using is connected to a computer network, UNIX can not only act as an operating system; it can also be a handy tool for electronic mail and other data communications.

1.3 Components of UNIX

A UNIX system consists in the main of three parts:

- the *kernel*,
- the *file system* and
- the *utility programs.*

(See figure 1.1.)

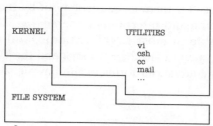

Figure 1.1

The *kernel* manages the input and output of data between the units of the system (terminals, external memory, main memory etc.). Another important function is to ensure that all users can make equal use of the computer's resources.

A *file* is a collection of related data which has been given a logical name. For example, a file may contain a text or a program. The *file system* can be compared to a store-room where files can be put away and picked out again when needed. It is possible, for example, to create new files, remove old files and print out the content of a file on the screen or on a printer. Every user can protect his or her files by assigning the files different levels of access permissions.

Every UNIX system includes several hundred *utility programs*. These 'utilities' consist partly of programs which are closely linked to the UNIX system itself, e.g. shells (command interpreters) and file-handling programs, and partly of other kinds of program from widely different areas of application, e.g. word-processing programs, programs for electronic mail and compilers. One of the central principles of UNIX is that the various utilities should be easy to combine with each other.

1.4 The X Window System

The X Window system has gained increasing importance in recent years, and works well in conjunction with UNIX. Nowadays, X is run on more and more workstations. X is network-oriented and operating system, hardware and supplier independent. This means that it does not have to be run under UNIX.

1.4.1 History

The development work started in 1984 and was carried out as part of *Project Athena* at MIT in collaboration with Digital and IBM. One of the aims of the project was to create a graphical user interface (GUI) which was not linked to any specific operating system or brand of computer.

In 1986 the first version, X10.4 (X Window Systems version 10 release 4) was distributed from MIT. Success was assured, as both commercial organizations and non-commercial institutions ordered the software and immediately set about producing application programs. Enthusiasm waned somewhat when X11.1 was brought out in September 1987. The reason was that the design had been modified and was no longer compatible with the first version. For this reason there was less demand. The mistakes were quickly rectified and by March 1988 X11.2 was available.

The same year, the so-called *X Consortium* was formed. The consortium is an interest group consisting of all the major computer suppliers. The organization is administered from the MIT Laboratory for Computer Science (LCM). The members either work on or direct the development process, or simply receive advance information on 'the direction things are taking' and regular updates of new versions.

A number of modifications and improvements were subsequently made to X11, and later versions (X11.3, X11.4 and X11.5) have since been issued.

In January 1989, Digital Equipment, Hewlett-Packard and others suggested that the graphical user interface in the Open Software Foundation's operating system OSF/1 should be based on the X Window System and use the *Motif* user interface. UNIX International's System V.4 is also based on X and uses a GUI called *OpenLook*.

One very popular X system is *OpenWindows*, which makes use of the OpenLook user interface. Along with UNIX, OpenWindows forms part of Sun's *Solaris* system, which is available in implementations for both workstations and IBM-compatible personal computers.

A major reason for the successful launch of X is the fact that all the major computer suppliers had chosen UNIX as a basis for their operating systems, but up to then there had been no user-friendly interface for UNIX comparable to that available on Apple's Macintosh.

1.4.2 X from the user's angle

X is a system which manages *windows* on what are known as *bit-mapped* monitor screens. These screens are composed of a large number of minute *pixels* (short for 'picture elements'), each of which can be separately controlled. Colour monitors can be used as well as monochrome. X has utility functions to produce lettering on the screen in different *fonts* (typefaces) and sizes and there are functions to produce graphical images. At each display desk there will be a monitor screen (or possibly several), a keyboard and a pointing device. The pointing device will usually be a *mouse* with three buttons.

A window is an area defined on the screen. Every application program (text editor, graphics program etc.) communicates with you, the user, by means of one or more windows. Several programs can be handled at the same time in different windows on the screen. The different application programs can write to the screen at the same time, independently of each other. It is possible, for example, to do word processing in one window, send electronic mail in another, display a clock in a third and so on.

Sometimes there can be so many windows on screen at the same time that it is difficult to make sense of them. To resolve this problem you can opt to convert the windows you are not currently working with to *icons*. An icon is a small picture representing the window.

The user can work intuitively, in a way which can sometimes be compared with working at an ordinary desk (which is why a GUI is sometimes called a 'desktop'). An example of what it can look like is shown in figure 1.2. This example is taken from the Sun OpenWindows X system.

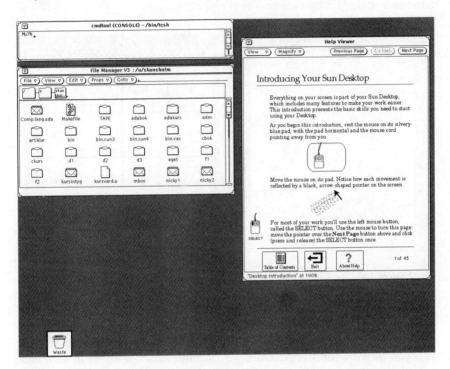

Figure 1.2

Programs need not necessarily be run on the local workstation, but can be run on any computer if the workstation is connected to a computer network.

A window manager is a special program which makes it possible to manipulate windows on the screen. Windows can be enlarged, reduced, moved, converted to icons etc. The window manager is an (application) program in its own right and *not* a part of the windows system.

A computer system will often provide access to several different window managers. The three most common are:

- *Tab Window Manager* from MIT, twm
- *Open Look Window Manager* from UNIX International, olwm
- *Motif Window Manager* from the Open Software Foundation, mwm

Which window manager you use is a matter of taste.

A window in X is really just the area within which an application program is being run. The window manager will *decorate* the window by surrounding it with a special *frame*. The appearance of this frame is different for different window managers. In figure 1.2 we saw what a window managed by `olwm` looks like. Figures 1.3 and 1.4 show windows managed by `twm` and `mwm` respectively.

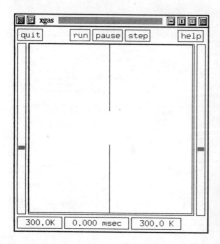

Figure 1.3

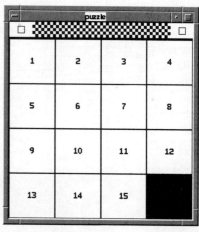

Figure 1.4

When you move the mouse, a special *mouse pointer*, most commonly a small arrow, will show you where you are on the screen. By pressing the buttons on the mouse you can do a wide range of different things: you can move windows around, for example, change them in size and turn them into icons. You can also cause *menus* to appear.

A menu is a list of different *options* you can choose from.

The exact details of the way windows are moved etc. vary a good deal, depending on which window manager is being used, and partly on how the user has customized it. In the next chapter we will be describing how to handle Motif and OpenLook windows in detail.

It is not usually difficult to learn the basics of using a certain window manager. Thanks to the graphical user interface (the desktop), you can easily feel your way forward and use your intuition. You don't always have to learn a particular command, as everything can be done using menus. However, you should avoid setting up more complicated customizations until you get used to the system. If you change the functions of the mouse buttons, for example, you may get some very odd effects.

1.4.3 A little about how X works

A basic concept in X is that of a *display*. A *display* usually consists of a physical terminal screen, a keyboard and a mouse. As a rule, then, a display is the same thing as a workstation. However, X is designed to be more general, and a display may have more than one screen. In an advanced graphics application, for example, the operator can be imagined surrounded by a number of screens run from the same keyboard and mouse.

Remember that the words 'display' and 'screen' do not mean the same thing.

In X, every display is controlled by a special program, the *X server*. There is exactly one X server to each display. As a rule, this means that there is one X server to each workstation. Special *X terminals* are also sold, which consist of a screen, a keyboard and a mouse, and which can only execute a single program internally, that is, the X server.

It is the X server which handles *all* the input and output of data at the display. This means it is the X server which creates and manages windows and produces text or graphics on the screen (or screens). The X server also takes care of all the input from the keyboard and the mouse. No other programs can access the physical units.

The X server program is often provided by the computer supplier, but, unlike similar programs in other systems, the X server is *not* part of the computer's operating system. As far as the operating system is concerned, the X server is simply a program like any other. It is this characteristic which makes X operating system independent. In principle, the X server can be run under any system.

The next important concept concerns the *clients*. The clients are all the programs wishing to communicate with the user at the display. A client, for example, may be a text editor or a spreadsheet program. The window manager is a client like other programs. The only actual difference is that the window manager does not have any windows of its own, but is concerned with *all* the windows on the screen.

As we have seen, client programs cannot directly read from or write to the physical units: all the communication is passed through the X server. Several clients can communicate with the X server at the same time. This is shown in figure 1.5. One client can also communicate with several X servers at the same time, on different computers—but this is less common.

When a client has some output it sends a *request* to the X server. The request may be, for example, to write a text in a specific window or to draw a line. Communication can also be directed from the X server to the clients. When something has occurred at the display which is of interest to a specific client (the mouse has moved into one of the client's windows, a key has been pressed on the keyboard, etc.), the X server sends an *event* to the client. The event provides details of what has happened.

DISPLAY

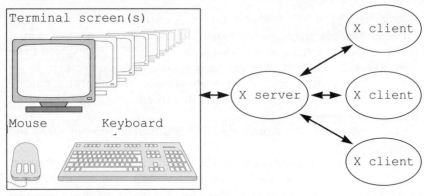

Figure 1.5

The communication route between the X server and a client is called the *connection*. All communication between server and client takes place according to a special *X protocol*. This is a set of rules determining what a request and an event will look like. The X protocol is independent of what the physical link between the server and the client program looks like and what underlying communication protocol is used. The X protocol is therefore unaffected by whether the the server and the client are being run on the same computer or different ones. This means that a program can be run on a remote computer but produce text in a window on the local workstation.

The X protocol and the X server take care of all physical input and output for the clients. The client programs will be totally hardware independent, so that a program which works in combination with one X server will work with another.

A library, *Xlib*, has been developed, and contains utility functions which can be used by those writing programs to be run under X. When a user program wishes to communicate with an X server, it can do this by using some appropriate function in this library. The utility will then generate the right message as prescribed by the X protocol. (In a way, Xlib could be said to define the X protocol.) Xlib was originally written in the C programming language, which means that most X programs are written in C, but since then Xlib has also been implemented in the Ada and LISP languages.

From a programming point of view, the Xlib functions are written at a very low level. For example, a simple program which does no more than write a text to a window may be a few pages long and include a large number of calls to different Xlib functions. This makes it by no means a trivial task to write X programs. To make all of this a bit easier, libraries of *toolkits* have been written, at a rather higher level. A library of this type is *Xt Intrinsics*: while this is not standard, it forms part of MIT's distribution of X. Xt Intrinsics contains basic functions for creating windows and the like, but does not include details of what the windows physically look like, or the layout of the menus, buttons and other components. To specify this, special program components called *widgets* are used. On the next level there is a set of widgets to create windows, menus etc. of a certain design. These will look different on the screen depending on which set of widgets the programmer has used. The various levels of utility functions are illustrated in figure 1.6.

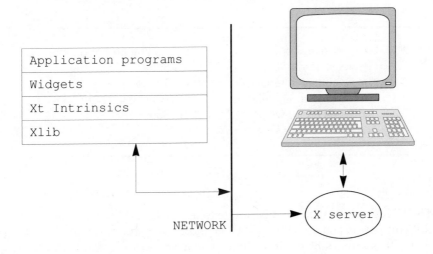

Figure 1.6

It is, in fact, the X protocol and nothing else which lays down the standards for X. Consequently, the standards are at a very low level and say nothing about what things will look like on the screen. This means that there can be a large number of different user interfaces which can all still be said to 'be X'. It all depends on which utilities ('widgets' or other 'toolkits') the programmer has used. The three most common user interfaces are *OpenLook*, *Motif* and *Athena*. (The last of these is based on the set of 'widgets' included in MIT's standard distribution.)

Two
The First Steps

The UNIX operating system is simple to learn and easy to use. The most difficult part is usually getting started and making the first experiments work. It is important to sit at the terminal and practise right from the beginning. In this chapter we describe how to log into and out of the system and how to use a password.

For users of the X Window system, there are also sections on how to start up X and how to begin running the window manager and the terminal windows. Some common X programs, and how to call them, are also covered. In particular, we have included a detailed look at the Motif and OpenLook user interfaces along with the OpenWindows X system.

The most important program for the user in a UNIX system is the *shell*—that is, the program which interprets and executes the commands given by the user. This chapter includes an introduction to shells. It shows how to write commands and how to correct wrong commands. Some common X programs are introduced in this context too.

In this chapter we also describe how to arrange for texts to be output by the UNIX system, both on screen and at the printer. Finally, we show you how to call up help texts when using the terminal.

Before we start, a few words should be said about the notation that will be used for examples in the book. To make it clear whether a certain piece of text has been produced by the user or the computer, we will be using two different styles of type. Everything written on the screen by the computer will be shown in light type:

```
produced by computer
```

and text typed in at the keyboard by the user will be shown in bold:

keyed in by user

(When you are actually working at the computer, of course, there will only be one style of type.)

When the UNIX system is ready to accept a command it displays a *prompt character* on the screen. If the shell being used is the Bourne shell or the Korn shell (there is more on shells below) the prompt is usually a dollar sign, and if the C shell or the TC shell is being used the prompt is usually a percent symbol. In this book, all four of these shells will be described, and for demonstration purposes we will therefore be using a neutral prompt character, $. This means that commands preceded in the book by this prompt apply to all four shells: the Bourne shell, the Korn shell, the C shell and the TC shell. When we wish to indicate that a certain command only applies to the Bourne shell and the Korn shell we will use the $ prompt and where we wish to indicate that a certain command only applies to the C shell and the TC shell we will use the % prompt.

Every user can easily change the prompt to suit his or her own preference, and this will be explained later. It is common, for example, to have a prompt consisting of a sequence of several characters giving the name of the computer.

2.1 Logging in and out

UNIX is a multi-user system, which means that a number of users can make use of the computer at the same time. For this reason, every user must have a unique name, the *user ID*, so that the system can keep track of who is who and who is doing what. Before you can start using the UNIX system, therefore, you must set up a user ID for yourself. This is supplied by the system administrator for the computer. He or she is the person with final responsibility for keeping the machine working.

In addition to the user ID, every user may also have a secret *password*. It is this that confirms the user's identity every time the system is used. Users can set up and change their own passwords using the passwd program (see below).

The first problem before you can log on is to make contact with the UNIX system. How this is done will depend on what type of hardware you are using and how this is connected to the UNIX system. The first thing to do is often to turn on the switch on the terminal. However, bear in mind that many types of personal computers and workstations are normally never switched off, they will be on even though the screen is dark. In this case, the terminal should not be turned off at the switch, but the screen should be activated by, for example, moving the mouse or pressing an 'appropriate' key on the keyboard.

If the terminal is directly connected to the UNIX system, the following text will show after a while on the terminal screen:

```
login:
```

(If the terminal is connected to a network, it will be necessary to give the name of the UNIX system you wish to run, using a system dependent procedure, before you get this far.) Now the UNIX system is ready to read in the user ID. Let us suppose that the system administrator has allocated you the name mike. Key in the name and finish your entry by pressing the <return> key. All UNIX commands are normally terminated by a press of the <return> key.

```
login: mike
```

Note that small letters should be used. (Make sure the 'caps lock' key on the keyboard is switched off.) If you enter your user ID in capital letters the UNIX system will deduce that the terminal you are using cannot write small letters, and all the text the computer gives you from then on will be in capitals.

The system checks that the user, mike in this example, is entitled to make use of the computer's resources, and if there is a password it will be asked for. For security reasons, the password is not shown on the screen.

```
login: mike
password:
$
```

If the password is correct, the UNIX system will output a prompt as in the example above. Once you are logged on you can enter the command:

```
$ who
```

to find out which other users are logged on to the system:

```
mike        tty021        Jan  8 09:42
linda       tty022        Jan  8 11:14
john        tty023        Jan  8 11:18
skanshol    tty024        Jan  8 08:11
torbjorn    tty025        Jan  8 12:05
```

Each line in the list consists of a user ID, the name of the user's terminal line and the time when the user logged into the system.

It is important that work at the terminal is terminated in a controlled manner, otherwise important information may be lost. Logging out of the system can be done in any of the following ways:

§ **logout**

or

§ **exit**

or, if preferred,

§ **<ctrl-d>**

(The form <ctrl-d> means that the control key and the 'd' key are pressed at the same time.) To create or change a password, enter the command:

§ **passwd**

You will then be asked first to enter your old password:

```
Changing password for mike
Old password:
```

The system will then ask for the new password:

```
New password:
```

In principle, a password can be made up from any characters you like. But only the first eight characters in the password are significant. For security reasons, nothing will be shown on screen whilst the old and new passwords are being entered. To prevent mis-keying, the system asks for the new password to be entered a second time:

```
Re-enter new password:
```

It is important not to forget your password, as you will not be able to get into the system without giving it. If you have forgotten it or you are unable to log in for any other reason, you must ask the system administrator for help.

2.2 Getting started under X

This section will describe what to do to start and stop the X Window System, and how to log in and out when running X. The description is general, and applies to all X systems. The following section covers the Motif user interface in detail, and section 2.4 the OpenLook user interface and the basics of how to use the OpenWindows X system. This includes how to start up OpenWindows, how to handle windows and what menus there are. Users of OpenWindows may skip directly to section 2.4 if they wish.

2.2.1 Starting up the system and logging on

If you want to use the X Windows System, you must *not* try to start up the system by typing x. Instead, you can start up using one of three different methods, which are described below. But first, we just need to discuss one basic condition.

Before you can run X, the 'environment variable' PATH must contain the name of the directory in which the X programs are to be found. If you get the message: Command not found when you try to run one of the X programs below, you need to add the X directory to the PATH variable. First find out the name of the X directory (ask the system administrator). Let us assume that it is called /usr/bin/X11 as in the MIT distribution. If the prompt is a dollar sign you are most probably running the Bourne shell or the Korn shell, so key in:

```
$ PATH=/usr/bin/X11:$PATH
$ export PATH
```

If the prompt is a percent sign you are likely to be running the C shell or the TC shell, in which case enter:

```
% path=(/usr/bin/X11 $path)
```

2.2.1.1   Start-up method 1

Following the first of the three methods, you will be doing everything yourself, starting at 'square one'. When you switch on your workstation, the X system will not be running and the workstation will look like an ordinary 'dumb' terminal. You will see the login: prompt on the screen. You can then log in exactly as described in the previous section of this chapter. When you have logged on and got into the UNIX system you can then start up X yourself by means of the xinit program:

```
$ xinit
```

When the xinit program is run, you will eventually be given a *terminal window* at the top left of the screen. You can enter normal UNIX commands in this window.

The first thing you need to do in the terminal window is to start up the window manager you wish to use. As we mentioned in chapter 1, the window manager is the program which takes care of moving and modifying windows on the screen. The command you give naturally depends on the window manager you have chosen. To run Motif Window Manager, mwm, for example, you key in

```
$ mwm &
```

2.2.1.2   Start-up method 2

When you call xinit you can instruct the program to initiate the system in a particular way, so that the window manager always starts up automatically and you are given the various windows you want, such as a terminal window and a clock. This will often have been prepared by the system administrator, who will have installed a new program called, for example, xstart, startx, x11, x11start, or openwin. This new program will in turn call xinit in the right way. Exactly which program you will use will depend on which variant of X you want to run and how things have been installed on your computer.

To start up using method 2, log on as if your workstation were a 'dumb' terminal and then key in, for example,

```
$ xstart
```

By the time the system has got itself running, the window manager will have been installed and you will have been given a number of windows on the screen, including a terminal window.

2.2.1.3   *Start-up method 3*

For the third log-in method, the X system is already running when you want to log on. The system administrator has started up a special X program called xdm. This program has displayed a box on the screen which looks more or less like figure 2.1. To log on, all you need to do is fill in your user ID and password.

```
Welcome to the X Window System
          Login:     |
          Password:
```

Figure 2.1

N.B. If your user ID is longer than eight characters you should only key in the first eight, otherwise your log-on will fail.

In chapter 4, in the context of 'start-up files', we will show you how you can design your own X environment, so that you always have exactly the windows you want when you start up X.

2.2.2 Logging out from X

When logging out, always make sure you have logged out completely and not just from the terminal window you have been working in. If you type logout, exit or, if preferred, <ctrl-d> in a terminal window, this will usually only kill this window. (In certain cases, however, the X session can be terminated by killing a certain terminal window, which is often called the console terminal window.)

Instead, to terminate your X session select from a root menu an option called exit, quit, logout or something similar. If you have logged on according to the third method described above (via xdm), you will also be logged out of the system. If you have logged on according to the first or second method, only the X system will have been terminated and the screen will look like a dumb terminal again. You will then have to log out in the usual way by means of logout, exit, or <ctrl-d>.

Some window managers have a menu option called Lock Screen or similar. This can be used as an alternative to logging out. This locks up the X system so that it will not allow anything further to be done until you have repeated your password. The advantage of this is that is it much faster if you want to continue the session next time. The X system will already be initiated and running. The drawback is that Lock Screen can only be used if you have a personal workstation, as it is not possible for anyone else to log on while the system is locked.

2.3 The Motif user interface

2.3.1 Starting up the system

To use the Motif user interface you must make sure that the Motif Window Manager, mwm, is started every time you start up the X system by means of one of the methods described in the previous section. In chapter 4, in the section on start-up files, we will be giving examples of start-up files which cause mwm to be run and which automatically give you the windows shown in figure 2.2. Four program windows are shown: a clock, a calculator and two terminal windows.

2.3.2 Window management

Figure 1.4 shows a Motif window. If you study this or one of the windows in figure 2.2 more closely, you will see that round every window there is a *window frame* (or *border*). At the top of the frame is the *title line*, which will usually contain the name of the application program. Also in the title line there are three buttons: the *Minimize button* (the one with a small square on it), the *Maximize button* (with a larger square) and the *Menu button* (with a horizontal line). The window frame and title line are generated by the window manager, not by the current X program. The window frame and title line (apart from the title itself) will therefore look the same and work in the same way for all Motif windows.

The background area, the space outside the windows, is called the *root window*. The root window does not belong to any particular application program, but is managed directly by the window manager.

The details of how the mwm window manager behaves, including which mouse buttons are used for what, and which menus are available,

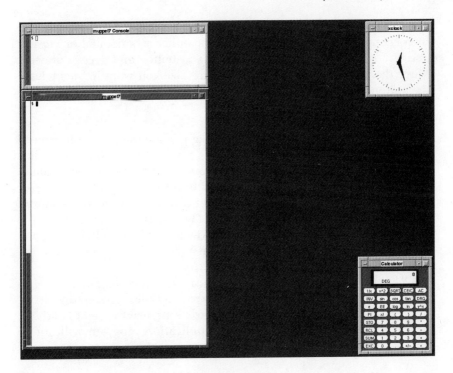

Figure 2.2

can vary a great deal, since each user is able to decide this individually in a number of ways. Besides this, the system administrator can give mwm a character particular to the individual installation (e.g.by means of the two system files /usr/lib/X11/system.mwmrc and /usr/lib/X11/app-defaults/mwm). What we will be describing here is mwm's default behaviour, that is, how it works if no special amendments have been made.

2.3.2.1   Moving windows and icons around

To move a window or an icon around on the screen, proceed as follows. Place the mouse pointer on the title line of the window or on the icon and press the left-hand button. Keep the button pressed, drag the pointer to the desired position on the screen and then release the button.

2.3.2.2   Changing the size of a window

To change the size of a window, place the mouse pointer on the outer edge of the window frame. If you want to make the window wider, place the pointer at the left-hand or right-hand side of the window; if you want to make it taller, place the pointer on the top or bottom edge; and if you want to change the width and the height of the window at the same time, place the pointer at one of the four corners. The pointer will then change its appearance and become either a horizontal or vertical line or a right angle. Press the `left-hand` button and keep it pressed. Move the pointer until the window is the size you want it, then release the button.

2.3.2.3   Bringing windows to the front
If two or more windows are overlapping one another and you want to see the the whole of a window which is partly concealed, you can click with the `left-hand` button (that is, press it and release it immediately) on the title line of the hidden window to lift it on top of the other(s). Naturally, this will not work if the entire title line of the window underneath is concealed. Instead, you would then need to place the mouse pointer somewhere on the window in front and select the option `Lower` from its window menu. (More on menus follows below.)

2.3.2.4   Converting a window to an icon (Minimizing a window)
A window can easily be converted to an icon by clicking with the `left-hand` mouse button on the small Minimize button at the right-hand end of the title line. The corresponding application program will not be aborted when this is done, but will continue running.

2.3.2.5   Restoring a window (Reconverting an icon)
Place the mouse pointer anywhere on the icon and double-click (click twice in rapid succession) with the `left-hand` button.

2.3.2.6   Maximizing a window
You can make a selected window fill the entire screen by clicking with the `left-hand` mouse button on the Maximize button on the title line. To restore the window to its normal size, click once more on the Maximize button.

2.3.2.7   Creating a window
A new window is created every time a new X application program is started. In the next section we will be seeing how to start an X program from a terminal window. It is also possible to set up root menus of your own, by means of which you can easily start new X programs.

2.3.2.8   Closing (terminating) a window
A window can be closed (and the corresponding application terminated) by double-clicking with the `left-hand` mouse button on the menu button in the title line. Note that in Motif the term *Close* is used for terminating a window and its program. The more usual term for this is *Quit*, which is used in most application programs and in OpenLook. (In OpenLook, *Close* refers to converting a window to an icon.)

2.3.3 Menus

A *menu* is a list of different options: an example is shown in figure 2.3. Depending on how menus are called up, they can be divided into two types: *pop-up menus* and *sub-menus*.

2.3.3.1 Pop-up menus

When X is being run, the various X programs are responsible for their own windows on the screen. Here, 'window' means the part inside the window frame. As mentioned earlier, the background area of the screen which is not inside any window is called the 'root window'. The window manager mwm is responsible for the root window and all window frames.

Many X programs operate in such a way that if the mouse pointer is placed somewhere inside the area the program is responsible for and a certain mouse button is pressed, a menu will appear. The particular menu you get will of course depend on where the pointer has been placed. Pop-up menus sometimes have a title at the top indicating the area to which they belong.

The menu shown in figure 2.3 is the menu which appears if the mouse pointer is placed in the root area and the right-hand button pressed. This menu is usually referred to as the *root menu*. On this menu, the option New Window means that a new window will be set up with the program xterm. The Refresh option can be used to redraw the screen if something has got out of kilter. The options Shuffle Up and Shuffle Down are there to deal with situations where several windows are overlapping.

The exact look of the root menu can vary, depending on how the system administrator or the user has set up the start-up files. There can be three different root menus, for example: one for each button.

Selecting an option from the menu in figure 2.3 is done in the following way. The right-hand button is pressed and held down. The mouse pointer is moved across the screen to the desired option and the

Figure 2.3

mouse button is released. If no option is desired, the mouse pointer can be drawn out of the menu before the button is released. The menu will then disappear again and nothing will happen.

Another example of a pop-up menu is shown in figure 2.4. This is what is known as the *window menu*, which appears when the mouse pointer is placed on the title line of a window and the `right-hand` button is pressed. The window menu can also be obtained by placing the pointer on the menu button at the left-hand end of the title line and pressing or clicking the `left-hand` button. The window menu contains a number of basic window-managing functions. In particular, there is the `Close` option, which removes a window and terminates the application program using the window; and the `Lower` option, which is used to re-position the window behind another window.

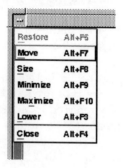

Figure 2.4

Options in window menus can be selected in the same way as in the root menu, by holding the mouse button down and moving the pointer to the chosen option, but there is also another way. If the window menu is called up by clicking with the `left-hand` mouse button on the menu button, the menu will remain on the screen. You can then place the pointer on the desired option and click with the `left-hand` button. If you do not want any of the options, click with the `left-hand` button outside the menu.

An icon also has a window menu. This can be obtained by placing the mouse pointer on the icon and either clicking with the `left-hand` button or pressing the `right-hand` button. Options can be selected in the same way as described above.

2.3.3.2   *Sub-menus*

Some menu options may have menus of their own, known as *sub-menus*. These are often indicated by small right-pointing triangles. As an example, figure 2.5 shows a 'home-made' root menu in which the two options `Window Options` and `MWM Controls` have sub-menus. If an option with a sub-menu is selected, a new menu will appear. An example of this is shown in figure 2.6, where `Window Options` has been selected.

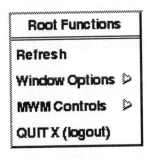

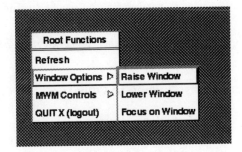

Figure 2.5   *Figure 2.6*

To select first a menu option with a sub-menu and then an option from this sub-menu, proceed as follows. Press the mouse button which causes the main menu to appear. (In the example in figure 2.5 this will be the `right-hand` button.) Hold down the button in question and move the mouse pointer to the option which has a sub-menu, e.g. the `Window Options` option in figure 2.5. Now the sub-menu will appear. Keep the mouse button pressed and move the mouse pointer to the right. Still keeping the button pressed, move the pointer to the option you wish to select from the sub-menu. Then release the mouse button. If you do not release the button, but move the pointer back to the main menu, the sub-menu will disappear and you can select another option from the main menu.

A sub-menu may itself contain one or more options producing sub-menus of their own. In this way, it is possible to have a chain of menus, which can have any number of levels.

2.3.4 Focus policies

What you enter via the keyboard will appear in the window which is currently *in focus*, that is, the active window. There are two *policies* (methods) for determining how the selection of the window in focus is carried out: the *pointer policy* (selection by pointing) and the *explicit policy* (selection by clicking).

Under the pointer policy, the window the mouse pointer is in will always be the one in focus. Under the explicit policy, it is not enough just to move the pointer to the window: to bring that window into focus, the mouse must also be clicked in the window.

You can decide for yourself which policy is to apply. One way (among several) of doing this is to indicate the preferred principle when starting up mwm. For example, if you want the pointer policy to apply, you can start up mwm with the command

```
$ mwm -xrm "Mwm*keyboardFocusPolicy: pointer"
```

If you prefer to choose the window in focus by clicking, enter instead the command

```
$ mwm -xrm "Mwm*keyboardFocusPolicy: explicit"
```

2.4 Introduction to OpenLook and OpenWindows

 OpenLook is a specification for a graphical user interface. It was drawn up by the UNIX International consortium and specifies how windows, menus etc. are to look. OpenLook also specifies a certain environment, a set of utility programs which are to be made available, e.g. the window manager and the file manager. This section provides a look at how the different elements on the screen are handled in OpenLook. We will be describing the interface as implemented in the OpenWindows X system, the most commonly-met X system following the OpenLook specification. As OpenLook closely specifies what the user interface is to look like, however, users of other systems based on OpenLook should be able to find their way around.

2.4.1 Starting up OpenWindows

When you switch on your workstation, the OpenWindows system will not usually be running: you will need to log on as if your workstation were an ordinary terminal. Follow the steps described in chapter 2.1. OpenWindows can then be started simply by entering the command

```
$ openwin
```

For everything to work, the two 'environment variables' OPENWINHOME and PATH must have been set up in the right way. OPENWINHOME must contain the name of the directory where the entire OpenWindows system has been installed. The name of this directory is usually /usr/openwin.

The two variables can be set up in the following way. It will vary a little depending on which shell is being used.

If the prompt is a dollar sign, you are probably running the Bourne shell or the Korn shell. In this case, enter

```
$ OPENWINHOME=/usr/openwin
$ PATH=$OPENWINHOME/bin:$PATH
$ export OPENWINHOME PATH
```

If you are running the C shell or the TC shell (in which case the prompt will be a per-cent symbol), enter instead

```
% setenv OPENWINHOME /usr/openwin
% set path=($OPENWINHOME/bin $path)
```

(The initiated reader will have noticed that $OPENWINHOME must be placed first in PATH so that the system will find the right version of the X programs.)

After this, it should be possible to start up OpenWindows without problems.

It would be best, of course, if you did not have to go through all this every time you want to start up OpenWindows. This can be avoided by including the above lines in your start-up file for the shell. Start-up files are described in chapter 4.6.

2.4.2 Managing windows

Once OpenWindows has started running, the screen is likely to look like the one shown in figure 1.2. Three application programs are running: a terminal program, a file manager and a program to display help texts. Each of the application programs has its own window. In addition, there is an icon which is connected to the file manager.

If you study a window more closely—see, for example, the one illustrated in figure 2.7—you will see that it is surrounded by a *frame*. At the top of the window frame there is a *title line*, which will usually contain the name of the application program. The window frame and the title line are generated by the window manager, not by the application program. The frame and the title line (apart from the title itself) will therefore look the same and work in the same way in all windows encountered in OpenWindows.

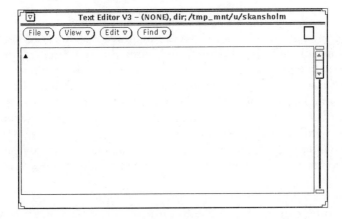

Figure 2.7

The background area, which is not part of any of the windows, is called the *Workspace* in OpenWindows. (This is the area of the screen more generally called the 'root window' in most X contexts). The workspace does not belong to any particular application program, but is managed directly by the window manager.

Before we go into how windows are moved around the screen etc., a few words should be said about the use of the mouse buttons. In OpenWindows documentation, the three buttons are called *SELECT*, *ADJUST* and *MENU*. The reason for this is that it is possible to redefine the use of the mouse buttons in a special start-up file so that the user can decide for himself or herself which button is to be used for what. In the following paragraphs, however, we will assume that the reader has not redefined the mouse buttons in this way, but kept to the default uses with which the mouse buttons are initialized. To keep things simple for the reader, we will refer to the *SELECT*, *ADJUST* and *MENU* buttons quite simply as the `left-hand`, `middle` and `right-hand` buttons.

2.4.2.1   Moving windows and icons around

To move a window to a new position on the screen, proceed in the following way. Place the mouse pointer on the window frame or the title line and press the `left-hand` button. Hold the button down, drag the window to its desired position and then release the button.

Icons are moved in the same way as windows: the mouse pointer can be placed anywhere on the icon.

2.4.2.2   Changing the size of a window

To change the size of a window, the mouse pointer should be placed at one of its four corners. The pointer will then change its appearance and turn into a circle. Press the `left-hand` button and keep it pressed. Move the pointer until the window is the size you want, then release the button.

2.4.2.3   Moving windows behind and in front of each other

If two or more windows are overlapping and you want to see all of a window which is partly concealed, you can click (that is, press and immediately release) the `left-hand` button with the pointer on the title line of the part-hidden window to raise it to the front. This will not work, of course, if the entire title line of the covered window is hidden. In that case, you can instead place the mouse pointer anywhere in the upper window and press the `Front` `(L5)` key on the keyboard. The front window will then become the back one. The `Front` key can also be used to raise a partly concealed window to the front.

2.4.2.4   Closing a window - converting it to an icon

A window can be changed into an icon simply by clicking with the `left-hand` button on the small square 'button' in the top left-hand corner of the window, on the title line. When this is done, the corresponding application program will not be aborted, but will continue as before.

2.4.2.5   *Opening a window - changing it back from an icon*
Place the mouse pointer anywhere on the icon and double-click (press and release twice in rapid succession) on the `left-hand` button.

2.4.2.6   *Creating windows*
A new window is created every time a new X application program is started up. One way of doing this is to select a program from the workspace menu (see below). As we will see, an X program can also be started from a terminal window or by means of the OpenWindows file manager.

2.4.3   Menus

A menu is a list of different options. An example of a menu is shown in figure 2.8. Depending on how a menu is called up, it can be assigned to one of three types: *button menus, pop-up menus* and *sub-menus.*

Figure 2.8

2.4.3.1   *Button menus*
All the buttons on the screen which contain a small down-pointing triangle are called *menu buttons*, and a menu called up by means of a menu button is known as a *button menu*. There are two kinds of menu button, oblong menu buttons with text and small square menu buttons with no text. (In the documentation, the latter type are called *abbreviated menu buttons*.) The window shown in figure 2.7, for example, includes five menu buttons. Four of these, File ▼, View ▼, Edit ▼ and Find ▼, contain text and can be found inside the window itself, in what is known as the *control area*, the area where buttons and other window controls (e.g. boxes and sliders) are usually collected. These five menu

buttons are positioned *inside* the window and have therefore been created by the application program. Different application programs, of course, are likely to have different menu buttons inside their windows, and therefore different button menus.

The fifth menu button in figure 2.7 does not have any text and can be found at the left-hand end of the window's title line. It is identified on the screen by the symbol $\boxed{\text{V}}$.

As the title line is created by the window manager and not by the application program, all windows will have an abbreviated menu button of this type on the title line, and the menu called up by this button will look similar for all windows. We call this menu the *window menu*: figure 2.9 shows what it looks like. The window menu contains a number of basic window-managing functions, in particular the Close option, which converts a window to an icon, and the Quit option, which removes a window and terminates the application program using the window.

To call up a menu and to select an option from the menu, proceed in one of the following two ways.

- Place the mouse pointer on the menu button. Click on the right-hand button. A menu will now appear and remain on the screen. Now place the mouse pointer on the menu alternative you want and click with the left-hand or right-hand button. If you do not want to select an option after all, click the left-hand or right-hand button outside the menu. The menu will then disappear and nothing will happen.

- Place the mouse pointer on the menu button. Press the right-hand button and keep it pressed. Move the mouse pointer to the option you want and then release the button. If you do not want to select any of the options you can move the mouse pointer outside the menu before releasing the button.

2.4.3.2   Pop-up menus

As we mentioned, the background area of the screen outside all of the windows is called (in OpenLook) the *workspace*. A rectangular area inside a window used by the application program to display data is known as a *pane*. There may be several different panes inside one window. If the mouse pointer is placed in the workspace, in a pane, on the window frame or at any other point on the screen not occupied by a menu button or other window control, and the right-hand button is then pressed, a *pop-up menu* will appear. The appearance of the menu will of course depend on the position of the pointer. Every pop-up menu will have a title at the top indicating which area it belongs to. For example, the menu shown in figure 2.8 is the frequently used pop-up menu called from the workspace, and is therefore known as the *workspace menu*.

Pop-up menus can be handled in the same way as button menus. In other words, when you call a pop-up menu you can either click with the `right-hand` button to cause the menu to stay put while you make your choice, or you can hold the `right-hand` button pressed and move the pointer to the option you want.

2.4.3.3　Sub-menus

Some of the options in a menu may be marked with a small triangle pointing to the right. In figure 2.8, for example, the options `Programs` and `Utilities` are marked in this way. The triangle indicates that there is a *sub-menu* to this option, which means that a new menu will appear if this option is selected. To select first an option with a sub-menu and then choose an option from this sub-menu, proceed as follows. Using the `right-hand` button (as described above for button menus and pop-up menus) select the option with a sub-menu, e.g. the `Programs` option in figure 2.8. Keep the `right-hand` button pressed and move the mouse pointer to the right. A sub-menu will now appear. Figure 2.10 gives you an idea of what this may look like: this is the sub-menu for `Programs`. Still keeping the `right-hand` button pressed, move the pointer to the option you want in the sub-menu. Then release the button. If you decide not to select an option, you can release the button when the pointer is no longer inside one of the windows. If you do not release the button, but move the pointer back inside the main menu, the sub-menu will disappear and you can choose a different option.

Figure 2.9

Figure 2.10

A sub-menu may include one or more options with their own sub-menus. In this way, it is possible to have a chain of menus, which can have any number of levels.

2.4.3.4   *Pushpins*

Some menus, for example the sub-menu in figure 2.10, are provided with a *pushpin*. This can be used to 'fix' the menu on the screen so that it remains visible as long as you want it and options can be selected from it without the need to call it every time. To fix a menu, call it as described above and select the pushpin, exactly as if it were one of the menu options. (That is to say, the mouse pointer should be placed on the pushpin as you make your choice.)

Once the menu has been 'fixed' with the pushpin, you can then select options using the left-hand or right-hand button as described earlier.

To 'take down' a menu which is 'pinned' to the screen, simply click on the pushpin with the left-hand button and the menu will disappear.

2.4.3.5   *The default option*

Most menus have a *default option*. The default option is marked by being enclosed in a ring. In the window menu in figure 2.9, for example, Close is the default option, and in the sub-menu in figure 2.10 the default option is Command Tool.

On a button menu, the default option will be selected automatically if you click on the menu button with the left-hand button instead of the right-hand one. A window can be closed, for example (using the Close option) by simply clicking with the left-hand button on the abbreviated menu button ▼ in the title line of the window.

The default option is also of interest in sub-menus. If you use the left-hand button instead of the right-hand button to select a menu option which has a sub-menu, this means that the default option in the sub-menu will automatically be selected. For example, if we have 'pinned up' the workspace menu and click on the Programs option with the left-hand button, the Command Tool option will be selected.

If desired, the default option can easily be changed to another option. First open the menu in the usual way by holding the right-hand button pressed. Keep the button pressed and move the mouse pointer to the option you want as the new default option. Then press the Control key on the keyboard and release it again. Finally, release the right-hand mouse button.

2.4.4 Bringing a window into focus

When you are working at the keyboard, whatever you have keyed will appear in the window which is currently *in focus*, that is, the active window. There are two techniques using the mouse to determine which window is to be in focus. One is to move the mouse to the desired window and click in it or on its frame: we can call this the Click

SELECT method. The other is simply to move the mouse into the window: this becomes the window in focus without the need to click. We can call this the Move Pointer method.

It is easy to specify which of these methods is to apply. Select the Properties option from the workspace menu. A new window will then appear, with an abbreviated menu button, $\boxed{\text{V}}$, next to the wording **Category**. Call the menu activated by this button and select the option Miscellaneous. Yet another window will appear, which includes the heading **Set Input Area**. You can now click in the box for the focussing method you want to apply. Finally, click in the $\boxed{\text{Apply}}$ box.

2.4.5 Deleting, moving and copying text

Many application programs work with ordinary text. Examples of programs of this type are the terminal program cmdtool, the text editor textedit and the mailtool electronic mail program. Many programs also make use of input lines, where input data is expected to be entered in text form, as a filename, for example. When working with text, the mouse makes it easy to erase, move or copy sections of text which have been marked. Text can also be moved or copied between different windows.

The first thing to do is to mark the text which is to be deleted, moved or copied. This can be done in any of the following ways:

- *Mark text, alternative 1.* Place the mouse pointer at the start of the text you want to mark and press the left-hand mouse button. Keep the button pressed and move the mouse to the end of the text to be marked. The selected text will now be shown in a different colour in the window. Release the button once the correct section of text is marked.

- *Mark text, alternative 2.* Place the mouse pointer at the start of the text you want to mark. Click with the left-hand mouse button. Place the mouse pointer at the end of the text to be marked. Click with the middle button. The selected text will now be shown in a different colour in the window. The selected text can easily be changed by moving the mouse pointer and clicking with the middle button again.

- *Mark a word.* Place the mouse pointer on the word and click twice with the left-hand button (double-click).

- *Mark a line.* Place the mouse pointer anywhere on the line and click three times with the left-hand button (triple-click).

- *Mark the entire text.* Place the mouse pointer anywhere in the text to be marked and click four times with the left-hand button.

If you change your mind and don't want any text marked, all you have to do is move the mouse pointer to some other part of the window in focus and click with the left-hand button: the text marking will disappear.

After a section of text has been marked, you can choose whether to erase it, move it somewhere else or copy it.

- *Delete marked text.* Press the Cut key (L10) at the left-hand end of the keyboard.

- *Move marked text, alternative 1.* Press the Cut key (L10). Then place the mouse pointer at the point to which you want to move the marked text and click with the left-hand button. Finally, press the Paste key (L8) on the keyboard.

- *Move marked text, alternative 2.* Place the mouse pointer anywhere within the marked section of text and press the left-hand button. The pointer will now take on a special appearance, like a target with a piece of text. Keep the left-hand button pressed while you move the target to the point you want to move the marked text to, then release the button.

- *Copy marked text, alternative 1.* Press the Copy key (L6). Then place the mouse pointer at the point where you want a copy of the marked text and click with the left-hand button. Finally, press the Paste key (L8) n on the keyboard.

- *Copy marked text, alternative 2.* Place the mouse pointer anywhere within the marked section of text. Press the Control key on the keyboard. Keep the key pressed and press the left-hand mouse button. The pointer will take on a special appearance, like a target with a piece of text. Keep the left-hand button pressed while you move the target to the point where you want a copy of the marked text, then release the button.

You can always change your mind and reverse your last operation by pressing the Undo key (L4) on the keyboard.

If you prefer to work entirely with the mouse, most programs working with text have a menu called Edit. This menu will have alternatives corresponding to the Cut, Copy, Paste and Undo keys. Often, the Edit menu will be provided with a pushpin so that it can be left in a convenient position within the text being worked on. In the cmdtool terminal program, for example, the Edit menu is a sub-menu called from the pop-up menu in the terminal window, and in textedit the Edit menu is under a special menu button.

2.4.6 The scroll bar

Most application programs which display text are provided with a *scroll bar* at the right-hand side of the window to enable the user to scroll forwards and backwards within the text—see the window shown in figure 2.7 for example. Programs which show various kinds of graphical information rather than text may also have scroll bars. Nor does the scroll bar have to be at the right-hand side, but can be on any edge of the window—the bottom, for example, if the scrolling is carried out horizontally. The following operations on the scroll bar can be useful:

- *Move text up and down.* Place the mouse pointer in the middle of the scroll bar (on the light-coloured square between the up and down arrows), hold down the `left-hand` button and drag the scroll bar up or down. The text in the window will move in the same direction.

- *Move one line up or down.* Place the mouse pointer on the up or down arrow and click with the `left-hand` button. If the pointer is on the up arrow, you will move up the text by one line, and if the pointer is on the down arrow, you will move down the text by one line.

- *Move one page up or down.* To move one page up in the text, place the mouse pointer on the vertical line (the 'slot') immediately above the up arrow on the scroll bar and click with the `left-hand` mouse button. To move one page down, place the mouse pointer on the vertical line under the down arrow.

- *Move to start or end of text.* To move to the start of the text, place the mouse pointer on the small square at the very top of the scroll bar section and click with the `left-hand` button. In the same way, placing the pointer on the small square at the bottom and clicking will take you to the end of the text.

2.4.7 Some workspace menu utilities

We will briefly mention here some of the most important utility programs available from the workspace menu (see figure 2.8). The first option, `Programs`, produces a sub-menu offering a number of handy application programs forming part of the OpenWindows system. The most important of these programs, such as the terminal program, the file manager and the text editor, will be described later in this book.

The next alternative on the workspace menu, `Utilities`, also brings up a sub-menu. The three most interesting options on this are `Refresh`, `Save Workspace` and `Lock Screen`.

`Refresh` can be used to redraw the screen if something has gone wrong (fault messages from low-level system programs may be displayed across the middle of the screen, for example).

When you have been using OpenWindows for a while, you will start to develop your own preferences as to what the screen should look like when you log on (which programs should be running and where the different windows should be positioned). To make sure things are always the way you like them, the first thing to do is arrange the screen exactly the way you want it. Then select the option Save Workspace. The next time you log on it will be just as you left it.

If you are going to be leaving your workstation for a short time you can select Lock Screen. Everything on the screen will then disappear and a moving pattern will be displayed instead. However, OpenWindows will not be shut down, and all the programs you are running will continue to run. When you return, simply press any key and the system will come alive again. You will have to enter your password, but after that the screen will resume its former arrangement and you can continue where you left off.

If you select the Properties option in the workspace menu, you will be able to customize some aspects of OpenWindows. For example, you can change colours, and alter the positioning of icons and scroll bars. We cannot go into it all here, but refer interested readers to the user manuals.

The final option in the workspace menu is Exit. This is used to terminate OpenWindows. After OpenWindows has been terminated, the workstation will operate as an ordinary plain terminal again and all the application programs that were being run under OpenWindows will be terminated. However, you will not be automatically logged out from the UNIX system. You will need to do this yourself by entering

```
$ logout
```

2.5 Terminal windows

X When you have started X up using one of the three methods described earlier, you will usually have one or more windows on the screen. At least one of these will generally be what we call a *terminal window*. Every terminal window will function as a standard terminal at which X commands can be entered. Several windows can be maintained on the screen, with different UNIX programs running in them at the same time. The different windows can also have programs in them running on different computers. (See chapter 5.)

We will be describing here two common terminal programs for X: xterm, which forms part of the MIT distribution of X and can be found in most X systems, and cmdtool, which is a terminal program included in OpenWindows and is most commonly used when this system is being run.

2.5.1 `xterm`

You can easily open a new terminal window by entering the command:

$ **xterm &**

or by selecting an option called `xterm`, `shell`, `command` or something similar from a root menu.

Here, we will be giving some details of how `xterm` works. Most things in X can be altered. For example, you can decide for yourself which mouse buttons should be used for what. Here, we describe the 'default arrangement': the way it works if you have not made any changes of your own.

Figure 2.11 shows you what an `xterm` window looks like. If you make sure the `xterm` window is in focus, you will be able to enter commands in it just as you would on an ordinary terminal. Everything you key in will appear on the bottom line and the text will disappear upwards at the top of the window to be replaced by fresh lines at the bottom. It is possible to look at the lines that have disappeared by scrolling using the *scroll bar* at the side of the window.

```
                                    xterm
PASS1.sed    c4.mm         halsa.c        psfix
PASS2.sed    c5.mm         halsa.o        psfix2
PASS3.sed    c6.mm         hej2           psinit
PASS4.sed    c7.mm         hello.c        psinit.fix
baksida      c8.mm         hello2.c       raster
bokheader    c9.mm         hello2.o       rasterbilder
c0.mm        eps2bilder    makefile       skrivare
c1.mm        fig5.18       old-bokheader  spool
c2.mm        gamla_figurer profile.mm     temp9
c3.mm        go            ps1bilder
% date
Wed Aug 12 21:33:38 CET DST 1992
% ▮
```

Figure 2.11

Often the system will have been initiated in such a way that the terminal window is always automatically given a scroll bar—but if a terminal window does not have one it can be added in the following way: Move the mouse pointer into the `xterm` window. Hold down the `<ctrl>` key and press the `middle` mouse button at the same time. This will give you a pop-up menu holding various 'options' for `xterm`. Hold down the `middle` button and move the pointer to the line containing the words 'Enable Scrollbar'. Release the button.

Another way of producing a scroll bar in an `xterm` window is to add the argument `-sb` when you create it:

$ **xterm -sb &**

The dark section of the scroll bar shows you which section of the overall text is displayed in the window. If the dark section is right at the top, the start of the text is being displayed, and if it is right at the bottom the display shows the end of the text. If the dark section is somewhere in the middle, a section from the middle of the text is being displayed. The size of the dark section also indicates how large a part of the overall text is being shown in the window. If the dark section is small, a small part of the whole text is being shown, and if it is large you can see a large part. A special case is if the entire scroll bar is dark. In that case the entire text is shown in the window.

Using the scroll bar, you can scroll backwards and forwards in the text and move up and down. The following three operations are useful:

- *Scroll text up or down.* Move the mouse pointer into the dark section of the scroll bar. Press the `middle` button and hold it down. If you move the mouse up or down the section of the text displayed in the window will move through the text in a corresponding way.

- *Move forward one page.* Move the mouse pointer to the bottom of the scroll bar and press the `left-hand` button.

- *Move back one page.* Move the mouse pointer to the bottom of the scroll bar and press the `right-hand` button.

Whenever you enter something at the keyboard—for example, when you key in a fresh UNIX command—the text in the `xterm` window will automatically move up so that what you key will appear on the bottom line. The same applies if a program starts to produce output in the `xterm` window. Its output will also appear at the bottom.

In `xterm` it is easy to mark or copy a specified section of text using the mouse buttons. This can be useful when entering UNIX commands—for example, to copy a previous command or a long filename. To mark the section of text to be copied, for example, you can choose one of the following methods.

- *Mark a chosen section of text, alternative 1.* Position the mouse pointer at the start of the text to be copied and press the `left-hand` button. Hold the button pressed and move the mouse to the end of the text to be copied. The chosen section of text will then be marked in the window. Release the button when the correct text is marked.

- *Mark a chosen section of text, alternative 2.* Position the mouse pointer at the start of the text to be copied. Press the `left-hand` button and release it. (This is generally called 'clicking'.) Then position the mouse pointer at the end of the text to be copied. Press the `right-hand` button. The chosen section of text will be marked. You can easily change the chosen section of text by moving the mouse pointer and pressing the `right-hand` button again.

- *Mark a word.* Position the mouse pointer on the word and press the `left-hand` button twice (double-click).

- *Mark a line.* Position the mouse pointer on the line and press the `left-hand` button three times (triple-click).

The text marked in the above way can be copied to the end of the command you are entering. This is done by pressing the `middle` button. The text will then be copied to your typing position exactly as if you had typed it in at the keyboard.

X also allows you to copy text from one window to another. In other words, the text you have marked does not have to be in the `xterm` window, but can be in a different window. When you want to copy over the marked text, all you have to do is make sure that you have moved the mouse pointer into the window you want to copy the text into before you press the `middle` button.

2.5.2 `cmdtool`

When OpenWindows is started up, there will normally be a small terminal window at the top left of the screen, as shown in figure 1.2. This window is where the `cmdtool` terminal program runs. In the window, `cmdtool` has been initialized as what is called a console terminal, which means that the system uses the window to display any error messages.

The console terminal window can be used to enter UNIX commands. However, if you want to enter your own UNIX commands it can be better to open a new terminal window which is a bit larger and where you won't be disturbed by error messages from the system. (However, the console terminal window should not be removed, as error messages could then appear right across the screen.)

The simplest way to open a new terminal window is to call the workspace menu and select the `Programs` sub-menu. From this menu, select the `Command Tool` option. A new `cmdtool` window will then be set up. Figure 2.12 shows what it might look like.

```
┌─────────────────────────────────────────────────────┐
│ ▽        cmdtool – /bin/tcsh                          │
├─────────────────────────────────────────────────────┤
│ % ls                                                  │
│ PASS1.sed      c4.mm        hej2          psfix2       │
│ PASS2.sed      c5.mm        hello.c       psinit       │
│ PASS3.sed      c6.mm        hello2.c      psinit.fix   │
│ PASS4.sed      c7.mm        hello2.o      raster       │
│ baksida        c8.mm        makefile      raster2      │
│ bokheader      c9.mm        old-bokheader skrivare     │
│ c0.mm          gamla_figurer profile.mm   temp9        │
│ c1.mm          go           ps1bilder                  │
│ c2.mm          halsa.c      ps2bilder                  │
│ c3.mm          halsa.o      psfix                      │
│ % date                                                 │
│ Wed Aug 12 17:11:37 CET DST 1992                       │
│ % ▲                                                    │
└─────────────────────────────────────────────────────┘
```

Figure 2.12

Everything you enter in a cmdtool window will appear at the bottom, and text for which there is no more room will disappear at the top. The bottom line of the window is known as the *command line*: this is where you enter your UNIX commands. On the command line you will see a cursor in the shape of a dark triangle, which indicates the *entry point*. What you enter at the keyboard will always appear at this point, immediately to the left of the cursor. The entry point will usually be at the right-hand end of the command line, but it is easy to move the entry point to edit a command you have written before pressing the return key to send it to the system.

One way of moving the entry point is to indicate the new cursor position with the mouse pointer then click with the left-hand button. Alternatively, the left and right arrow keys or <ctrl-b> and <ctrl-f> respectively can be used to move the cursor to left and right. Keying <ctrl-e> or <ctrl-return> brings the entry point back to the end of the line. In addition, the cmdtool window will scroll forwards so the command line can be seen. This can be useful if a terminal window has been scrolled and entry of a UNIX command is then required. If the cursor position is not at the end of the line, always press <ctrl-e> or <ctrl-return> before sending the command with the return key.

There are a number of commands to delete characters that have been keyed in the command line by mistake. Backspace will delete the character to the left of the cursor position and <shift-backspace> will delete the character to the right. Everything on the line to the left of the cursor position can be deleted by keying <ctrl-u> and everything to the right of the cursor position can be deleted similarly by keying <ctrl-shift-u>.

The editing commands we have described are summarized in table 2.1.

Some cmdtool editing commands	
<ctrl-f> →	move one character to the right
<ctrl-b> ←	move one character to the left
<ctrl-e>	move to end of line
<ctrl-return>	move to end of text
<backspace>	delete character to left of cursor position
<shift-backspace>	delete character to right of cursor position
<ctrl-u>	delete to start of line
<ctrl-shift-u>	delete to end of line
x	insert character x to left of cursor position

Table 2.1

There are more editing commands than we have shown in the table. If you choose to have an editable `cmdtool` window, it will work by and large in the same way as in the `textedit` text editor. The editing facilities available there are described in chapter 6.3. (The `cmdtool` window can be made editable by using the `Term Pane` pop-up menu, which is called with the `right-hand` mouse button. From the pop-up menu, you should select `History` and from there the `Mode` option. You can now choose between making the terminal window `Editable` or `Read Only`.)

One way of editing the command line is to copy text from somewhere else in the `cmdtool` window or from another window. This is useful, for example, if you need to repeat a command you entered earlier or if the command requires a long filename you have already used. The way copying like this works is described in section 2.4.5.

2.6 Calling an X program

There are a number of programs designed to be run under X. We have already mentioned one, `xterm`. A couple of others are `xclock` and `xcalc`. If you enter

> $ **xclock &**

in a terminal window, you will get a new window containing a clock. The command

> $ **xcalc &**

gives you a new window containing a calculator you can do calculations on. A special X program is `xkill`. This is used for removing X windows. After you enter the command

> $ **xkill**

the mouse pointer will take on a special shape. You can then move this pointer to the window you wish to remove and click on the `left-hand` button.

Another program which can sometimes be useful is `xrefresh`, which redraws everything on the screen. It is handy to be able to do this if you have had some error messages you want to be rid of, from the communications system, for example. All you need to do is enter the command

> $ **xrefresh**

When you start up an X program you can enter a number of arguments to specify how you want everything to look on the screen. Many of these arguments are standardized and are entered in the same way for different X programs. An example of these arguments is

-geometry, which controls how large a new window will be and where it will be positioned on the screen. For example, you can key

$ **xclock -geometry 250x350+500+50** &

The first two figures give the width and height of the window respectively. For most X programs, this is given as the number of pixels, but for some programs, e.g. xterm, it is given as the number of characters instead. The last two figures indicate whereabouts on the screen the window is to be placed. For this, pixels are always used. The last figure but one gives its horizontal position and the last gives its vertical position. If the third figure is preceded by a plus sign, as in this example, it indicates that the left-hand edge of the window is to be positioned that number of pixels from the left-hand edge of the screen. If, instead, it is preceded by a minus sign, this means that the right-hand edge of the window is to be positioned the given number of pixels from the right-hand edge of the screen. In a similar way, a plus sign in front of the last figure means the figure gives the distance in pixels between the upper edge of the window and the top of the screen, and a minus sign means the figure indicates the distance between the lower edge of the window and the bottom of the screen. It is permissible to omit the size or the position, in which case the default (standard) values will be assumed. Let us look at some examples:

$ **xterm -geometry 80x60+0+0** &
$ **xclock -geometry 80x80-0+0** &
$ **xcalc -geometry -0-0** &

Here, a terminal window 80 characters wide and 60 characters high has been created in the top left-hand corner. A clock has been placed in the top right-hand corner, and will be 80 pixels square. The bottom right-hand corner has been occupied by a calculator in the default size.

Another two standard arguments for X programs are -iconic, which indicates that the window is to appear at first as an icon, and -title, which can be used to specify the title which appears at the top of the window frame. There are many other standard arguments—for example, you can specify the text font and colour. For a full description, you should refer to the X manual.

For an X program to work, it must know where its windows are to be shown. In most cases, it gets this information from the environment variable DISPLAY. If X programs do not work as described above, it may well be because this variable was not set correctly. DISPLAY will include the name of the display (see section 1.4.3). This name comes in three parts: a machine name, a display number and a screen number. The last two will in most cases be zero. The display name for a workstation or X terminal with the name odin, for example, would be odin:0.0. To set the environment variable DISPLAY, key in

```
$ DISPLAY=odin:0.0
$ export DISPLAY
```

if the prompt is a dollar sign (Bourne shell or Korn shell) or

```
% setenv DISPLAY odin:0.0
```

if the prompt is a percent mark (C shell or TC shell)

X programs can of course be started in this way in OpenWindows
too. Instead of selecting the `Calculator` option from the workspace
menu's `Programs` sub-menu, you can, for example, enter the name of
the program directly in a terminal window:

```
$ calctool &
```

OpenWindows will also let you run general X programs which are
not specific to OpenWindows. The X programs demonstrated in this
section will run without problems, for example. If for any reason you
happen to prefer `xterm` to `cmdtool` as a terminal program, this will
also run perfectly well under OpenWindows.

2.7 Shells

The program in a UNIX system which reads and interprets the
commands entered by the user is called the *shell*. There are several
different shells for use in a UNIX system. The two most common are the
Bourne shell (abbreviated to `sh`) and the *C shell* (abbreviated to `csh`), the
C shell being rather more advanced. Two other shells in common use are
the *Korn shell* (`ksh`) and the *TC shell* (`tcsh`). These are expanded
versions of the Bourne shell and the C shell respectively, and include a
number of useful enhancements. The differences between the various
shells are not great as far as the manner of writing ordinary commands
is concerned. You can generally tell which shell is being used by the
prompt character. If the system produces a percent symbol `%` it is most
probably the C shell or the TC shell that is being used; and if it writes a
dollar sign `$` it is likely to be the Bourne shell or the Korn shell.

It is an easy matter to choose for yourself which shell you are going
to use. If you are running on a system which normally uses the Bourne
shell, for example, but you would like to run the C shell instead, you can
test for it by keying the command `csh`. If the C shell is installed this will
result in the system changing to it. In a similar way, you can enter the
command `sh` to change from the C shell to the Bourne shell, `ksh` if you
prefer the Korn shell and `tcsh` for the TC shell. Some systems allow you
to specify for yourself which shell should automatically be used when
you log on. Simply use the command `chsh`. The name of the old shell
will then be written out and you will be asked to enter the name of the
new one.

When a command is entered, the shell assumes that the first word in the command line is the name of the program to be run. The command is sent to the shell as soon as the <return> key is pressed:

$ *program* **<return>**

Once the program (the command) has been run in the computer system the shell will again give you a prompt character on the screen. As a simple example, suppose we run the program date, which displays the current date and time:

```
$ date
Fri Mar  8 14:25:59 MET 1992
$
```

A number of programs sometimes require one or more arguments:

$ *program argument*$_1$ *argument*$_2$ ... *argument*$_n$

The two most common types of argument are options and filenames. Options always start with a minus sign and are used to control the behaviour of the program. (For example, it is often possible to choose between different forms of output.) The exact arguments available vary from program to program. For instance, we can add the option -u to the date command to get the time in Greenwich Mean Time (GMT) instead of local time:

```
$ date -u
Fri Mar  8 13:25:59 GMT 1992
$
```

The program name and any argument for the program are input in *free format*, which means that the program name and arguments must be separated by at least one space.

When keying in long commands which will not fit on one line at the terminal, the command can be continued on a second line provided the backslash character \ is keyed immediately before the <return> at the end of the first line. The shell will then read it as if it had all been keyed on one line:

$ *program argument*$_1$ *argument*$_2$ *argument*$_3$ *argument*$_4$\
    argument$_5$ *argument*$_6$

We will be using this format in this book if a command we wish to demonstrate does not fit on a single line.

If you try to run a program which is not on the computer, the shell will report this by giving an error message:

```
$ dte
dte: command not found
$ date-u
date-u: command not found
$
```

The shell distinguishes between capitals and small letters. This means that every program name entered must be exactly right in terms of capitals and small letters:

```
$ DATE
DATE: command not found
$
```

Another simple program you can try out is cal, which produces a calendar:

```
$ cal 9 1992
     September 1992
 S   M  Tu  W  Th   F   S
            1   2   3   4   5
 6   7   8   9  10  11  12
12  14  15  16  17  18  19
20  21  22  23  24  25  26
27  28  29  30
$
```

A calendar for September 1992 will be displayed on the screen. To obtain a calendar for the whole of the year 2000, you can enter the command:

```
$ cal 2000
```

As an example of a simple program, we can also mention the clear program. The following command clears the screen:

```
$ clear
```

On certain systems, you will need to enter instead:

```
$ tput clear
```

If the program does not work, it will be because the system does not know what type of terminal you are working at.

It is possible to enter several commands on the same line by keying a semi-colon between the different commands. The commands will then be executed one after the other in sequence. For example, to start by wiping the screen, then write out the current date followed by a calendar for 1993, key in:

```
$ clear; date; cal 1993
```

When keying in a command line, mistakes often slip in. These can be corrected provided <return> has not been pressed. You can either use the 'erase' key, which will delete the last character keyed, or the 'kill' key, which will delete the entire input line. Which actual keys on the keyboard correspond to the 'erase' and 'kill' keys may vary, and you can choose for yourself which keys are used. The most common arrangement is for the 'erase' key to be assigned to the <backspace>,

\<delete\> or # key and the 'kill' key to be given by \<ctrl-u\> (control key and u at the same time) or the @ character.

The simplest way to find out where the 'erase' and 'kill' keys are is to try it out; but you can also enter the command

$ **stty -a**

The response may then be, for example,

erase = ^h   kill = ^u

which means that 'erase' and 'kill' are given by \<ctrl-h\> and \<ctrl-u\> respectively. N.B.: \<ctrl-h\> and \<backspace\> are the same thing.

If you want to change the 'erase' or 'kill' key, you can enter the commands

$ **stty erase** *erase_character*
$ **stty kill** *kill_character*

We will shortly be seeing that the more advanced Korn and TC shells offer more editing facilities than 'erase' and 'kill'. If X is being run, there will also be some extra editing commands in whichever terminal program is being used.

Sometimes you have a reason for stopping the program before it has finished. (For example, it may turn out that the print-out you are getting is far too long, or the program is taking too long to run.) In that case, you can press the 'interrupt' key. This is usually assigned to the \<delete\> key or to \<ctrl-c\> (control and C together). (The stty -a can be used here, too, to find out where it is.)

2.8 Text output

The majority of information handled by computers consists of ordinary readable text. This text may comprise articles and books, for example, or texts connected with computer programs. Text is stored in a computer system in the form of *text files*. Every text file has a name and can contain text of any length. (The text you are reading at this moment, for example, is held in a text file called c2.mm.)

A program called cat can be used in its simplest form to display the content of a text file on the terminal screen:

```
$ cat c2.mm
.H 2 "Text output"
The majority of all information handled by
computers consists of ordinary readable text.
This text may comprise articles and books, for
example, or texts connected with computer
programs. Text is stored ...
```

(The curious line beginning with a full stop contains an editing command for the text formatting program `troff`.)

The abbreviation `cat` stands for 'catenate', as the program can be used more generally to join files on to the end of each other. For example, the command

$ `cat c1.mm c2.mm c3.mm`

will write the contents of the files `c1.mm`, `c2.mm` and `c3.mm` to the screen in sequence.

A problem with writing to the screen using the `cat` program is that the text is displayed on the screen at such a speed that you can't read anything but the last page. To prevent this, the program `more` can be used instead:

$ `more c2.mm`

This program displays one page on the screen at a time, stopping at the end of each page so that you have time to read it. Each time it stops, the program is waiting for a command telling it to continue. The most common commands for `more` are given in table 2.2. Note that only the last of these commands needs to end with `<return>`.

Commands for `more`	
`<space bar>`	Display next page.
`b`	Display previous page.
`h`	Help. Gives information on commands.
`q`	Terminate screen program.
`/xxx`	Search for text string 'xxx'.

Table 2.2

Instead of `more`, certain versions of UNIX have a similar program called `pg`. This is called in a similar way:

$ `pg c2.mm`

The most common commands for `pg` are shown in table 2.3. Note that all commands for `pg` must end in `<return>`.

Commands for `pg`	
`<return>`	Display next page.
`-1`	Display previous page.
`h`	Help. Gives information on commands.
`q`	Terminate screen program.
`/xxx`	Search for text string 'xxx'.

Table 2.3

SV

To print text on the printer in System V, the program `lp` can be used. For example, the command

```
$ lp letr
request-id is laser-1234 (1 file)
```

generates a print-out of the file `letr` on the printer. The printer system returns an ID number for the print-out (in this example *laser-1234*).

If more than one printer is connected to the system, you can choose which printer to send the text to by adding the option `-d`:

```
$ lp -dprinter3 letr
request-id is printer3-1235 (1 file)
```

When the `lp` command is issued, the print job will join the end of the selected printer's queue. If you change your mind and decide not to have a print-out, you can use the `cancel` program. The argument for this program is the ID number returned by `lp`. We can cancel the first print job above, for example, by giving the command

```
$ cancel laser-1234
```

If you have forgotten the ID number given to the job, you can use the program `lpstat` (details are given in the manual).

OSF BSD

In the BSD and OSF systems, output on the printer is generated by means of the program `lpr`. To print out the file `letr`, for example, enter the command

```
$ lpr letr
```

The option `-P` can be used to indicate which printer is to be used:

```
$ lpr -Pprinter3 letr
```

The `lpr` program will add the print job to the selected printer's queue. You can see the situation in the printer queue by issuing the command

```
$ lpq
```

You will then be given a list of all the jobs waiting to be printed. If you change your mind and don't want the print job you have sent, you can use the `lprm` program. As a parameter, this program needs the job number for the print job to be removed from the queue, which will be found in the messages returned by the `lpq` program. For instance, if the print-out of the `letr` file was given the job number 54, you can cancel the print job by keying

```
$ lprm 54
```

Open

In OpenWindows there is an application program, `printtool`, which provides the user with a convenient way of printing files on different printers. The `printtool` program is started up by selecting `Print Tool` from the `Programs` sub-menu accessed from the workspace menu. Once `printtool` is running you will see a print window like the one shown in figure 2.13. The line next to the heading

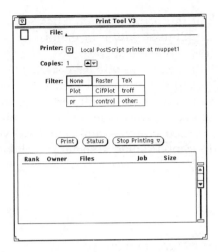

Figure 2.13

Printer in the window gives the name of the printer which will be used. If there is more than one printer in the system, there will be an abbreviated menu button $\boxed{V}$ next to this heading. You then have the option to select another printer by placing the mouse pointer on the menu button and pressing the `right-hand` mouse button. You will then see a list of printers and can select the one you prefer.

One way to specify the file to be printed is to enter the name of the file on the top line of the window, against the heading **File**. The full pathname for the file must be entered, starting from your own home directory. (Filenames and pathnames are explained in chapter 3.) If the name of the file appears in another window on the screen, it can be copied instead of being re-entered, using the method described in section 2.4.5. Once the name of the file has been entered against **File**, the mouse pointer can be placed on the $\boxed{\text{Print}}$ button and the `left-hand` mouse button clicked. Printing will then start.

However, OpenWindows also provides a much easier way to print out a file than to enter the pathname. This uses a technique called *drag and drop*. In chapter 3 we will be describing the OpenWindows file manager program, and we will see that every file can be displayed graphically on the screen by means of a symbol. To print out a certain file, you simply place the mouse pointer on the symbol for the file you want to print and then press the `left-hand` mouse button and keep the button pressed while you move the pointer to the small rectangular 'target' box at the top left of the print window. There you 'drop' the file by releasing the mouse key. Printing will then start automatically.

The drag-and-drop technique can be made even simpler if, after selecting the printer you want, you convert the print window to an icon. You can then simply drop the file you want printed anywhere on the icon.

To take a look at the printer queue, click with the `left-hand` mouse button on the Status button in the printer window. You will then see a list of all the jobs in the queue.

You can halt all the print runs you have started by calling the menu under the Stop Printing ▽ button and then selecting the option `All Print Jobs`. If you only want to halt certain of the print jobs, the mouse pointer should be moved to the list of print jobs, where you can click with the `left-hand` button against the job(s) you want to stop. You can then call the Stop Printing ▽ menu and choose the `Selected Jobs` option.

2.9 How to get help

If you want to run a program but you are unsure how the program should be used, most UNIX systems will provide you with direct help on the screen. This simply writes out the manual instructions for the different programs. The simplest way of doing this is by using the `man` command. For example, to see the page of the manual for the `stty` program, enter the command:

```
$ man stty
```

If the manual page does not exist, the following message will be displayed:

```
No manual for stty
```

Otherwise, the page in the manual will be output to the screen:

```
NAME
  stty - set or alter the options for a terminal
SYNOPSIS
  stty [ -ag ] [ option ]
DESCRIPTION
  stty sets certain terminal I/O options for the
  device that is  the  current  standard
  output. Without arguments, it reports the
  settings of ...
```

An alternative way of using the `man` program is to search for all the information linked to a specified keyword. If, for example, you key in

```
$ man -k password
```

you will be given a short summary of all the commands etc. concerned with passwords.

The `more` program is normally used internally by the `man` program to produce the text output itself. Accordingly, when reading output from `man`, the same commands described for `more` above can be used to move around in the text.

Under X, an alternative to man is the program xman. This is run by means of the command

     $ **xman &**

or else xman or similar can be selected from a suitable root menu.

The xman program is mouse-controlled. When it is called you will see a window like the one shown in figure 2.14. If you click on Help you will get a help text describing how to use the program. To get information on the different commands, click on Manual Page.

Figure 2.14

You will then see a window like the one in figure 2.15. (In some cases you will not be given a window like the one shown in figure 2.14, but the window in figure 2.15 will be displayed directly.) The simplest way of searching for a manual page for a particular program is to select the Sections menu from the window shown in figure 2.15 and then the option User Commands in this menu. You will then be given a list of all the programs and you can mark the program you want with the mouse. If you are looking for the manual page for an X program, select instead the option X program from the Sections menu.

Another way to search for a manual page for a specific program is to select the Options menu and then the Search option. You will then be

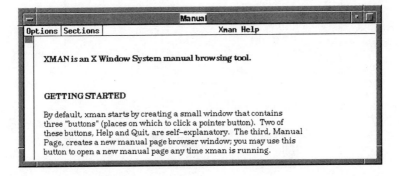

Figure 2.15

given a small window. In this window you can enter the name of the program you are interested in, then click on [Manual Page].

The `Search` option is also useful if you want to know the commands connected with a particular keyword. In this case, key in the keyword instead and click on [Apropos].

If, for example, you want to know which commands are involved in electronic mail, key in 'mail' as the search key.

When reading a manual page, you can use the scroll bar to move around the text in the same way as for `xterm`.

In OpenWindows there are two separate, easy-to-use systems to provide the user with help, *Spot Help* and *Help Handbooks*. Spot Help can be used when information is required on a window or a menu specific to OpenWindows. The user places the mouse pointer on the item for which information is required and presses the `Help` key on the keyboard. This produces a Spot Help window with a brief explanatory text. This window is 'fastened' with a pushpin, and when the user has seen enough he or she can click on the pushpin with the `left-hand` mouse button to get rid of it. Some Spot Help windows have a button at the bottom marked [More]. Clicking on this takes the user to the other help system and an appropriate handbook.

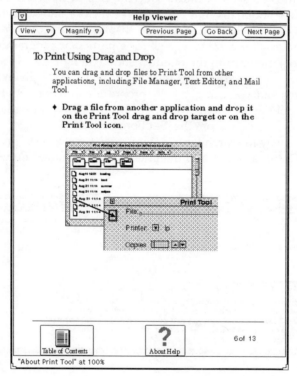

Figure 2.16

The more detailed help system consists of a number of handbooks. Figure 2.16 shows what a page of these handbooks looks like. The program which displays the handbooks can be run by selecting the `Help` option in the workspace menu. This produces a window containing a list of the titles of all the handbooks available. The first of these, `Introducing Your Sun Desktop`, is rather special in that it is designed to be read from 'cover to cover'. The other handbooks are more like reference books, where you can look up what you want to know and read only the relevant pages.

To select a specific handbook, double-click on its title with the `left-hand` mouse button. You will then see a contents list for the selected handbook so that you can choose the section you are interested in by double-clicking against the right heading. If you want to return instead to the full list of handbooks, double-click on the `More Handbooks` box.

After double-clicking against a heading, you will be presented with a text and you will be able to read as many pages as you need. The `Next Page` and `Previous Page` buttons are used to page forward and back. The `Go Back` button is used to return to the last page you read. You can always return to the contents list of the handbook you are reading by double-clicking in the `Table of Contents` box at the bottom. From the contents list you can return to the full list of handbooks, as described above.

Finally, we must mention a technical point regarding the manuals. The `man` and `xman` programs can of course also be used in OpenWindows. However, the manual pages for the programs included in OpenWindows, such as `cmdtool` and `textedit`, are located in a special directory. To enable `man` and `xman` to find these manual pages, they must therefore be told where to look. This is done by making sure that the environment variable `MANPATH` has been correctly set up. The best way to do this is to include the lines below in the start-up file for your shell program (see chapter 4.6); but you can also enter the commands directly.

If you are running the Bourne shell or the Korn shell, enter

```
$ set MANPATH=$OPENWINHOME/man:/usr/man
$ export MANPATH
```

and if you are running the C shell or the TC shell, key

```
% setenv MANPATH $OPENWINHOME/man:/usr/man
```

If you are using the `xman` program, you will now find the manual pages for your X programs under the `Open Windows Clients` option in the `Sections` menu.

2.10 Summary

Some basic UNIX programs	
who	list users logged on
logout exit <ctrl-d>	log out
passwd	change password
date	display current date and time
cal [*month*] *year*	display calendar
clear tput clear	wipe screen
stty -a	give information on keys
stty erase *erase_char*	set 'erase' key
stty kill *kill_char*	set 'kill' key
sh	install Bourne shell
ksh	install Korn shell
csh	install C shell
tcsh	install TC shell
chsh	change 'default' shell
cat *filename* ...	write files to screen
more *filename* ... pg *filename* ...	write files to screen (halt after every page)
lp [-d*name*] *filename*	send files to printer, System V
cancel *print_job_ID_number*	cancel printing, System V
lpstat	display printer queue, System V
lpr [-P*name*] *filename*	send files to printer, BSD/OSF
lpq	display printer queue, BSD/OSF
lprm *print_job_number*	cancel printing, BSD/OSF
man *program*	write out manual page for *program*
man -k *keyword*	give information on *keyword*

Table 2.4

Some basic X programs	
xinit	install X system (start-up method 1)
xterm [-sb] &	install a new terminal window
cmdtool &	install a new terminal window in OpenWindows
xclock &	install a clock
xcalc &	install a calculator
xkill &	kill a window
xrefresh &	redraw screen
xman &	run program to display manual page
printtool &	install printer program in OpenWindows

Table 2.5

Three
The File System

One of the most important components in the UNIX operating system is the *file system*. The file system is organized as a *tree*, where the individual elements of the tree are *files*. A file is a quantity of data which has been given a logical name and a type. The most common types of file are:

- *plain files* (or just '*files*')
- *special files* or *device files*
- *directory files* (or *directories*)

This chapter describes the structure of the file system and the different types of file. It deals particularly with how *filenames* are entered (simple filenames, full pathnames, filename patterns and automatic filename completion). Various operations on the file system will be described, for example, how to move around the tree structure, how to output information on files in the tree and how to remove and add files. Finally, some programs are introduced which are useful in handling files. We will see, among other things, how to compare files, look for files, sort files and look for a particular text in files.

3.1 Plain files

A plain file contains data or information which has been created, for example, by:

- a word processing program,
- a text editor,
- a compiler.

It can thus contain either normal text or data intended as input to another program (which is difficult for human beings to read). Examples of the latter are files containing executable code or object programs. For plain files, there are no special requirements as regards the structure of the contents. A file can be any length. Once a file has been created, it will stay in the file system until it is removed.

Examples of plain files are:

```
/etc/passwd
/etc/group
/etc/hosts
.login
.profile
```

These files contain ordinary text. Examples of files containing the binary, executable code which is 'downloaded' and run in the computer are:

```
/bin/cal
/bin/who
/bin/date
/bin/passwd
```

3.2 Special files

Special files provide the links between the system's various physical units (terminals, tape drives, hard disk(s) etc.) and the logical, hierarchical file system. Every computer unit handling input and/or output data is represented in the file system by a logical name. For example, we can regard a terminal as a plain file for which writing means displaying characters on the screen and reading is carried out at the keyboard.

3.3 Directory files

Directory files link together the different levels of the hierarchical file system. They enable plain files and special files to be organized in a logical and hierarchically arranged manner. A directory file is in fact no more than a table containing names and references for the files belonging to the current directory (the directory you are currently working in).

The hierarchical model of file organization has many parallels with the way people organize information using folders, card indexes and the like. One type of card index, for example, is found in many homes in the form of a recipe set. The recipes are generally grouped in such a way that all the starters are filed after a special index card, all the sweets after another, and so on. (See figure 3.1.)

Figure 3.1

Information can be organized in a similar way in a hierarchical file system. This is illustrated in figure 3.2.

Figure 3.2

Ring binders with index sheets, as shown in figure 3.3, are another way we organize our information in human life.

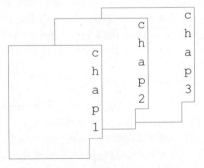

Figure 3.3

Using a hierarchical file system, the ring binder and its index cards can be modelled as shown in figure 3.4

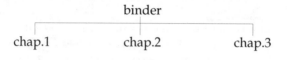

Figure 3.4

In a UNIX system, the / symbol stands for the root of the file system. The root directory contains a number of plain files along with some directory files. The directory files, in turn, contain plain files, special files and directory files, and so on. An example of what this might look like is shown in figure 3.5.

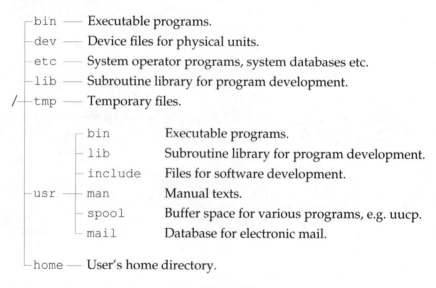

Figure 3.5

At any given time when you are running a UNIX system, the system will be keeping track of the *current directory* you happen to be working in for the time being. Searches for files you refer to will usually start in the current directory. To find out the names of the files in the current directory, you can enter the command

$ **ls**

As we will see later, there are easy ways of moving around the file tree and changing the current directory. When you log on you will automatically be in your *home directory*. Every user will normally have a home directory of his or her own. The location of the home directory in the file system is decided by the system administrator. Users' home directories are most commonly located in a sub-directory called /home, /u or /user.

The /bin directory contains executable standard programs, e.g.:

```
cal
cat
date
who
```

The /dev directory contains a large number of device files. These files represent ports to the terminals, hard disks, tape drives etc.

A large number of databases and programs for system administration are stored in the /etc directory. One of the most important system databases, for example, is /etc/passwd, in which the users of the computer system are defined.

The /tmp directory is where application programs create temporary files. Temporary files normally last only as long as the program is running. The lib directory is a library of subroutines used in the development of software. If the manual is available through the machine, it will be stored in the sub-directory man. Electronic mail sent to users is stored in the mail directory.

3.4 Filenames

3.4.1 Simple filenames

The name given to a file within a particular directory is called a *simple filename* or simply a *filename*. A simple filename can consist of any number of characters. The following characters should be avoided as they have special meanings in some contexts:

```
(space)   |   <   >   &   ~   #   ?   ^   @
$   "   '   `   !   *   {   }   [   ]   ;
```

The filename will often have an *extension*, a suffix indicating which type of file it is. The extension goes at the end of the filename after a full stop. The UNIX system does not require extensions to be used: it is more a matter of convention. As well as this, different compilers and other programs may demand that the names of files holding input data to the program have specific extensions. Some examples of extensions are:

```
test.c       text of a C program
prog.ada     text of an Ada program
ex1.o        a compiled object program
chap1.mm     a text document
```

3.4.2 Pathnames

A file in the hierarchical file system can always be identified by its full *pathname*. The pathname includes all the directory names starting from the root directory, and ends with the simple filename. The names are separated by / characters (slashes).

> */directory/directory/ ..... /directory/filename*

It is perfectly possible, for example, to run the date program by using the full pathname:

> $ **/bin/date**

Files in the current directory are generally referred to without giving the full pathname.

Suppose we have the file structure shown in figure 3.6 and the current directory is mike, which is marked in bold in the figure.

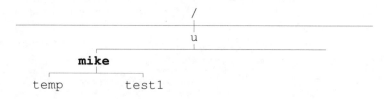

Figure 3.6

If we now wish, for example, to see the contents of the file temp we can enter the command

> $ **cat temp**

Of course, we can equally well use the full filename:

> $ **cat /u/mike/temp**

3.4.3 Filename patterns (filenames with wildcards)

Certain UNIX programs, for example cat and more, allow the input of a list of files as the argument, and not just a single file. When calling programs of this sort, we can use certain special characters called *wildcards* to enter a *pattern* showing what the filenames making up the argument are to look like. This means that a pattern of this type can be used to specify not just *one* file, but a *list of files* whose names match the pattern given. This is best explained with a few examples.

The simplest wildcard is a question mark. If a question mark is included in a filename, this means that any single character at all is acceptable in its place. The command

> $ **cat chap?**

will produce at the terminal the contents of all files with names of five characters of which the first four are chap. For example, if there are files called `chap1`, `chap7` and `chaps` the content of these files will be displayed. On the other hand, files called `chap12`, `chap` or `chapter3` will not be included, as their names do not follow the pattern given.

There can be more than one question mark in a pattern—for example:

$ **cat e????e**

This will display the contents of all files with names which are six characters long and start and end in an 'e'.

The wildcard most often used in filenames is the asterisk *. An asterisk can be matched by any number of characters in a row. The command

$ **cat chap***

will display the contents of all files whose names start with `chap`. If, as in the example above, there are files called `chap`, `chap1`, `chap12`, `chap7`, `chaps` and `chapter3`, the contents of all these files will be displayed on the screen. However, the files `chpt3`, `ch5` and `newchap3` will not, of course, be displayed.

Here are some more examples. The command

$ **ls *.ada**

can be used to obtain a list of the names of all files in the current directory containing Ada programs; and

$ **ls *font***

will list the names of all the files with the combination 'font' as part (or all) of their names. If the filename consists only of an asterisk, it will match *all* filenames.

$ **cat ***

will therefore display at the terminal the contents of all files in the current directory.

The third type of special character comprises the square brackets [and]. As we have seen, a question mark will match with any single character. Square brackets are used to indicate a match with one of a number of single characters if not all characters are desired. The brackets are used to enclose the only characters that are to be allowed. For example, to get a list of all the files whose names start with one of the letters i, j, k, l or m we can enter the command

$ **ls [ijklm]***

Alternatively, we can enclose in the square brackets a range within the alphabet. We could then type, instead of the command above,

$ **ls [i-m]***

All filenames ending in a capital letter can be found using

$ **ls *[A-Z]**

3.4.4 More on filenames in the Korn shell

In the Korn shell, the ~ character (tilde) has a special meaning when specifying the name of a directory. If ~ is entered by itself, it indicates the name of the user's own home directory. To see the contents of a file called `info` in your home directory, therefore, whatever the current directory may be, you can key in the command

$ **cat ~/info**

The tilde can also be combined with a user ID. For example, ~sarah would denote the name of Sarah's home directory (if she has been given `sarah` as her user ID). To print out on screen a file called `projectinfo` in Sarah's home directory, we would then key

$ **cat ~sarah/projectinfo**

You can also decide for yourself whether or not filename patterns (also known as 'global filenames') are to be allowed. This is controlled by a 'variable' called `noglob`. As a rule, filename patterns are allowed initially, but if this is not the case it can changed by entering the command

$ **set +o noglob**

To exclude the use of filename patterns, enter

$ **set -o noglob**

In the Korn shell there is a mechanism which makes it unnecessary to key in the whole of the filename in commands. If the start of the filename is keyed, followed by the keys <esc>\, the shell will automatically complete the remainder of the name. For example, if we have a file called `project_information` in the current directory, we can enter the command

$ **cat proj<esc>**

If there are no other files whose names begin with `proj` the shell will automatically complete the filename:

$ **cat proj**ect_information

Suppose there are also files called `prog1` and `prod` in the current directory. If we now enter the command

$ **cat pro<esc>**

there will be three files matching the unfinished filename. The shell will then be unable to complete the name. We must then add one or more characters until the truncated filename is unique.

There is also a facility to see all the files with names starting in a particular manner while a command is actually being entered. For this, <esc>= is keyed instead of <esc>\. The command

$ **cat pro<esc>=**

for example, will result in the output

```
1) prod
2) prog1
3) project_information
$ ls -l pro
```

The Korn shell is now in what is called *command mode* (see chapter 4.5). We now have to switch to *input mode* to be able to continue entering the command. The simplest way of doing this is to press the a key. We can then complete the command we have started:

$ ls -l pro**ject_information**

An alternative to this is to find out the name of all files starting with a particular sequence of characters. The command

$ **cat pro<esc>***

will expand the command line in the following way:

$ **cat pro**d prog1 project_information

If we do not want the contents of all the files displayed, the command line must be edited (see chapter 4.5). Editing of the command line is initiated by pressing <esc>. The h is then used to move the cursor to the left and l to move it to the right. To delete a character, the cursor is placed on the character before pressing the x key.

To gain access to automatic filename completion as described above, enter the command

$ **set -o vi**

The mechanism can be switched off by the command

$ **set +o vi**

3.4.5 More on filenames in the C shell and the TC shell

In the C shell and the TC shell, the ~ sign (tilde) has a special meaning when you specify the name of a directory. If you key ~ by itself, it denotes the name of your own home directory. So, to look at the contents of the file info in your home directory, irrespective of what the current directory is, you can key in the command

% **cat ~/info**

The tilde can also be combined with a user ID. For example, you can type ~sarah for the name of Sarah's home directory (if she has been given sarah as her user ID). To print out on screen the file project_info in Sarah's home directory, we can enter

% **~sarah/project_info**

You can decide for yourself whether filename patterns (also known as 'global filenames') are acceptable or not. This is governed by a 'variable' called noglob. As a rule, filename patterns are permissible from the start, but should this not be the case you can enter the command

% **unset noglob**

which will enable the use of filename patterns. To exclude the use of filename patterns, enter the command

% **set noglob**

In later versions of the C shell there is a mechanism relieving the user of the need to key filenames in full. You can get away with keying the start of the name and then pressing the <esc> key. (This mechanism also exists in the TC shell, although the <tab> key is normally used instead of <esc>.) The shell will then complete the rest of the name for itself. If we have a file called project_information in the current directory, for example, we can key the command

% **cat proj<esc>**

If there is no other file with a name beginning in proj, the shell will automatically complete the name:

% **cat proj**ect_information

Suppose the current directory also contains the files prog1 and prod. Now, if we enter the command

% **cat pro<esc>**

there will be three files matching the unfinished filename. In this case, the shell will be unable to complete the name, and instead generates a beep at the terminal. We can then add one or more characters to the name so that it becomes unique.

There is also a facility to see all the files with names starting in a particular manner while a command is actually being entered. For this, <ctrl-d> is keyed instead of <esc>. The command

% **cat pro<ctrl-d>**

for example, will result in the output

```
prod/ prog1 project_information
% cat pro
```

and we can then carry on finishing the command we have started on. (the / sign after prod indicates that the file is a directory.)

To be able to access the filename completion mechanism, enter the command

% **set filec**

The mechanism can be switched off by

% **unset filec**

(This is not necessary in the TC shell.)

3.5 Operations on the file system

There are a number of programs which make it possible to create files, copy files, and move files from one place in the file system to another. There are also programs to create and delete directories. Other types of program allow for modification of the owners, group allocations and access permissions listed for files.

3.5.1 Current directory

As mentioned above, the directory the user is working in at any given time is known as the current directory. With the help of the program pwd, the full pathname of the current directory can be displayed.

    $ **pwd**
    /u/mike

There is a simplified way of entering the name of the current directory. Simply key a full stop.

    $ **cat ./temp**

thus means the same as

    $ **cat temp**

3.5.2 Moving around the tree with cd

Using the program cd, you can climb around in the branches of the tree. Suppose that the file tree looks like figure 3.6, which we saw earlier. The current directory is /u/mike and you want to move to the directory /u.

    $ **cd /u**

The current directory will be changed and we will have the situation shown in figure 3.7.

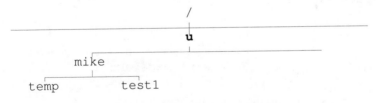

Figure 3.7

However, you can also move relative to the current directory. We could equally well have typed the command above as

    $ **cd ..**

This is because a double full stop is used in UNIX as a simplified way of entering the 'parent directory' of the current directory.

You can get back to the sub-directory `mike` with the command

$ **cd mike**

or by keying the full pathname

$ **cd /u/mike**

The simplest way of getting back to your home directory is by entering the command

$ **cd**

without any argument. If there is no argument it is always assumed that you mean your home directory.

3.5.3 Displaying access permissions with `ls`

All files have three categories of access permissions. A report on access permissions can be obtained by keying the command:

$ **ls -l**

or

$ **ls -al**

The option `-l` means, as we have seen, that full information is displayed. If we add `-a`, files whose names begin with '.' (full stop) will be included.

```
$ ls -al
total 9
drwxr-xr-x   2 doc        32 Sep 18 06:41 .
drwxr-xr-x   3 doc       528 Sep 18 06:41 ..
-rw-r--r--   1 mike      146 Sep 17 09:53 temp
-rw-r--r--   1 mike     2144 Sep 17 09:10 test1
```

Each line begins with a group of ten characters. This group in fact consists of three sets of three characters plus an extra character indicating the file type:

```
drwxrwxrwx
|                    File type
 | | |               Access permissions for file owner
    | | |            Access permissions for user group
       | | |         Access permissions for other users
```

The most common file types are listed in table 3.1.

File types	
–	plain file
d	directory file
c	special file (hardware communicating by characters)
b	special file (hardware communicating by blocks)
l	symbolic link to file located elsewhere

Table 3.1

The most common symbols for access permissions are given in table 3.2

Access permissions for files	
–	no access permission
r	file may be read
w	file may be written to
x	file may be executed (run)

Table 3.2

When examined, the full information for the file `temp`
```
-rw-r--r--   1 mike        146 Sep 17 09:53 temp
```
begins with the access permissions:

–	plain file,
r	file owner can read file,
w	file owner can write to file,
–	file owner cannot execute (run) file,
r	group can read file,
–	group cannot write to file,
–	group cannot execute file,
r	all other users can read file,
–	other users cannot write to file,
–	other users cannot execute file.

The rest of the line tells you the following:

1	file has only one link,
mike	file owner,
146	number of characters in file,
Sep	month,
17	date in month and
09:53	time when file was last modified,
temp	name of file

3.5.4 Modifying access permissions using chmod

Access permissions to files can be modified using the program chmod (change mode). The program requires the access permissions and the filename to be specified. The access permissions can be given absolutely or symbolically.

$ **chmod** *access_permissions file*

When access permissions are given in absolute form, an octal pattern is used. Each of the columns of figures in table 3.3 is added up.

Octal values for access permissions	
400	file may be read by owner
200	file may written to by owner
100	file may be executed (run) by owner
040	file may be read by group
020	file may written to by group
010	file may be executed (run) by group
004	file may be read by all users
002	file may written to by all users
001	file may be executed (run) by all users

Table 3.3

If, for example, we want to amend the access permissions for the file temp to give read and write permissions to the group and all other users, we would enter the following command:

```
$ chmod 666 temp
$ ls -l temp
-rw-rw-rw-    1 mike      146 Sep 17 09:53 temp
```

The symbolic method of changing the access permissions is based on the three categories of user:

```
u    owner,
g    group,
o    others,
a    all in above categories;
```

the following operations:

```
+    add access permissions,
-    cancel access permissions,
=    absolute allocation of access permissions;
```

and the access permission symbols:

```
r    read,
w    write,
x    execute (run).
```

As an example:

```
$ chmod a=rw temp
$ ls -l temp
-rw-rw-rw-    1 mike      146 Sep 17 09:53 temp
```

The following command adds execution permissions for the owner of the file temp:

```
$ chmod u+x temp
$ ls -l temp
-rwxrw-rw-    1 mike      146 Sep 17 09:53 temp
```

This command cancels execution permissions for the owner of temp:

```
$ chmod u-x temp
$ ls -l temp
-rw-rw-rw-    1 mike      146 Sep 17 09:53 temp
```

The chmod program can be used to amend access permissions for both plain and directory files.

3.5.5 Creating sub-directories with mkdir

The program mkdir is used to create new sub-directories.

Suppose the current directory is /u/mike. We can now create a sub-directory called manual by keying in the following command:

```
$ mkdir manual
```

You can check that the directory has been created by requesting a list of the files in the current directory. For this, you can use the program ls. As we saw earlier, the option -l means that we want the full information on the files:

```
$ ls -al
total 7
drwxr-xr-x    2 mike       32 Sep 18 00:54 manual
-rw-r--r--    1 mike      146 Sep 17 09:53 temp
-rw-r--r--    1 mike     2144 Sep 17 09:10 test1
```

If the first character in the line giving the information for a particular file is a d, the file is a directory. (In this example, therefore, manual is a directory file.) The overall arrangement is illustrated in figure 3.8.

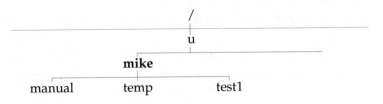

Figure 3.8

3.5.6 Removing sub-directories using `rmdir`

Sub-directories can be removed from the file system using the program `rmdir`.

The sub-directory `manual` can be removed by keying the command:

$ **rmdir manual**

The current directory cannot be removed. This would be the same as sawing off the branch you are sitting on.

3.5.7 Removing plain files using `rm`

Using the program `rm`, it is possible to remove plain files. Suppose the situation is as shown in figure 3.8. The files `temp` and `test1` can be removed from the file system by the command:

$ **rm temp test1**

It should be pointed out that the `rm` program used with a * will wipe *all* the files in a directory.

If we want to remove both the plain files and the sub-directory we can use the command:

$ **rm -r manual temp test1**

3.5.8 Changing filenames or moving files using `mv`

Files can be moved from one directory to another by using the program `mv`:

$ **mv** *filename directory*

Suppose the file `/u/mike/temp` is to be moved to the directory `/u`:

$ **mv /u/mike/temp /u**

More than one file can be moved at the same time:

$ **mv /u/mike/temp /u/mike/test1 /u**

Here, both files -`/u/mike/temp` and `/u/mike/test1`—are copied to the directory `/u`. A group of files can also be moved by using a filename pattern. For example, all the files with names ending in `.c` can be moved from the current directory to the directory `/u` by means of the command

$ **mv *.c /u**

We can change the name of a file in the current directory very easily by using `mv`:

$ **mv** *old_name new_name*

The command can also be used to change the name of a directory.

3.5.9 Copying files with `cp`

A file can be copied using the program `cp`. The following command

```
$ cp file1 file2
```

copies the contents of `file1` to the file `file2`.

One or more files can be copied into another directory at the same time with the command

```
$ cp file1 file2 /tmp
```

The copies are given the same names as the original files in the source directory (`/tmp/file1` and `/tmp/file2`). In a similar way, all files containing C programs can be copied to the directory `clib` using a special character:

```
$ cp *.c clib
```

3.5.10 Creating links to files using `ln`

When the `cp` program is used, and exact copy of the original file is created. For example, if we have a file called `file1` and enter the command

```
$ cp file1 file2
```

there will afterwards be two files, `file1` and `file2`, identical in content but with different names.

Instead of creating several copies containing exactly the same information, we can create what are known as *link*. Creating a link to a file means creating an additional name for an existing file. Any number of links can be created to one and the same file. In other words, we can have any number of names all referring to the same physical file. By means of the command

```
$ ln file2 file3
```

for example, we create a link called `file3` to `file2`.

If two filenames refer to the same file, we can see this by including the option `i` in the `ls` command. This will cause the number of the *i-node* to be displayed. Filenames referring to the same physical file will always have the same i-node number. If we also include the `l` option, we can see how many links, or filenames, there are to each physical file.

```
$ ls -li fil*
total 7
48111 -rw-r--r--    1 linda users    95 May 18 10:21 file1
57519 -rw-r--r--    2 linda users    95 May 20 22:52 file2
57519 -rw-r--r--    2 linda users    95 May 20 22:58 file3
```

Here we see, as expected, that the i-node number (`57519`) is identical for `file2` and `file3`. We can also see that the number of links to `file2` and `file3` is 2.

Links to a file can be created as one of two types: *hard links* and *soft links*. Unless otherwise specified, hard links will be created as in the example above. All hard links to a file are equal in status. In other words, there is nothing special about the first name referring to a file. This means that if we want to remove a physical file with more than one link to it, we need to remove `all` the links to the file. For example, if we were to enter the command

```
$ rm file2
```

the physical file would not be removed. It would remain in place, and could be accessed via the name file3. To get rid of the file itself, we would also need to enter the command

```
$ rm file3
```

There are a few limitations to hard links. Firstly, only the system administrator can set up hard links to directory files. (This affects the structure of the file tree.) Secondly, hard links can only be set up within the same 'physical file system'. (For practical reasons, the file tree is generally constructed from several physical file systems.) An information listing of the physical file systems in the machine can be obtained with the command

```
$ df
/          (/dev/root      ) :    88246 blocks    44391 files
/proc      (/proc          ) :        0 blocks       68 files
/dev/fd    (/dev/fd        ) :        0 blocks        0 files
/stand     (/dev/dsk/0s10  ) :     6264 blocks        0 files
/home      (/dev/dsk/1s10  ) :   451880 blocks    95395 files
```

Each line represents a physical file system.

As we have seen, all hard links are equal in status, and refer *directly* to the physical file (by means of the i-node number). A *symbolic link* (or soft link) can be seen as an *indirect* reference to a file. A symbolic link is a pointer which points to a hard link to the file. So, for files with only one hard link, we can say that a symbolic link points to the name of the file. Using symbolic links, links can be created not only within the same physical file system but also between different physical file systems. Symbolic links can also be set up referring to directory files.

To create a symbolic link, give the `ln` command the argument `-s`. To create a symbolic link called `file4` to the `/usr/bin` directory, for example, use the command

```
$ ln -s /usr/bin file4
```

The `ls` program provides information on symbolic links:

```
$ ls -l fil*
```

```
-rw-r--r-- 1 linda users 95 May 18 10:21 file1
-rw-r--r-- 2 linda users 95 May 20 22:52 file2
-rw-r--r-- 2 linda users 95 May 20 22:58 file3
lrwxrwxrwx 1 linda users  8 May 20 23:53 file4 -> /usr/bin
```

The first character on each line gives the file type, as we mentioned above. The character l tells us that file4 is a symbolic link. As well as this, the text file4 -> /usr/bin indicates which file it points to.

If you go to a directory by means of a symbolic link, you cannot return via the link, as the following example shows.

```
$ pwd
/home/linda
$ cd file4
$ cd ..
$ pwd
/usr
```

3.6 The file manager in OpenLook and OpenWindows

The specifications of the OpenLook user interface include the way a *file manager* is to look and work. The file manager is a graphical program which allows the user to look after his or her files in a simple and clear manner. By means of the mouse, and without using any UNIX commands, the user can carry out nearly all the operations on the file system described earlier in this chapter. It is also possible to run application programs in a simple way direct from the file manager. In practice, this means that many OpenLook users can get by for quite a long time without knowing much about UNIX at all.

We will be describing the file manager filemgr supplied with the OpenWindows system. Usually, the file manager will be run automatically as soon as OpenWindows is started up, but if this does not happen it can easily be started by selecting the File Manager option from the workspace menu's sub-menu Programs.

3.6.1 Displaying files

Figure 3.9 shows what the screen might look like when the file manager is started up. Files in the current directory are shown in the main 'pane' of the file manager window. (If the file manager has been started from the workspace menu, the current directory is the user's home directory.) The files are shown as icons of different sorts, depending on the type of file. Text files, for example, are shown as a sheet of paper with one corner folded over, as shown by the file c7.mm in the figure. In the file manager program, directory files are called *folders*, and an example of this is the file called gamla_figurer.

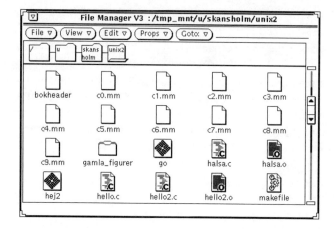

Figure 3.9

Files in the current directory can be shown in a number of ways. Figure 3.9 illustrates the usual, standard way. To change the type of display, we can use the [View ▽] menu button. If we want to see the files as icons we can select either Icon by Name, which sorts the files by name, or Icon by Type, which sorts them so that all the folders are together, all the text files are together, etc.

If there are a large number of files in the directory, it can be useful to show the files as a list instead. In this case we would select one of the options List by Name, List by Type, List by Size or List by Date from the [View ▽] menu. The only difference between these options is the sorting order. The files will then be shown as small icons, of which there are only two types: folders and other files.

If you wish to see more information about the files than the names, you can choose the Customize option from the [View ▽] menu. This allows you to specify what information should be displayed. (You can get the same information as in the UNIX ls command.) You can choose, for example, to have the access permissions and owners displayed for the files. You can also choose whether or not hidden files—files with names starting with a full stop—should be displayed.

3.6.2 Moving around the file tree

It is a simple matter to move around between different directories in the file tree. This can be done two ways. In the file manager window, in the smaller pane beneath the menu buttons, there is a display showing the current directory. Either the path from the root directory to the current directory is shown, or the entire tree structure. The option you prefer can be entered via the [View ▽] menu, where you can choose between Show Path and Show Tree.

The simplest way to change the current directory and move around the tree is to double-click with the left-hand mouse button on the icon for the directory you want. This icon may be either in the larger pane where the files in the current directory are displayed, or in the smaller pane above it showing either the path or the tree structure. This technique therefore allows you to move either upwards or downwards in the file tree.

If the directory you want is not shown, you can use an alternative technique. Enter the name of the directory on the line to the right of the Goto: V menu button, then click on this menu button with the left-hand mouse key. If no directory name has been entered when you click on the Goto: V button, you will find yourself in your own home directory.

There is a third way to display the contents of a directory. Place the mouse pointer on the icon for the directory you want, press the left-hand mouse button and keep it pressed whilst you drag the icon into the workspace, outside the file manager window. Then release the button. The contents of the selected directory will then be shown in a separate window, 'fastened' with a pushpin. The current directory in the file manager window will not be changed.

3.6.3 Changing the name of a file

Click with the left-hand button on the name of the file, which will then be marked. Then enter the new name, using the same editing commands as used to edit the command line in the cmdtool program (see table 2.1 in section 2.5.2).

3.6.4 Creating new directories and files

When you wish to create a new plain file or a new directory, first move to the directory in which you wish to keep the new file. Then select either the Create File option or the Create Folder option from the File V menu, depending on whether the new file is to be a plain file or a directory. The new file will automatically be given the name NewDocument or NewFolder. The name can then be changed using the technique described above.

3.6.5 Moving files

It is simple to move a file from one directory to another. Even entire directories can be moved. Place the mouse pointer on the file you want to move, press the left-hand button, hold the button down, drag the file to the folder representing the directory you want to move the file to and release the button (the 'drag-and-drop' method).

3.6.6 Copying files

Mark the file you want to copy by placing the mouse pointer on it and clicking with the left-hand button. (If you wish to copy several files, place the pointer on each of them and click with the left-hand button each time.) Then press the Copy key on the keyboard. Alternatively, you can call up the file manager's File Pane pop-up menu by pressing the right-hand button and select Copy in that menu. If the file is to be copied within the same directory you can then press the Paste key on the keyboard or select the Paste option in the file manager's pop-up menu. The new file will then have the same name as the old one, but with with .1 added. If the file is to be copied to a different directory, first open this directory and place the pointer in it before pressing Paste.

3.6.7 Removing files

A file can be removed by dragging it to the icon showing a waste paper basket (Waste) using the drag-and-drop technique described above. Alternatively, the file can be marked by clicking with the left-hand button, after which the Cut key on the keyboard can be pressed. In either case, the file will not be 'actually' deleted, but will be moved to the .wastebasket directory in the home directory. This means that you can reclaim files which have been deleted by opening the waste basket (by double-clicking on the icon with the left-hand button) and dragging the file back.

When you want the files in the waste basket to be finally deleted, you can open the waste basket, call up its pop-up menu and select the option Empty Wastebasket using the right-hand button. It is also possible to delete individual files in the waste basket.

If you do not want to use the waste basket, that is, if you want files you have removed with the Cut key to be actually deleted, you can call up the Props ▽ menu in the file manager. There, you should select the File Manager option. In the window which then appears, click in the really delete square against the **Delete** heading.

3.6.8 Changing the access permissions for a file

First specify the file you want by clicking on it with the left-hand mouse button. Then go to the Props ▽ menu and select the default option, File. This will produce a menu with a variety of information on the file you have selected. In the window there are squares in which you can easily enter the read, write and execute permissions which are to be assigned to the file.

3.6.9 Searching for files

You can search for one or more files using the Find option in the File ▽ menu. When this option is selected, a window appears in which the user can indicate the file or files to be searched for and where the search should start. At the top of the window, enter the name of the directory in which the search is to begin. Against the heading **Filename:** enter the name of the file which is the object of the search. Filename patterns can be used here to indicate that more than one file is wanted. For example, if the search is to find all files with names ending in .mm, the entry against the **Filename:** heading can be *.mm. The search is started by clicking on the Find button.

3.6.10 Running programs

Executing programs designed to run under X from the file manager is very easy. It is simply a matter of double-clicking with the left-hand button on the symbol representing the program file in the file manager window. If you move to the /usr/openwin/bin directory, for example, you will find a number of such programs. If you wish to run the xman program, for example, simply find its symbol and double-click on it.

Text files, that is, files containing readable text, constitute a special case. If you double-click on one of these, a text editor will automatically be run. The text editor usually run in OpenWindows is called textedit and will be described later in this book. If you happen to prefer a different text editor, e.g. vi, it is possible to change text editors by means of the File Manager option in the Props ▽ menu.

3.7 Some useful programs for use on files

3.7.1 Find the differences between two files with diff

Using the diff program, we can compare the contents of two files:

```
$ diff file1 file2
```

If the argument consists of the names of plain files, the program will produce a report showing the differences between the files. All the differences in the first file will be marked with a < symbol and all the differences in the second file with a > symbol to the left of the line. If the contents of the two files are identical, the program will produce no text.

3.7.2 Searching for files using find

UNIX's hierarchical directory structure is both powerful and flexible. On the other hand, it can be awfully easy to forget where files, programs and collections of data are being kept. The program find helps you to locate the position of files in the file system.

For example, you can find out the location of the file prog1.c in the file system by using the command:

$ **find . -name prog1.c -print**
./project/cbib1/prog1.c

The arguments to the find program indicate how the search and presentation of the result are to be carried out.

.	start search from current directory and downwards,
-name	search for file with name,
prog1.c	prog1.c,
-print	display result on terminal.

The following command asks for information on all files containing C programs, starting from the current directory. Note that a backslash \ is needed before the asterisk so that the filename will be interpreted as a filename pattern.

$ **find . -name *.c -print**

If you wanted to look for a file using find and started from the root directory, it would be a very time-consuming process. This should be avoided.

In some systems there is an alternative way of using the find program, known as 'fast find'. Here, you can use a simplified call with the form

$ **find** *text*

The program will use a special database to run a quicker search for a file with the string *text* anywhere in its pathname. (The database is updated every so often during system servicing, so it will not record the very latest changes in the file tree.) For example, to see whether, and if so where, the TC shell is held in the file system we can enter a command like

$ **find tcsh**

which will list the names of all files with names containing the string 'tcsh'. Often this will give you an extremely long list of filenames. To avoid this, always try to use a *string* which is as unique as possible.

3.7.3 Reporting the content of a file using file

The program file analyses the contents of a file and attempts to decide what type of file it is. Suppose the file main.c contains a C program and the file a.out contains an executable program:

```
$ file main.c a.out
main.c:      c program text
a.out:       mc86k executable
```

3.7.4 Counting lines, words and characters using wc

The following command counts the number of lines in the file c3.mm and displays the result.

```
$ wc -l c3.mm
218 c3.mm
```

The argument -l stands for 'lines'. If we want to count the number of words, we key instead

```
$ wc -w c3.mm
1504 c3.mm
```

('Words' means anything separated by spaces, tab characters or line endings.) The argument -c correspondingly indicates characters. If no argument is entered before the filename, the number of lines, words and characters will all be counted:

```
$ wc c3.mm
218      1504      9984 c3.mm
```

The program wc can take a list of files as its argument. In that case, the count will be carried out separately for each file. In addition, there will be an overall total at the bottom. The command below displays the number of lines, words and characters for all files with names ending in .mm:

```
wc *.mm
 171       910      7593 c1.mm
 494      2481     16572 c2.mm
 218      1504      9984 c3.mm
 839      3577     28124 c4.mm
 241      1148      9753 c5.mm
1963      9620     72026 total
```

3.7.5 Searching for text strings using grep

Another program you will find useful is grep, which can be used to find all occurrences of a text string in one or more files. The first argument for grep is the text string you want to search for; then follows a list of the names of the files you want to search through. As an example, we will search for all the places where the string 'UNIX' occurs in the file c1.mm:

```
$ grep 'UNIX' c1.mm
```

All lines containing the string 'UNIX' will then be displayed. In its most general form, `grep` allows the string you want to search for to be specified as what is termed a 'regular expression'. In these we can use various special characters which can match different characters (in a corresponding way to the use of wildcards in composing filename patterns). We will not be going into detail on this here. For the moment, however, note that the characters . * [ ] \ ^ and $ are regarded as special characters. If you are not intending to work with regular expressions, therefore, you should avoid including them in the text string you are searching for. The single quotes enclosing the text string in our example are not in fact necessary, but it can be safer to include them, as this will avoid the surprise of the shell program interpreting characters in the text string in some way that had not occurred to you.

There are a few different arguments to `grep` which it can be useful to know of. In the example above we were given a display of the lines including the search string. If we want to know the number of the line as well, we key in

```
$ grep -n 'UNIX' c1.mm
```

The argument `-i` can be used to indicate that small letters and capitals are to be treated as the same thing. The command

```
$ grep -ni 'UNIX' c1.mm
```

for example, will display all lines (with their line numbers) containing any of the strings 'UNIX', 'unix', 'Unix' etc. If you only want to know how many lines contain a certain string, you can use the argument `-c`.

```
$ grep -c 'UNIX' c1.mm
21
```

You can search through a number of files. If you enter the command

```
$ grep 'UNIX' *.mm
```

you will be given all the lines containing the string 'UNIX' in files with names ending in .mm. In front of every line shown, you will also see the name of the file in which the text string has been found. If you only want to know which files contain a certain text string, you can use the argument `-l`.

```
$ grep -l 'UNIX' *.mm
```

3.7.6 Sorting lines using `sort`

The `sort` program reads one or more files, sorts the lines it has read and displays the result on the screen. (The result of the sort can also be written to a file, of course. See, for example, section 4.1, dealing with redirection.) The file or files which are read are not affected, and will be unchanged after the sorting process.

If the only arguments you give the `sort` program are the filenames, the sort will be carried out on a purely alphabetical basis, and the lines will be compared starting at the first character. Alphabetical order in this case is determined by the ASCII codes for the different characters. (This means, among other things, that figures and most special characters are regarded as lower in value than capital letters, which in turn are lower than small letters.) For example, if the file `file1` contains the lines

```
mike1234
Mark24345
freda1990
fred493
 steve1255
```

(note the space at the start of the last line), the command

$ **sort file1**

will produce the result

```
 steve1255
Mark24345
fred493
freda1990
mike1234
```

To treat small letters and capitals as the same, we can enter

$ **sort -f file1**
```
 steve1255
fred493
freda1990
Mark24345
mike1234
```

Now look at the file `file2`, which contains flat numbers, phone numbers and names for a number of people living in the same block (with sub-fields separated by TAB characters).

```
10      1234    mike
-1      2345    mark
8       1990    julie
4       1493    louise
```

If we try to sort:

$ **sort file2**
```
-1      2345    mark
10      1234    mike
4       1493    louise
8       1990    julie
```

If we want the lines in order of flat numbers, we have to use numeric sorting.

```
$ sort -n file2
-1      2345    mark
4       1493    louise
8       1990    julie
10      1234    mike
```

On the other hand, if we want the list sorted into phone number order, we have to indicate that the second subfield of each line is the sort key. The subfields are numbered starting with zero, so the phone number is subfield 1.

```
$ sort +1 -2 file2
10      1234    mike
4       1493    louise
8       1990    julie
-1      2345    mark
```

Here, +1 indicates that the first sort key is field 1 and -2 that the last sort key is the field before field 2 (which is also field 1).

Subfields on a line are not always separated by spaces or tabs. In that case you can use the argument −t to specify the separator. In the file file3, for example, a colon is used to separate the fields:

```
10:1234:mike
-1:2345:mark
8:1990:julie
4:1493:louise
```

If we want to sort by name, we enter

```
$ sort -t: +2 -3 file3
8:1990:julie
4:1493:louise
-1:2345:mark
10:1234:mike
```

and to sort by flat number we have to indicate that field 0 (the first field) is to be sorted numerically:

```
$ sort -t: +0n -1 file3
-1:2345:mark
4:1493:louise
8:1990:julie
10:1234:mike
```

Other facilities are available in the sort program. For further details see the manual.

3.8 Summary

Programs and built-in commands	
pwd	reports current directory
cd [*directory*]	move around tree
ls [-al]	list file information
chmod *access filename*	allocate *access* rights to file
mkdir *director*	create directory
rmdir *director*	remove directory
rm [-r] *filename*	remove files
mv *old_name new_name*	change filename or move files
cp *original_file copy_file*	copy files
ln [-s] *filename new_filename*	create a link to a file
diff *file1 file2*	difference between two files
find *search_criteria*	look for files
file *filename*	report contents of files
wc [-lwc] *filename*	count lines, words, characters
grep [-nicl] *text_string filename*	search for text strings in files
sort [-fn] *filename*	sort files
filemgr &	start File Manager in OpenWindows

Table 3.4

Filename patterns	
*	matches any number of characters, each may be any character
?	matches one character, may be any character
[ ]	matches one character, may be any of those shown in the square brackets

Table 3.5

Four
More about Shells

The shell is the user's principal interface with the UNIX system and the program which is always run when the system is used. Learning how to master the shell is therefore essential for successful and effective use of a UNIX system. In previous chapters, we have learned the basics of how shells are used, how commands are entered etc. In this chapter some further important features of shells are described.

We will see how, with the help of what is known as *redirection*, input and output data can be guided in and out of the program so that it is not always read from the keyboard or written to the screen, but can be read from or written to actual files or be directly sent on to another program.

UNIX is a multi-user system, which means that a number of users can run on the computer at the same time. Each user can also have several activities—known as *processes*,—in operation at the same time. This chapter describes how it works.

When we run a UNIX program we don't always want it to behave in the same way. Sometimes, for example, we want the print-out to be on one printer, and sometimes on another. In this chapter we will see how, by means of *environment variables*, information can be given to UNIX programs and how, by using *shell variables*, we can get the shell to operate in a specific way. In this context, we will also be describing *start-up files*, which can be used to customize the UNIX system to the user's preferences, so that it looks exactly the way you want it every time you log on.

For users of X, a few special start-up files are described, which can be used to customize the X system. The user can for example determine which X windows will automatically appear on the screen every time X is run.

Sometimes we want to repeat an earlier command without having to re-key it, and sometimes we make a mistake and want to correct the previous command and re-run it. Here we can use the *editing* and *history mechanisms* available in the Korn shell, the C shell and the TC shell, which are described in this chapter.

4.1 Redirection

It is a feature of many UNIX programs that they can read input data from what is known as the *standard input* file and write output data to the *standard output* file. Any error messages are often written to a file called *standard error*. Normally, *standard input* is connected to the keyboard and *standard output* and *standard error* to the screen, which means that the program can read and write at the terminal. See figure 4.1.

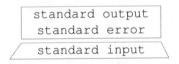

```
standard output
standard error
standard input
```

Figure 4.1

When starting a program which reads files, the names of the files are usually given as arguments on the command line. It is usual for the program to be designed to read from the keyboard if the filename is omitted. The program sort is such a program. It is normally used to sort a specified file, but in its simplest form it will read input data from the *standard input*. This can appear as follows.

```
$ sort
mike
john
linda
anne
<ctrl-d>
anne
john
linda
mike
$
```

The user enters four lines of input data, then indicates that the data from the *standard input* is complete by keying <ctrl-d> at the start of a fresh line. Note that this way of indicating the end of the input data ('end of file') is very common in a UNIX context. (Exactly which character is used to mark the end of the input data can be controlled by the program stty, but the usual character is <ctrl-d>.)

This is illustrated in figure 4.2 by filtering a stream of data from the keyboard through the program sort to be written out on the screen:

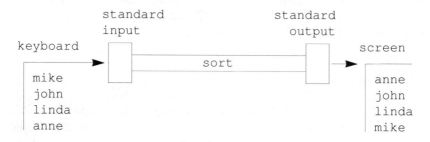

Figure 4.2

A program need not necessarily use both *standard input* and *standard output*. The program who only uses *standard output*. This is shown in figure 4.3.

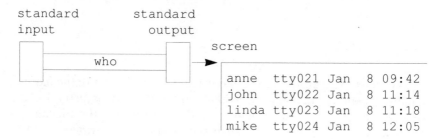

Figure 4.3

4.1.1 Redirection of output data

With the help of the command operator >, output data from a program can be redirected from the screen to be written instead to a file chosen by the user. Data output to the *standard output* can thus be stored directly in a 'proper' file instead of being written to the screen.

The following example shows how output data from the who program can be written to a file called temp:

```
$ who > temp
```

This gives us the situation in figure 4.4.

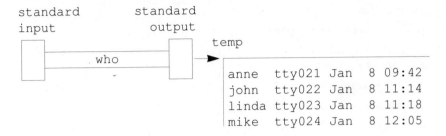

Figure 4.4

Later, the contents of the file `temp` can be written to the screen by using, for example, the program `cat`:

```
$ cat temp
anne   tty021 Jan   8 09:42
john   tty022 Jan   8 11:14
linda  tty023 Jan   8 11:18
mike   tty024 Jan   8 12:05
```

This is shown in figure 4.5.

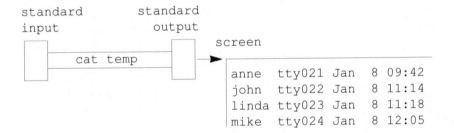

Figure 4.5

In the Korn shell, existing files can be protected against being destroyed by the redirection of output data. The relevant command is:

```
$ set -o noclobber
```

If there is already a file called `temp` and the user now attempts to enter the command

```
$ who > temp
```

the result will be the error message

```
ksh: temp: file already exists
```

Existing files can also be protected against being destroyed by the redirection of output data in the C shell and the TC shell. The relevant command is:

> % **set noclobber**

If there is already a file called `temp` and the user now attempts to enter the command

> % **who > temp**

the result will be the error message

    temp: File exists.

4.1.2 Redirection of output data to the end of an existing file

Output data from a program can be redirected to go on the end of an already existing file by using the command operator **>>**.

The following example shows how output data from the program who can be placed at the end of the already existing file `temp`:

> $ **who >> temp**

This is shown in figure 4.6.

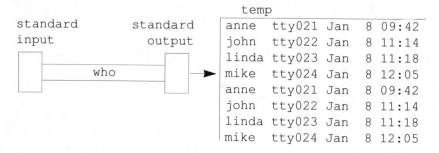

Figure 4.6

4.1.3 Redirection of input data

Input data to a program can be redirected from the keyboard to be read instead from a chosen file. This is done by using the command operator **<**.

The following example shows how the contents of a file `temp` can be redirected to become input data for the `sort` program:

```
$ sort < temp
anne   tty021 Jan  8 09:42
anne   tty021 Jan  8 09:42
john   tty022 Jan  8 11:14
john   tty022 Jan  8 11:14
linda  tty023 Jan  8 11:18
linda  tty023 Jan  8 11:18
mike   tty024 Jan  8 12:05
mike   tty024 Jan  8 12:05
```

This is demonstrated in figure 4.7

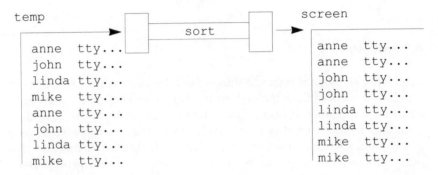

Figure 4.7

4.1.4 Pipelines

Using the command operator |, output data from one program can be redirected to become input data to another program. This is called creating a *pipe*. For example, we can key in the command

```
$ who | sort
anne   tty021     Jan  8 09:42
john   tty022     Jan  8 11:14
linda  tty023     Jan  8 11:18
mike   tty024     Jan  8 12:05
```

This can be illustrated as in figure 4.8.

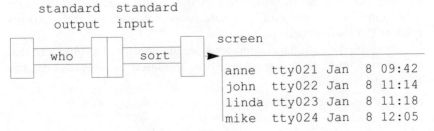

Figure 4.8

As many commands as you like can be linked together by means of the pipeline operator:

```
$ who | sort | grep mike | wc
```

(The programs grep and wc read from the *standard input* in the same way as sort if no input data file is specified in the command.) See figure 4.9.

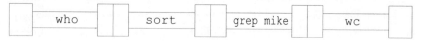

Figure 4.9

4.2 Processes

In a UNIX system a number of things can take place at the same time. A number of users can use the system and each user can have a number of activities happening at once. Each activity is called a *process*. Like files, processes form a tree structure, which means that every process has a *parent process* (except the first one, when UNIX is started up) and that every process can create one or more *child processes*. Every process has a unique *process number*. In each process a specific program is being executed. Only one program at a time can be executed in a process, but within a process we can switch so that first one program, then another is being run.

The shell is a program, and is therefore executed in a process. To find out the number of the process in which the shell is being run, we can enter:

```
$ echo $$
812
```

When a command is given to the shell, e.g.

```
$ man sh > tempfile
```

this results in a new child process being created and the specified program, in this example man, being executed in this new process. (An exception is formed by what are known as built-in commands: see below.) The process in which the shell is being executed *sleeps* until execution of man is finished. The child process then dies and the process holding the shell reawakens.

By using the command operator **&** we can specify in a command that we do not want the process holding the shell to sleep whilst the command is executed:

```
$ man sh > tempfile &
```

The program man is run in a new child process. However, the shell does not sleep, but the system answers directly with the message

    1234

or

    [1] 1234

depending on which shell is being used. The figure 1234 in this example is the process number for the new child process in which the program man is being executed. The shell is then ready to accept new commands immediately. It is usual to say that the program man is running in the *background* and the shell in the *foreground*.

As a further example, we can illustrate the program sleep, which waits a specified number of seconds:

    § **sleep 120 &**

Active processes can be shown on the screen by means of the program ps (process status). The display looks something like this:

    § **ps**
     PID TTY   TIME COMMAND
     812 console   0:02 ksh
    1234 console   0:01 lpr
    1257 console   0:01 sleep
    1281 console   0:02 ps

Each line corresponds to one process, where PID is the process number, TTY reports the terminal line the background process was initiated from, TIME tells you how long the command has been executed for and COMMAND shows the command. For further information refer to the manual page for ps.

The ps program will normally show you only your own processes. If you want a complete list of processes, your own and other users', and you are running System V, you will need to add the argument -e:

    § **ps -e**

In BSD and OSF, use instead the argument -ax:

    § **ps -ax**

to achieve the same thing.

The program kill has the effect you would expect. The argument for the program will be a list of process numbers:

    § **kill 1257**

Sometimes it can be difficult to kill off a process. Try this out by entering kill with the option -9:

    § **kill -9 812**

A special program which normally runs in the background without the need to use the command operator &, is at. The program can be used to carry out one or more commands at a specified time. For example, if you want to set off two long print runs in the middle of the night you can enter:

```
$ at 0300
at> lpr list1
at> lpr list2
<ctrl-d>
```

As shown, the input data for at is a list of the commands that are to be executed at the stated time. The list is terminated with <ctrl-d>. (The program at itself produces the at> prompts.) Another useful program which is available in BSD and OSF is leave, which can be used to set an 'alarm clock' to tell you when it is time to stop work on the computer:

```
$ leave 1700
```

At the programmed time, you will then be given a reminder to finish; if you continue you will get repeated reminders.

It should be pointed out here that certain common commands, e.g. cd, are *built in* as part of the shell. This means that they are executed by the shell itself. If no & is entered for one of these commands, no child process will be created when these commands are run. Which commands are built in varies from one shell to another. As a rule, it makes no difference to the user whether a command is built in or not. It looks exactly the same when they run.

It is possible to terminate the shell and pass its processes to another program. To do this, the command exec is used. For example, if we are in the Bourne shell we can enter:

```
$ exec csh
%
```

What happens in this example is that the Bourne shell is terminated and does not restart. The process is taken over by the C shell. If, instead, we keyed:

```
$ exec who
```

the process would die after the program who had finished running. The program login, for example, functions in the same way. Once a user has logged on and login has done its job, it passes the process to the shell which is going to be run.

In the Korn shell, the C shell and the TC shell there are, in addition to process numbers, identifiers called *job numbers*. A list of the background processes can be obtained by means of the command jobs:

```
$ jobs
[1]   - Running     lpr c4.mm
[2]   + Running     sleep 120
$
```

Alternatively, the *job number* can be used to remove a background process:

```
$ kill %1
[1]      Terminated lpr c4.mm
$
```

There must always be a percent sign in front of the job number in a command.

A program being executed in the foreground can be stopped temporarily by keying <ctrl-z> at the terminal. This returns the user to the shell, where any command can be entered. For example, if you are in a text editor, you can sometimes want to break off editing for a while to go out to the shell. For this, you can key <ctrl-z> while you are in the editor. Once you are out in the shell, you can then enter the command jobs to see what jobs are running:

```
$ jobs
[1]  + Stopped     vi c4.mm
$
```

(Here we are assuming you are using the vi text editor.)

To take another example: you may have started the compilation of a program and decided to run other commands while the compilation is in progress. You can key <ctrl-z> so that the compiler temporarily stops. A stopped job can be resumed either in the foreground or in the background. The command fg causes a job to be executed in the foreground:

```
$ fg %1
```

and the command bg causes it to take place in the background:

```
$ bg %1
```

4.3 The environment

Every UNIX process runs in a specific *environment*. An environment consists of a table of *environment variables*, each with an assigned value. Note that each process has its own table. Environment variables have unique names, which are conventionally written in capitals. Examples of environment variables are TERM and HOME. The value of an environment variable is a text string. TERM, for example, may have the value vt100.

When the program login is run, which happens every time you log on, this program will initialize the table holding the environment variables for its process. Then, when login passes the process to the shell, the table will be accessible to the shell.

When a process starts up a child process, such as when you start up another program from the shell, the new process will be given a copy of the parent process's table. The newly started program can read the values in the environment table and in certain cases change values of variables and add or remove variables. A text editor, for example, can read the environment variable TERM to find out what type of terminal the user is working at. It can then make sure it is displaying the right number of lines etc. on the screen.

Remember, though, that a process can only change its own table of environment variables. For example, if a new terminal window is set up in X with the command

$ **xterm &**

a new process is created. The table of environment variables for the new process will start off as a copy of the parent process's table, but if changes are made to the environment variables in any of the terminal windows these changes will not affect the other terminal window.

The environment variables with which login initializes the table include LOGNAME, HOME, SHELL, TERM and PATH. The environment variable LOGNAME will hold the user's login name (e.g. mike). In BSD UNIX there is an environment variable called USER instead of LOGNAME.

HOME contains the name of the user's home directory (e.g. /u/mike), and SHELL the name of the shell the user wishes to use (most often /bin/sh or /bin/csh). login takes the information it needs to initialize HOME and SHELL from the file /etc/passwd, which is managed by the system administrator. The environment variable TERM will hold the name of the type of terminal being used (e.g. vt100 or xterm).

When a command is entered, e.g.

$ **xyz**

this means, as we have seen, that a program called xyz is to be run. To be able to start up this program, the shell must find it somewhere in the file tree. The environment variable PATH is used to give information to the shell about where in the file tree it should look for the program the user wants to run. The value of PATH is a list of the full pathnames of all the directories which are to be looked through. To separate the different directory names in the list, a colon is used before each directory name. Unless otherwise specified, login will initialize PATH to the value :/bin:/usr/bin (or something similar). This means that a search for the program that has been asked for will be carried out in the directories /bin and /usr/bin. (The search will be carried out in the order the directories are listed in PATH).

Built-in commands, as we have seen, are executed by the shell itself, so it does not have to search in the file tree for these.

You can get a list of all your environment variables and their values by entering the command

$ **env**

In the next section, which deals with *shell variables*, we will explain how environment variables and shell variables are related to each other and how individual environment variables can be read and altered.

4.4   Shell variables

The shell maintains a set of internal variables, known as *shell variables*. These variables are used to cause the shell to work in a particular way. An example might be that the shell is required to use a prompt identifying which computer it is being run on. Every shell variable has a unique name, and the value of a variable usually consists of a text string. In the Bourne shell and the Korn shell, the name of the variable is usually given in capitals, whilst the C shell and the TC shell use small letters. Shell variables are variables kept internally by the shell for its own use, and their values cannot be accessed by any other program. There are a number of predefined shell variables and it is also possible for the user to define variables of his or her own.

Shell variables are handled a little differently in different shells. In addition, they are linked to the environment variables in different ways. For this reason, we will for the most part be dealing separately with each of the two families of shells—the Bourne/Korn shell and the C/TC shell.

We go about discovering the values of shell variables, however, in the same way in all the different shells. We will therefore be describing this first.

4.4.1   How to find out the values of variables

The command set without any argument can be used to obtain a display of all the shell variables.

    $ **set**

It is also possible to check the value of each shell variable individually. The following example assumes that we have defined a shell variable computer which has the value sun and a shell variable priority with the value medium. (How this is done is described in the next section.)

The value of a variable is obtained by keying a dollar sign in front of the variable's name. The expression $computer thus has the value sun and the expression $priority has the value medium. This can be demonstrated with the command echo, which simply echoes its argument when it is called.

    $ **echo $computer**
    sun
    $ **echo computer**
    $computer

Note the difference between keying a dollar symbol and not keying one. If you want to join together a variable value and some other text without a space between, you can enclose the name of the variable in braces:

```
$ echo ${computer}4
sun4
```

If a dollar sign appears in a text enclosed in single quotation marks, or if the dollar sign is immediately preceded by a \ character, it will be treated as a normal character:

```
$ echo '$computer $priority'
$computer $priority
$ echo \$computer
$computer
```

However, if the text is enclosed in double quotation marks the value of the variable will be substituted:

```
$ echo "$computer $priority"
sun medium
```

4.4.2   Shell variables in the Bourne shell and the Korn shell

To define your own shell variables in the Bourne shell and the Korn shell, follow the example below:

```
$ priority=medium
```

Here a variable with the name `priority` is defined and given the value `medium`. (Note that there must not be any spaces next to the equals sign.) If you want the value of a variable to include spaces, it will need to enclosed in single quotes:

```
$ computer='IBM PC'
```

The value of a variable can be altered at any time simply by issuing a new value:

```
$ computer=sun
```

In the Bourne shell and the Korn shell, a variable can be protected against being changed by entering the command `readonly`:

```
$ readonly computer
```

There are a few variables which are pre-defined and which are used to give information to the shell itself. Two of these are `PS1` and `PS2`. The variable `PS1` has as its value the prompt used by the Bourne shell or the Korn shell: the default value is a dollar sign followed by a space. You can give the prompt any value you like, for example two plus signs:

```
$ PS1="++ "
++
```

or the name of a computer:

```
$ PS1="computer1: "
computer1:
```

If a command line is entered which the shell considers to be incomplete (the line might contain an unfinished text string, for instance) the shell will display a special continuation prompt indicating that the user is invited to finish the command. The way this prompt will look is given by the variable PS2. The default value is a > sign followed by a space.

Another pre-defined variable in the Bourne shell and the Korn shell is the one called ?—that is, a question mark. This contains the return code from the last command to be executed. A command which has terminated normally will give the value zero, but a different return code is given if the command has not terminated normally. To find out the value of the variable, a dollar sign is entered in front of the name, as before:

```
$ echo $?
0
```

So how are shell variables and environment variables related to each other? When the Bourne shell or the Korn shell is started up, the shell reads the information in the table of environment variables and defines itself a shell variable for every environment variable. The shell variables will have the same names as the corresponding environment variables, and the values of the environment variables will be copied to the shell variables. This means that the shell will have shell variables called LOGNAME, TERM, HOME and PATH, among others. (In BSD UNIX there is a variable called USER instead of LOGNAME.) It is these local shell variables that the shell refers to afterwards for its own use. For example, when you enter the command cd without parameters, you will find yourself in the directory given in the shell variable HOME:

```
$ cd
$ pwd
/u/hilary
```

and when a command has been issued it will be the list of directories held in the shell variable PATH that will determine where the Bourne shell or the Korn shell looks for the desired program. Needless to say, the value of the variable PATH can be altered. For example, if PATH was given the value /bin:/usr/bin when the shell was started up and we also want the search to include the directory /etc/bin, we can enter the command:

```
$ PATH=$PATH:/etc/bin
```

The variable PATH will now have the value /bin:/usr/bin:/etc/bin, as $PATH denotes the old value and /etc/bin has been added to the end.

When the Bourne shell or the Korn shell calls another program, the program that is called will have the same environment as the shell itself had when it was started up. The shell variables are local and cannot be accessed from any other program. This means that none of the changes or additions that have been made to the local shell variables will have any effect on the environment given to the program that has been called. To change its environment we need to issue a special command, `export`, which indicates that the value of a specified variable is to be exported to the corresponding environment variable. If, for example, we want to change printers before using the `lp` program in System V to obtain a printout, we can do the following:

```
$ LPDEST=Printer2
$ export LPDEST
$ lp article
```

In BSD or OSF we would key instead:

```
$ PRINTER=Printer2
$ export PRINTER
$ lpr article
```

If the command `export` had not been, the printing would have been done on the old printer. Note that the `export` command must be entered for every variable that is to be exported. If you also want the programs called to be aware of changes to the variable `PATH`, for example, you need to enter the command

```
$ export PATH
```

There are a large number of predefined variables used to provide information to the Bourne shell and the Korn shell. Some examples of these shell variables are shown in table 4.1.

Some common shell variables in the Bourne/Korn shell	
PS1	defines what prompt looks like
HOME	defines home directory
PATH	defines shell's search paths
SHELL	name of file containing executable code for shell

Table 4.1

The shell's prompt, for example, can be changed by means of the command

```
$ PS1="computer1> "
computer1>
```

Shell variables can be removed using the command `unset`:

```
$ unset PS1
```

In the Korn shell, the values of the variables are not limited to being single text strings, as described above. The value can also be a list of any length, with each individual element in the list being a text string. To give the variable a value made up of a list of this sort, we use the built-in shell command `set` and the option `-A` (for 'array') as in the following example:

```
$ set -A names david sarah hilary
$ echo ${names[*]}
david sarah hilary
```

Individual elements can be pulled from the list by means of indexing:

```
$ echo ${names[0]}
david
$ echo ${names[1]}
sarah
$ echo ${names[2]}
hilary
```

Note that the first element in all lists is numbered as 0 and the last element in the above example is numbered 2.

When defining a list, you can also find out how long the list is using the following command:

```
$ echo ${#names[*]}
3
```

As well as the usual shell variables, the Korn shell includes a number of *flags*. All we are interested in with regard to these is whether they have been set or not. A few examples of these flags are shown in Table 4.2.

A few common Korn shell flags	
`vi`	initiates command line editing using the built-in text editor `vi`
`ignoreeof`	if this flag is set the shell cannot be terminated by (accidentally) entering `<ctrl-d>` (eof=end of file): it must be terminated using `exit`
`noclobber`	indicates whether existing files are prevented from being destroyed by the redirection of output data
`noglob`	indicates whether filename patterns are illegal

Table 4.2

To set the flag `vi`, for example, you type

```
$ set -o vi
```

and to unset the same flag, you type

```
$ set +o vi
```

(Flags are described in detail in chapter 4.5.1.)

4.4.3   Shell variables in the C shell and the TC shell

In the C shell and the TC shell, use the command `set` to define your own shell variables. For example, to define a variable with the name `priority` and the value `medium` you will need to enter

    % **set priority=medium**

A variable's value can include spaces, but then the value must be enclosed in single quotation marks:

    % **set computer='IBM PC'**

The `set` command can also be used to allocate a new value to a variable which is already defined:

    % **set computer=sun**

The values of the shell variables are mostly ordinary text strings, as shown above. (Numeric variables are described in chapter 7.) In the C shell and the TC shell the value of a shell variable can also be a list of any length, where the elements in the list are text strings. If the value of a shell variable is to be a list, brackets are used as in the following example:

    % **set names=(david sarah hilary)**
    % **echo $names**
    david sarah hilary

Individual elements can be pulled from the list by means of indexing:

    % **echo $names[1]**
    david
    % **echo $names[2]**
    sarah
    % **echo $names[3]**
    hilary

Note that the first element in any list will be given the number 1 and that the last element in the list above is number 3. It is also possible to produce a partial list:

    % **echo $names[2-3]**
    sarah hilary

When a list is defined, a variable giving the length of the list is also automatically defined. The name of this variable is the same as the name of the list, but with an extra # character first. In our example, this means that we will have a variable called #names. The value of the variable can be obtained in the usual way, with a dollar sign at the beginning:

    % **echo $#names**
    3

We can see the last person on the list, for example, by means of the command:

```
% echo $names[$#names]
hilary
```

There are a large number of predefined variables which are used to pass information to the C shell and the TC shell. These can be divided into two categories: variables whose values are of interest and those whose values are not. In the latter case, all we are interested in knowing is whether or not they have been set.

Some examples of shell variables in the first category are shown in table 4.3.

Some common C shell and TC shell variables	
prompt	indicates what the prompt is to look like
home	specifies the home directory
path	specifies search paths for shell
shell	name of file containing executable code for the shell.
cwd	name of current directory

Table 4.3

The prompt can be changed, for example, with the command

```
% set prompt="computer1> "
computer1>
```

Table 4.4. shows some examples of *flag*, that is, variables in the second category, where we are only interested in knowing whether or not the variables are set.

Some common C shell and TC shell flags	
filec	indicates whether completion of filename using <escape> key is allowed.
ignoreeof	if this is set it is impossible to terminate the shell by (accidentally) keying <ctrl-d> (eof = end of file): it must be done by exit
noclobber	indicates whether existing files are prevented from being destroyed by the redirection of output data
noglob	indicates whether filename patterns (global filenames) are allowed.

Table 4.4

To set the variable `ignoreeof`, for example, the command is

% **set ignoreeof**

Shell variables can be removed using the command `unset`:

% **unset ignoreeof**

Note that shell variables and environment variables are not the same thing. Shell variables are only known internally to the shell itself, while environment variables are accessible from all UNIX programs and are used to provide global information. In the C shell and the TC shell it is possible to read off the values of the environment variables directly in the same way as for the shell variables by keying a dollar sign in front of the name of the environment variable:

% **echo $LOGNAME**
hilary
% **echo $PATH**
/bin:/usr/bin

To see what environment variables there are and what values they have, we can enter the command

% **env**

We can also change the value of an environment variable or add new environment variables. To set the default printer to 'printer3' in System V, for example, we can key in the command

% **setenv LPDEST printer3**

In BSD and OSF the default printer is given by the environment variable PRINTER. Here we key instead

% **setenv PRINTER printer3**

Note that there should not be an equal sign in the `setenv` command. In addition, if no other argument to `setenv` is given, the value of the environment variable will be a blank text. The environment variables LOGNAME, TERM, HOME and PATH should not be altered. If this should be necessary, the corresponding shell variables should be changed instead. (See below.)

It is also possible to remove an environment variable completely:

% **unsetenv MINVAR**

We have seen that there are predefined environment variables called LOGNAME, TERM, HOME and PATH. In the C shell and the TC shell there are four important predefined shell variables which have not been described earlier. These are `user`, `term`, `home` and `path`. When the shell is started up, these are automatically initialized to contain the same values as the corresponding environment variables. If a change is made to one of these four shell variables, the corresponding environment variable will also be changed.

The shell variable `path` differs from the corresponding environment variable `PATH` in that it is defined as a list. We can have, for example

```
% echo $path
. /bin /usr/bin /u/hilary/bin
```

In the C shell and the TC shell we can add a new directory at the end of the search path by altering `path`. As the value of the variable is a list, we must set up a new list consisting of the old list followed by the name of the new directory. Suppose we want to add the directory `/usr/etc`. In that case we enter:

```
% set path=($path /usr/etc)
```

Note that the automatic link to the corresponding environment variable only exists for the four shell variables `user`, `term`, `home` and `path`. All other shell variables are completely local and do not affect the environment. This means that the shell variables are not accessible from any program other than the shell itself.

If we want to change the environment for other programs that are to be called, and it is not one of these four variables that is involved, we therefore need to alter the environment variable directly using the command `setenv` described above.

4.5 Editing and history mechanisms

Sometimes we wish to amend a long command we are in the process of entering to the computer, without re-keying the whole of the command. We may also want to repeat and perhaps modify a command we have entered earlier. Here, we can use the editing and history mechanisms provided in the Korn shell, the C shell and the TC shell.

4.5.1 Editing and history mechanisms in the Korn shell

In the Korn shell there are two separate mechanisms that can be used in this context: the built-in editor and the `fc` command. The built-in editor uses more or less the same commands as the `vi` text editor described in chapter 6. (In some systems there may also be a built-in editor using commands taken from the `emacs` text editor.)

To enable the user to repeat and perhaps edit earlier commands, the Korn shell must remember a number of old commands. If nothing specific is entered, the last 128 commands given will automatically be stored. To get the Korn shell to remember a different number of commands, the shell variable `HISTSIZE` can be assigned a positive integer number n. We can key, for example

```
$ HISTSIZE=256
```

All commands that are given will be stored by default in a file called
`.sh_history` in the user's home directory. (If you want the history list
to be stored in a different file, you can define this by means of the
environment variable `histfile`.)

4.5.1.1   *The built-in editor*

Before you can edit commands using the built-in, `vi`-like editor, the
editing mechanism must be initialized. This can be done with the
following command:

    $ **set -o vi**

To avoid having to input this command manually every time you
log in to the system, it should be included in the shell's set-up file.
Alternatively, the environment variable `VISUAL` or `EDITOR` can be given
the value `vi`.

    $ **VISUAL=vi**
    $ **export VISUAL**

(If both environment variables have been given values, VISUAL takes
priority over EDITOR.)

Once the built-in editor has been switched on, the Korn shell will be
in either *command mode* or *input mode*. Initially, it will be in input mode.
In this mode, the shell behaves exactly as usual, and commands can be
entered just as described earlier in this book. For example, the 'erase'
and 'kill' keys can be used to delete the last character entered or the
whole line.

To be able to do more advanced editing and access old commands
using the built-in editor, we must switch to command mode. We do this
by pressing the <esc> key. This gives access to a host of interesting
commands. Using the h and l keys, we can move around on the
command line to the point or points where we need to amend, then
make additions or erase or alter what is there. A number of commands,
such as the command a, which is used to insert text after the cursor,
result in a return to input mode. If we wish to do further editing after
inserting text, we have to press the <esc> key again. Once all the
editing is complete, pressing the <return> key executes the command.
This is the same whether it is keyed from input mode or command
mode.

Table 4.5 provides a summary of the commonest editing commands
in the built-in editor. (In this table, the term 'plain word' means a word
containing only the characters a-z, and the term 'word' means a
sequence of characters separated by spaces.)

Editing commands in the Korn shell	
`<esc>`	switch to command mode
`<space>`	move cursor one character to the right
`l`	
`h`	move cursor one character to the left
`^`	move cursor to start of line
`0`	
`$`	move cursor to end of line
`w`	move cursor one plain word to the right
`W`	move cursor one word to the right
`b`	move cursor back one plain word (to the left)
`B`	move cursor back one word (to the left)
`a`	enter ('add') text to right of cursor
`A`	enter ('add') text at end of line
`i`	enter ('insert') text to left of cursor
`I`	enter ('insert') text at start of line
`x`	delete character at cursor
`dw`	delete plain word
`dW`	delete word
`D`	delete rest of line
`dd`	delete entire line
`r`	amend character at cursor to new character
`cw`	amend ('change') one plain word
`cW`	amend ('change') one word
`C`	amend ('change') rest of line
`cc`	amend ('change') entire line
`u`	undo last editing command
`U`	undo all edits to line
`<return>`	execute command

Table 4.5

The built-in editor can also be used when you want to scroll back through the history list and pull out an old command. To do this, you must first press the `<esc>` key to switch the shell into command mode. After this you can use the commands shown in Table 4.6 to scroll through the history list. For example, you can scroll backwards or forwards through the history list using the – and + keys or search for the last command containing a specified text. If you want to find the latest command including the string `cc`, for example, you can enter the command

    $ **/cc**

Scrolling commands in the Korn shell	
k −	scroll back through history list
j +	scroll forward through history list
/*xxx*	search backwards for text string *xxx*
?*xxx*	search forwards for text string *xxx*
/	repeat previous search backwards
?	repeat previous search forwards
*n*G	go to command No. *n*

Table 4.6

When you have found the command you are looking for you have two possibilities. If you want to repeat the command as it stands, simply press <return>. If you want to make some changes to the command before it is sent to the shell for execution, you can use the editing commands shown in Table 4.5 above.

We have not shown all the commands in the built-in editor. In chapter 6 there is a detailed description of the vi text editor, and most of the commands described there are also available in the Korn shell's built-in editor.

4.5.1.2   *The* fc *command*

The fc (fetch commands) command can be used on the one hand to get a list of old commands and on the other to pull out an old command and execute it again. In the latter case, there is also a facility to edit the old command. Editing can be carried out either directly using the fc command or with the aid of any text editor.

The command fc -l will produce a list of the last 16 commands given:

```
$ fc -l
6      date
7      cal 1993
8      xterm &
9      clock &
10     uptime
11     ruptime
12     rwho
13     cd ub
14     ls
15     lpstat -t
16     lp -dpsl -otroff c4.mm
17     clear
```

```
18     set -o vi
19     VISUAL=/usr/bin/vi
20     export VISUAL
21     fc -l
```

An alternative is the command `history`, which is an alias (another name) for the `fc -l` command.

$ **history**

The general form of the command to list selected sections of the history file is

fc -l *first*

or

fc -l *first last*

If, for example, you want to list all the commands in the history file starting from No. 18, you can enter:

```
$ fc -l 18
18     set -o vi
19     VISUAL=/usr/bin/vi
20     export VISUAL
21     fc -l
22     fc -l 18
```

Instead of referring to commands by the numbering, they can be located with their program names, e.g.:

```
$ fc set export
18     set -o vi
19     VISUAL=/usr/bin/vi
20     export VISUAL
```

or by 'just enough' characters to identify each program name:

```
$ fc se ex
18     set -o vi
19     VISUAL=/usr/bin/vi
20     export VISUAL
```

We will now demonstrate a number of different ways to repeat an old command. The following command, for example, repeats the previous command:

$ **fc -e -**

Alternatively, the command `r` can be used in place of `fc -e -`.

$ **r**

As another example, this command repeats the last command starting with the characters `cc`:

$ **fc -e - cc**

or

    $ **r cc**

This can be a handy way of repeating the last compilation of a C program. (More on this in chapter 8.)

When an earlier command is repeated, it is also possible to make changes. For example, if we enter

    $ **r ex1=prog2 cc**

the last command containing the text string cc will be executed again, but with the text prog2 replacing ex1. To repeat the last command with an alteration, the final argument is omitted, as in the following example:

    $ **r pront=print**

In its most general form, fc allows a text editor to be given as an argument. The specified text editor will be called to edit the selected command, and when the text editor is terminated the selected command will be executed. For example, the command

    $ **fc -e emacs**

will call the emacs text editor to edit the previous command. The name of the text editor can be given in the environment variable FCEDIT, in which case the name of the text editor to be used need not be entered in the fc command. If we have previously entered

    $ **FCEDIT=/usr/pd/emacs**
    $ **export FCEDIT**

for example, and enter the command

    $ **fc 18 20**

emacs will be called to edit commands 18 to 20. (All of this is on the assumption that emacs is installed at the location given.) In these circumstances, all we need to enter to use emacs to edit the last command containing the text cc is:

    $ **fc cc**

4.5.2 The editing and history mechanism in the C shell and the TC shell

Giving the shell variable history a positive integer number *n* enables the C shell and the TC shell to remember the last *n* commands entered. We can key, for example

    % **set history=50**

We can now use the command history to produce a list of the last commands entered:

```
%  history
    1                set history=50
    2                history
```

We can repeat the last command entered in the following way:

```
%  !!
history
```

To repeat command No. 2 in the history list, we can enter:

```
%  !2
history
    1                set history=50
    2                history
    3                history
```

Another way to repeat a command is to enter 'just enough' characters of the name of the program. For example, to execute the latest command beginning with the character sequence his we can enter

```
%  !his
history
    1                set history=50
    2                history
    3                history
    4                history
```

As another example, the following command will repeat the last command which began with the characters cc:

```
%  !cc
```

This can be a convenient way of repeating the latest compilation of a C program. (More on this in chapter 8.)

It is also possible to repeat an earlier command with changes. To repeat the last command but amend the first occurrence of the text xx in the command to yy we can enter

```
%  ^xx^yy
```

(The texts represented here by xx and yy do not have to be the same length.) For example, if we had entered the command

```
%  cd mu_proj
```

and this should really have been my_proj, we can key

```
%  ^u^y
cd my_proj
```

There is also a facility to re-run an earlier command with changes. However, the rules for doing this are rather complicated, and it is not used very much.

The TC shell has a history mechanism that is very easy to use. For this reason, if you have access to the TC shell we recommend that you use it instead of the C shell. Here is a brief description of how the history mechanism in the TC shell works.

The basic idea is that the user can scroll through the list of commands executed earlier. To scroll back through the list we enter `<ctrl-p>` (previous) and to scroll forwards `<ctrl-n>` (next). Sometimes the arrow keys can also be used, in which case the 'up' arrow scrolls back and the 'down' arrow forwards. To get the last command we therefore press `<ctrl-p>` (or the 'up' arrow) once.

When we have found the command we want to repeat we can run it precisely as before, that is, unchanged, by simply pressing `<return>`. Before pressing `<return>`, we can also make changes to a command—either to an old one we have scrolled to or to a new one we are in the process of keying. There are quite a number of editing commands in the TC shell, but we will mention only the most common ones here.

To move the editing cursor within a command, we can use `<ctrl-b>` and `<ctrl-f>` to move one step backwards or forwards, `<ctrl-a>` to move the cursor to the start of the line and `<ctrl-e>` to move to the end of the line. As an alternative, it is sometimes possible to use the left and right arrow keys.

To delete the character at the editing cursor, we can press `<ctrl-d>` and the character immediately before the cursor can be deleted with the `<delete>` key or sometimes the `<backspace>`. New characters can be added to the command by simply keying them in the right place. A new character which is entered will appear immediately before the editing cursor.

Let's look at an example. Supposing that some time ago we entered the command:

```
cp /usr/lib/systemx/sub1 temp1
```

and we now want to enter the similar command:

```
cp /usr/lib/systemx/sub2 temp2
```

We scroll using `<ctrl-p>` or the 'up' arrow if available, until the old command appears. The editing cursor will then be at the end of the line. We change the final '1' into a '2' by first pressing `<delete>` and then keying a '2'. Then we press `<ctrl-b>` or the left-hand arrow until the editing cursor is immediately to the right of the first '1'. The character is removed by keying `<delete>` and a '2' is keyed in its place. The command can then be executed by pressing `<return>`.

Table 4.7 gives a summary of the editing commands in the TC shell which we have just described.

Editing commands in the TC shell	
`<ctrl-p>` ↑	scroll backwards (previous command)
`<ctrl-n>` ↓	scroll forwards (next command)
`<ctrl-f>` →	move cursor forward one character
`<ctrl-b>` ←	move cursor back one character
`<ctrl-a>`	move cursor to start of line
`<ctrl-e>`	move cursor to end of line
`<ctrl-d>`	delete character at cursor
`<delete>`	delete character to left of cursor
x	Insert character *x* to left of cursor

Table 4.7

4.6 Start-up files

In UNIX, the user can customize the environment to his or her own personal liking so that it will always look the way it is wanted when the system is used. To do this, a personal *start-up file* must be created. A start-up file is a text file which will be included in the home directory and which can be used to contain commands which are to be executed automatically every time you log on. Often a number of definitions of environment and shell variables are also included. Advanced UNIX users will generally have quite complicated commands in their start-up files. A start-up file is in fact an example of a *shell script* or *command file*: these are dealt with more fully in chapter 7.

4.6.1 Start-up files for the Bourne shell and the Korn shell

If you are running the Bourne shell or the Korn shell you will create a start-up file called `.profile` in your home directory. Note that the filename begins with a full stop. When you log on, the shell will read the commands in this file and execute them, exactly as if they had been entered at the keyboard. An example of what this file might look like is:

```
echo "Hello $LOGNAME and welcome to UNIX"
date
PS1="? "
export PS1
PATH=.:$HOME/bin:/usr/bin/X11:$PATH
export PATH
stty erase <erase_key>
```

This will give you a welcome message on the screen every time you log on, followed by the current date. After this, the prompt will be changed to a question mark and the variable PATH will be expanded so that searches for commands are also carried out in the current directory (given by the full stop at the beginning) and in the user's own directory bin (given by $HOME/bin). The command also adds the directory containing all the programs concerned with X. This must be included to enable X to be run.

The commands in the .profile file will only be executed after logging on, that is, once per session. When running the Korn shell a second start-up file can be used. The UNIX commands in this file will be executed *every time* the Korn shell is started up, that is, when the user logs on, when the Korn shell is started up by the command

> $ **ksh**

or when a new terminal window is opened. If you want to have a second start-up file of this type, you will need to specify this by placing the name of the file in the environment variable ENV. It is usual to call the start-up file .kshrc, as this follows the UNIX conventions. It is easiest to arrange for the ENV variable to be initialized automatically at log-on: this is done by including the following lines in .profile:

```
ENV=$HOME/.kshrc
export ENV
```

The .profile file should contain commands relevant to log-on information, whilst the .kshrc file should be given lines concerned with environment and shell variables. An example of what .profile can look like is:

```
echo "Hello $LOGNAME and welcome to UNIX"
date
```

This results in a welcome message and a display of the date every time the user logs on.

The .kshrc file could have the following contents:

```
stty erase <erase_key>
PS1="? "
PATH=$PATH:/usr/bin/X11:$HOME/bin:.
HISTSIZE=256
set -o vi
alias d="date +%m/%d/%y"
alias t="date +%H:%M:%S"
```

Here, the prompt is changed to a question mark and the current directory (the full stop), as well as the directories /usr/bin/X11 and $HOME/bin, are added to the list in PATH. The Korn shell is also instructed to remember the last 256 commands and told that the user wishes to use the built-in vi editor.

The last two lines in the file are an example of the use of the `alias` command. This is used to enter an alternative name for a (long) command. The form of the `alias` command is:

$ **alias** *alias_name=actual_command*

The result of the `alias` commands in the `.kshrc` shell above, therefore, is that every time the command

$ **d**

is entered from now on, the effect will be exactly as if the command entered had been

$ **date +%m/%d/%y**

and the command `t` similarly acts in the same way as

$ **date +%H:%M:%S**

4.6.2   Start-up files for the C shell and the TC shell

If you are running the C shell or the TC shell, there are two start-up files that you can use, `.login` and `.cshrc` (note the full stops). Every time you log on the shell will execute the commands in the file `.login` if it can find it. This only happens once per session. If the file `.cshrc` exists, the commands in this will be executed *every time* the shell is started up. This happens when you log on, but also when the shell is started up explicitly by entering the command

$ **csh**

or, if you are running X, by opening a new terminal window. If both the files `.login` and `.cshrc` exist, all the commands in both files will be executed when you log on, with the commands in `.cshrc` executed first.

If you are using both files, you should include in `.login` the commands concerned with logon information, while lines concerning environmental and shell variables are included in `.cshrc`. An example of what `.login` can look like is:

```
echo "Hello $LOGNAME and welcome to UNIX"
date
```

This will result in a welcome message and the date being displayed every time you log on.

The file `.cshrc` might have the following contents:

```
stty erase <erase_key>
set prompt="? "
set path=(. $HOME/bin /usr/bin/X11 /bin /usr/bin)
set noclobber
set history=50
alias d date +%m/%d/%y
alias t date +%H:%M:%S
```

Here, the prompt is altered to a question mark and extra directories are added to the standard ones in the `path` list, `/bin` and `/usr/bin`: the current directory, indicated by a full stop; the directory `/bin` in the user's home directory, given by `$HOME/bin`; and the directory containing all the programs concerned with X. Additional commands are included indicating that existing files are not to be destroyed by redirection of output data and instructing the shell to remember the last 50 commands.

The last two lines are examples of the command `alias`, which is used to enter alternative names for (long) commands. The command `alias` has the form:

> % **alias** *alias_name actual_command*

The effect of including the `alias` lines above is thus that every time the command

> % **d**

is entered from now on, the effect will be exactly as if the command entered had been

> % **date +%m/%d/%y**

and the command `t` similarly acts in the same way as

> % **date +%H:%M:%S**

A final mention should be made of the file `.logout`. If this is included in your home directory, the shell will execute the commands in this file when you log off. The file might for example include:

```
echo "Bye bye $LOGNAME - Call again soon!"
```

4.7   Start-up files in X

 When X is being run, there are three types of start-up file which are of special interest: *initialization files, resource files* and *start-up files for the window manager*. We will consider each of them in turn.

4.7.1   Initialization files

Initialization files contain UNIX commands and are used to make sure the screen looks the way it is wanted every time X is started up. These include commands to start up the preferred window manager and the other X programs the user wishes to have running, for example a terminal program.

If the X system has been started up using *start-up method 1*, as discussed in chapter 2, by entering the command

§ xinit

without an argument, the program xinit will check to see whether there is an initialization file with the name .xinitrc in the user's home directory. If this file is found, xinit will execute the UNIX commands in the file instead of creating a terminal window. The file .xinitrc should therefore include commands to start up the X programs you want to be running every time you start up X. An example of how the .xinitrc file might look is:

```
xclock -geometry 100x85-0+0 &
xcalc -geometry -0-0 &
xterm -ls -geometry 80x51+0+185 &
xterm -ls -C -geometry 80x10+0+0 -title "Console" &
mwm
```

First, a clock is created in the top right-hand corner. Then a calculator is placed at bottom right. Two terminal windows are opened on the left-hand side of the screen: a larger one with 51 lines and a small one with only ten lines. The small one is what is known as the 'console terminal window', which is given by the argument -C. This means that any error messages from the system will be displayed in this window. The argument -ls indicates that this terminal is to be what is known as a 'log-in terminal', which means that the .profile or .login file will be executed when this window is set up. The last line starts up the mwm window manager.

Note that all commands except the last are run as background processes. The way the program xinit works is that when the last command in the .xinitrc file has been executed, the running of X is completely terminated. It therefore makes sense for the last command to start up a window manager, in our example mwm. xinit passes its process to mwm by making use of exec. (See chapter 4.2.) Later, when mwm is interrupted, usually by selecting an option from a root menu, X will be terminated.

What we have described so far applies if start-up method 1 is used. If X is started by *start-up method 2*, that is, by use of a special start-up command, it is also sometimes possible to use an initialization file. In OpenWindows, for example, which is usually started by method 2, we can have an .xinitrc file of our own in our home directory. As a rule, however, no file of this type is set up. The system will then use instead a default file called $OPENWINHOME/lib/Xinitrc.

If *start-up method 3* is used (starting via xdm), it is usual to follow the convention of including an initialization file called .xsession (or .Xsession) in the user's home directory. The .xsession file will hold the commands required to initialize X the way it is required, exactly as described above. Here again, we need to make sure that the last command takes over the process so that X is not terminated. The example of an .xinitrc file above can also serve as an example of .xsession. If there is no .xsession file everything will take the default values when the system is started up.

A number of systems, e.g. OpenWindows, have utility programs which generate initialization files automatically. X can then be started up in the standard manner, after which the user can open the windows desired and position them at appropriate places on the screen. When this is finished, a suitable command can be chosen from a root menu. This command 'sees' how everything looks on the screen at the time and generates an initialization file, as a result of which the screen will be set up in the same way every time the system is started up.

As described in chapter 2, in OpenWindows the option Save Workspace is selected from the Utilities sub-menu reached from the workspace menu to generate an initialization file which will create the desired arrangement of the screen. The generated file will be placed in the home directory and is called .openwin-init. If no initialization file has been generated for the user, the appearance of the screen will be generated by the default file $OPENWINHOME/lib/openwin-init.

4.7.2   Resource files

X has a general mechanism to initialize the different X programs in the desired way. This uses a feature called *resources*. These can be used, for example, to select colours for various areas, the text font to be used and the size and position of windows.

A resource can be said to be the initial value of a particular characteristic of an application program (or a group of application programs). Resources must be specified according to particular rules, allowing the application program, characteristic and initial value to be given. For example, to specify that mwm should use the 'pointer policy' to determine which window is in focus, we can use the line:

    Mwm*keyboardFocusPolicy: pointer

and to indicate that the xterm program is to use a certain font we can use the line:

    xterm*Font: 8x13

When an X program is started up it searches in various places (following very complicated rules) to find the resources it is interested in. Resources can be kept in special text files, they can be keyed in as arguments on the command line and (using the xrdb program) they can be stored in a special database managed by the X server. Management of resources in X is a relatively complicated process, so an examination of this aspect falls outside the scope of this book.

It can be mentioned that the default values of resources for mwm can generally be found in the file /usr/lib/X11/app-defaults/Mwm and that the user can have a file of his or her own, Mwm, in the home directory, where the user's own resources for mwm can be kept.

In OpenWindows the default values for resources are held in the file $OPENWINHOME/lib/Xdefaults and there may be a file, .Xdefaults, in the home directory. However, the user must never edit this latter file. It is created automatically when the Properties option in the workspace menu is used to amend various characteristics.

4.7.3   Start-up files for the window manager

The third type of start-up file to be mentioned comprises files used to initialize the window manager. (In mwm this type of file is called a 'Resource Description File' and in OpenWindows a 'Menu File'.) In these window manager start-up files the functions of the window manager can be tailored to the user's own needs. The user can create his or her own menus, for example, or specify what is to happen when the mouse buttons are pressed. These files do not contain UNIX commands, but special commands designed specifically for the window manager concerned.

Standard   menus   for   mwm   are   held   in   the   file /usr/lib/X11/system.mwmrc and the user's own menus etc. can be stored in the .mwmrc file in the user's home directory.

In OpenWindows, the standard menus are held in the file $OPENWINHOME/lib/openwin-menu and if the user wishes to create individualized menus these can be described in a file called .openwin_menu in his or her home directory.

4.8   Summary

Programs and built-in commands	
sleep *seconds*	wait a specified number of seconds
ps [-ax]	status of background processes, BSD/OSF
ps [-e]	status of background processes, System V
kill *signal process*	kill background process
at *time*	execute command at stated time
leave *time*	reminder 'alarm clock'
echo	display text strings
env	list environment variables

Table 4.8

Command operators	
>	redirect standard output to any file
>>	redirect standard output to end of any file
<	redirect standard input to read from any file
|	pipeline
&	execute command in background

Table 4.9

Variables in the Bourne shell and the Korn shell	
variable_name=text_string	assign a shell variable
export *variable_name*	make value of shell variable accessible to environment
unset *variable_name*	remove a shell variable

Table 4.10

Variables in the C shell and the TC shell	
set *variable_name=text_string*	assign a shell variable
setenv *variable_name text_string*	assign an environment variable
unset *variable_name*	remove a shell variable
unsetenv *variable_name*	remove an environment variable

Table 4.11

Start-up files	
.profile	Bourne shell and Korn shell
.cshrc	C shell and TC shell
.login	
.xinitrc	initialization file in X (methods 1 and 2)
.xsession	initialization file in X (method 3)
.openwin-init	initialization file in Open Windows
Mwm	resource file for mwm
.Xdefaults	resource file in X
.mwmrc	start-up file for mwm
.openwin-menu	start-up file in OpenWindows

Table 4.12

Five
Communication

As we have seen, UNIX is an operating system which simplifies the application of a wide range of programs on your own computer. Even more interesting and useful possibilities open up if the computer is connected to a computer network. *Internetwork* or *Internet* is a mechanism whose aim is to offer users standardized services, independently of the underlying physical network type. In this chapter we present some of the services provided by the *TCP/IP Internet* .

As far as the user is concerned, TCP/IP consists of a number of utility programs. These utilities use the communication facilities of the network to access resources and services on other computers, but as an ordinary user you do not have to worry about the details. The utility programs offer the following services, among others:

Remote Log-in. It is possible to log on to other computers in the network.

Electronic Mail. Users can exchange mail with other users throughout the world.

117

File Transfer. It is possible to copy files between different computers. The system monitors access permissions, that is, checks for valid read and write permissions.

News. There is a worldwide system to provide messages and news on the network.

5.1   History

In the mid-'70s, the *Defence Advanced Research Projects Agency* (DARPA) in the United States began financing development work on what was christened an 'internetwork' (internet). The motivation for starting up the project lay in problems with the exchange of services and information between incompatible independent networks. The aim was to create standardized operations and mechanisms to 'iron out' the differences between different types of network.

By the end of the decade the design was beginning to take on its present shape, and the first TCP/IP-based computers were linked together in the early 80s. In January 1983 DARPA required all computers connected to the already existing ARPANET to start using TCP/IP. ARPANET was one of the first research projects in which data communication was studied. It was financed by DARPA's predecessor, the *Advanced Research Projects Agency* (ARPA).

To broaden and increase interest in TCP/IP, it was decided that colleges and universities would be able to buy the system at a modest price. Implementation and integration were carried out under BSD UNIX, as this was by then in use at 90% of all universities and colleges. Berkeley's TCP/IP became very popular since it not only offered standard protocols and programs but also new utility programs such as `rlogin`, `rcp` and `rwho`.

5.2   Names and addresses

In the development of this chapter we will be using the TCP/IP network shown in figure 5.1 as the basis for our examples. The network includes three computers, `thor`, `odin` and `balder`.

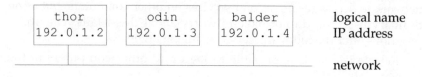

Figure 5.1

Any computer, X terminal or other device connected to a *network* will have a unique *IP address*, e.g. 192.0.1.4, which corresponds to a *logical name*, e.g. balder, which makes it easier for the user to remember.

To make it clear on which computer in the network commands are being executed, the shell prompt will include the logical name of the computer. For example, if a command is being executed on the computer called thor we will use the prompt

> thor$

The terms *host computer* and *remote computer* are defined in the following way:

the *host computer* is the computer or workstation at which the user first logs in;

a *remote computer* is any other computer in the network.

5.3   File transfer using rcp

This section introduces the program rcp (remote copy), which is used to copy individual files or entire directory structures between different computers. When the program is called, the argument to the command gives the name of the file to be copied and a name for the copy.

rcp [-rp] *filename filename*	
-r	copy directory structure
-p	retain modification time and access permissions

The names of files and the remote computer can be given in two different ways. The first way is to specify the computer name and filename as follows:

> *remote_computer:filename*

This method is used, for example, by a user wishing to copy his or her own files between two computers. Suppose, for example, that the user keith wants to copy the file main.c in his home directory on the host computer odin to his home directory on the remote computer balder. Before the copy process, the file trees on the two computers are as shown in figure 5.2.

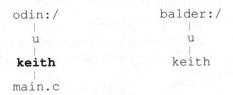

Figure 5.2

The command is then given:

odin$ **rcp main.c balder:**

or alternatively:

odin$ **rcp main.c balder:main.c**

The result will be a copy with the same name as the original. See figure 5.3.

Figure 5.3

If the copy is to be named differently, e.g. as prime.c, the command can be, instead:

odin$ **rcp main.c balder:prime.c**

and the result after the copy process will be as in figure 5.4.

Figure 5.4

The command can also use the full pathname, e.g.

odin$ **rcp /u/keith/main.c balder:/u/keith/prime.c**

Using the second way of specifying filenames on the remote computer, the user ID must be included before the names of the computer and the file. The command syntax is then:

user_ID@remote_computer:filename

This method is used where a user wants to copy files from or to another user's directory. The copy will only work, of course, if the user has valid write permission.

Suppose the user keith wants to copy the file main.c in his home directory on the odin computer to the directory belonging to the user john on balder. The file structures are shown in figure 5.5.

Figure 5.5

The copy can now be done by means of the command:

odin$ **rcp main.c john@balder:**

or, alternatively:

odin$ **rcp main.c john@balder:main.c**

The copy will then have the same name. See figure 5.6.

Figure 5.6

(This is of course on condition that keith has write permissions for john's home directory, which is not necessarily the case.) The rcp program can also copy entire directory structures between different computers. To instruct rcp to create directory structures, the option -r must follow the call. Suppose we have the file structures shown in figure 5.7 and that the directory structure book in the home directory of the user keith on the odin computer is to be copied to his home directory on balder.

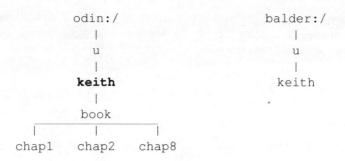

Figure 5.7

The command is then entered:

odin§ **rcp -r book balder:**

or, alternatively:

odin§ **rcp -r book balder:book**

Afterwards, there will be an exact copy of the directory structure book on the balder computer as well. See figure 5.8.

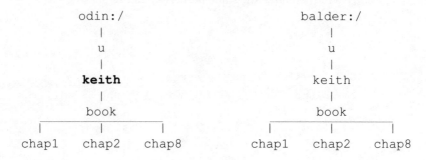

Figure 5.8

5.4   File transfer using ftp

This section describes the program ftp (file transfer program). The program is called with or without the name of a remote computer as argument.

ftp [*remote_computer*]	
remote_computer	Name of remote computer which
	files are to be copied from or to.

Once the program is running, a number of commands can be given. These are listed in table 5.1.

ftp-**commands**	
open	Set up connection to *remote_computer*
get	Transfer a file from remote computer to host computer
put	Transfer a file from host computer to remote computer
mget	Transfer multiple files from remote computer to host computer
mput	Transfer multiple files from host computer to remote computer
binary	Define binary file (e.g. a program) as file to be transferred
cd	Change directory on remote computer
dir	List contents of a directory on remote computer
mkdir	Create new directory on remote computer
quit	Terminate `ftp` session
?	List all `ftp` commands

Table 5.1

Suppose, for example, that the user `keith` wants to transfer the file `main.c` in his home directory on `odin` to his home directory on the remote computer `balder`. The file structures are shown in figure 5.9.

Figure 5.9

First, a connection to `balder` must be set up:

```
odin$ ftp
ftp> open balder
Connected to balder.
220 balder FTP server ready.
```

The remote computer then asks who is logging in. It displays the line:

```
Name (balder:keith):
```

It is usual to log in on the remote computer as the same user as on the host. In this case, the user can simply press <return>. The remote computer then asks for the user's password:

```
331 Password required for keith.
Password:
```

The user then enters the password. File transfer can now be carried out by means of the command put, and the program can be terminated with quit:

```
ftp> put main.c
200 PORT command successful
150 Opening data connection for main.c
226 Transfer complete.
local: main.c remote: main.c
63 bytes sent in 0.0037 seconds (17 Kbytes/s)
ftp> quit
221 Goodbye
odin$
```

Control is then returned to the shell on the host computer and a copy of the file main.c exists on the remote computer balder. This is shown in figure 5.10.

Figure 5.10

The copy need not have the same name as the original file, but can be given a different name in the copy command: we can enter, for example:

```
ftp> put main.c prime.c
```

in which case the file main.c will be copied to the local file system on balder and the copy will be named prime.c. The situation will be as shown in figure 5.11.

Figure 5.11

As ftp cannot transfer entire directory structures, we have to create these 'by hand'. The following example illustrates how this can be done. Suppose that the directory structure book in keith's home directory on odin is to be copied to his home directory on balder. This situation is as shown in figure 5.12.

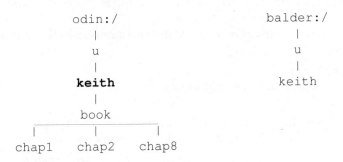

Figure 5.12

We enter the following commands:

```
odin$ cd book
odin$ ftp
ftp> open balder
...
ftp> mkdir book
...
ftp> cd book
...
ftp> mput chap1 chap2 chap8
...
ftp> quit
221 Goodbye
odin $
```

The result is shown in figure 5.13.

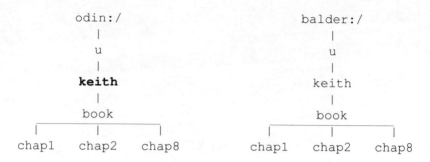

Figure 5.13

Finally, an example of how `ftp` can be used to copy software available free of charge from the University of California at Berkeley. To be able to emulate this example, your local TCP/IP-based network must also be linked up with the worldwide TCP/IP Internet. The software we are getting is a graphics management system.

First, open up a connection to the Californian university's computer, `ucbvax.berkeley.edu`.

```
odin$ ftp
ftp> open ucbvax.berkeley.edu
Connected to ucbvax.berkeley.edu
```

You can now log in using the ID `anonymous`. The password you should enter is your electronic mail address (see section 5.11).

```
Name (ucbvax.berkeley.edu:keith): anonymous
331 Guest login ok, send ident as password.
Password: <mail-address>
```

Then find your way into the directory `pub/tiff`, where software is stored:

```
ftp> cd pub/tiff
250 CWD command successful.
```

The contents of the directory can be listed using the help command `dir` or `ls`:

```
ftp> dir
200 PORT command successful.
150 Opening ASCII mode data connection for /bin/ls
total 1025
-r--r--r--  1 953 tty      546 Jun  1  1990 README
-r--r--r--  1 953 tty   333827 Jun  4  1990 v2.2.tar.Z
-r--r--r--  1 953 tty   688527 Jun  1  1990 v2.2pics.tar.Z
```

As you will be transferring software, which is stored in 'binary format', you must indicate this to ftp with the command

ftp> **binary**

After this you can copy each file separately using get or everything at one go using mget.

How do you get the software to work? Ah, well, that's a different story altogether.

5.5   Executing commands on remote computers using rsh

By means of the program rsh (remote shell), commands can be sent to other computers to be executed. Output data will be presented on the local terminal.

rsh *remote computer* [-1 *user_ID*] *command*	
remote_computer	Name of remote computer on which command is to be run.
-1 *user_ID*	Use *user_ID* instead of your own user ID to run the command on the remote computer.
command	Command to be executed on the remote computer.

The program is called from the command line with the name of the remote computer and the command to be executed, e.g.:

```
odin$ rsh balder cal 10 1992
      October 1992
   S   M Tu  W Th  F   S
                1   2   3
   4   5   6   7   8   9  10
  11  12  13  14  15  16  17
  18  19  20  21  22  23  24
  25  26  27  28  29  30  31
odin$
```

If a file on the host computer is to be used by the program on the remote computer this must be redirected to the remote command, e.g.:

```
odin$ rsh balder more < /etc/passwd
```

or alternatively:

```
odin$ cat /etc/passwd | rsh balder more
```

If output data from the program on the remote computer is to be saved to a file on the local computer, this can be redirected using the standard redirection operators > and >>, e.g.:

odin$ **rsh balder cat /etc/passwd > output**

By including the option -1 the command can be executed on the remote computer on accounts belonging to other users. Suppose, for example, that the user keith is running on odin. The following command allows him to write out the contents of the file /etc/group on the remote computer thor using john's account:

odin$ **rsh thor -l john cat /etc/group**

Which other computers it is possible to gain access from by means of the rsh command is determined locally for each computer. The system administrator can create a file called /etc/hosts.equiv which contains a list of other computers which the local computer 'trusts'. Computers that trust each other have the same registered users. If the local computer trusts a particular remote computer a user on the remote computer will be allowed to execute a rsh on the local computer using his own account. Each user can also individually list those users on other computers who are allowed to use his or her account on the local computer: this is held in a file called .rhosts in his or her home directory on the local computer. (This should be given only limited use.) Every line in the .rhosts file will contain the name of a computer plus a user ID. The command above, for example, is permitted if the home directory for john on the thor computer includes a .rhosts file which in turn contains the line

odin keith

Command operators to be sent to the remote computer must be enclosed in single or double quotation marks, otherwise they will be acted on by the host computer:

odin$ **rsh balder cd /etc; cat passwd**
cat: passwd: No such file or directory
odin$

If the aim is to access the directory /etc and then list the contents of the file passwd on the remote computer balder, the command should be laid out as follows:

odin$ **rsh balder 'cd /etc; cat passwd'**

It is not possible to use rsh to run interactive programs such as the vi text editor. Instead, log in using rlogin and start up the interactive program from there. Environment variables on the host computer are not exported to the remote computer when using rsh.

5.6   Logging in on remote computers using `rlogin`

By using `rlogin` (remote log-in), users can log in on other computers in
the network. Once properly logged in on a remote computer, commands
can be given in the usual way and the output will be presented on the
local screen. The environment variable TERM at the remote computer is
automatically given the same value as held by the host.

When calling `rlogin` you must give the name of the computer you
want to log in on. There are also a number of other arguments you can
add.

`rlogin` *remote_computer* [-l *user_ID*] [-8] [-e*c*]	
remote_computer	Name of remote computer to be logged into.
-l *user_ID*	Defines the user ID to be used on the remote computer. If this is left undefined, the same ID will be used as on the host.
-8	Transfers eight bits over the network instead of seven.
-e*c*	Defines a character *c* to be used as the 'meta' symbol instead of ~.

The command below, for example, will log you in on the `balder`
computer—provided you are registered as a user on the remote
computer.

```
odin$ rlogin balder
balder$
```

If you wish to log in on a remote computer under a different user
ID, you can indicate this by means of the option -l and a user ID:

```
odin$ rlogin balder -l keith
Password:
balder$
```

The `/etc/hosts.equiv` file, which we discussed above in
connection with the `rsh` command, is also checked for `rlogin` to see
which other computers a given computer 'trusts'. If two computers trust
each other, it is not necessary to give a password when using `rlogin`.
The `.rhosts` file in a given user's home directory lists the users on
other computers who are allowed to gain access on the user's account
via `rlogin` without giving a password. (Use this facility with caution!)

A session can be terminated by keying the `rlogin` command ~. at
the start of the command line:

```
odin$ rlogin balder
balder$ ~.
Closed connection.
odin$
```

Alternatively, the session can be terminated in the usual way, that is, by keying exit, <ctrl-d>, logout etc.:

```
odin$ rlogin balder
balder$ exit
Closed connection.
odin$
```

Sometimes the ~ character is needed in its own right. In this case, rlogin must be stopped from interpreting it. This can be done by keying the character twice. The ~ symbol can be switched for another character by means of the -e option. To change it to an exclamation mark, for example, we can enter

```
odin$ rlogin balder -e!
balder$
```

The function of the ~ can be switched off completely by leaving out the character after the -e option:

```
odin$ rlogin balder -e
balder$
```

As a rule, the program only transfers seven-bit codes, which can occasionally present problems. The -8 option tells rlogin to transfer eight-bit codes.

5.7 Logging in on remote computers using telnet

The telnet program allows you to log in on other computers in the network in much the same way as rlogin.

telnet [*remote_computer*]	
remote_computer	Name of remote computer to be logged in on.

The telnet program is called direct from the shell:

```
odin$ telnet
telnet>
```

After this you will be in telnet's own shell, from which it is possible to give a number of telnet-specific commands. These are shown in table 5.2.

telnet **commands**	
open *remote_computer*	Opens a connection to *remote_computer*.
quit	Terminates a `telnet` session.
?	Provides help texts for all `telnet`-specific commands.

Table 5.2

Once you are inside the `telnet` program and wish to connect to a remote computer you can enter the command `open`:

```
odin$ telnet
telnet> open balder
Trying 192.0.1.5 ...
Connected to balder.
Escape character is '^]'
```

You then have to log in in the usual way:

```
login: keith
Password:
balder$
```

Alternatively, you can enter the computer you want to log in on on the command line itself:

```
odin$ telnet balder
Trying 192.0.1.5 ...
Connected to balder.
Escape character is '^]'
login: keith
Password:
balder$
```

Once you are properly logged in on a remote computer, you can terminate the session and return to the host computer by entering `exit`, `<ctrl-d>` or `logout`:

```
balder$ exit
Connection closed by foreign host.
odin$
```

If you are in the `telnet` shell and decide to terminate the session, you can do so by keying the command `quit`:

```
odin$ telnet
telnet> quit
odin$
```

There are many more `telnet` commands than we have described in this section. You can see a short description of them by keying the ? command.

```
odin§ telnet
telnet> ?
```

5.8   Running on a remote computer under X

X When running X you can have several windows on the screen at the same time. Sometimes we will want to run a program on a remote computer but still have the result displayed in a window on the screen of the local computer, the host. Probably the most common way of doing this is to open a window which can then be used to give any necessary commands to the remote computer. In this section we will be explaining how to run the `xterm` program on a remote computer and display results in a window on the local one. We will be demonstrating two different ways of doing this.

One way is to open a terminal window on the local computer and then use this window to enter the command `rlogin` followed by the name of the remote computer. Suppose, for example, we are running on the local computer and wish to open a window to the remote computer `thor`. We can enter the command

```
odin§ rlogin thor
```

The window will then start up a shell executed on the remote computer `thor`. To enable us to use this shell to start up a new X program which will run on `thor` but display its window on the local computer `odin`, we must first set the environment variable `DISPLAY`. When the process of logging in on `thor` has been completed, therefore, we enter the command

```
thor§ setenv DISPLAY odin:0.0
```

The other, more direct, way to open a window to a remote computer is to use the program `rsh` to give the command `xterm` to the remote computer. It is important to include the display desk to be used as an argument to `xterm`. As you want the window to be on the computer you are working at, this is the one that should be specified. Suppose we are running on the `odin` computer and wish to open a window to the remote computer thor. In a terminal window on `odin`, we can enter the command

```
odin§ rsh thor /usr/bin/X11/xterm -T thor -ls \
      -display odin:0.0 < /dev/null &
```

Thus, `thor` is the computer on which the `xterm` program is to be run. The argument `-T thor` means that we want the title line of the new window to bear the wording thor and the option -ls indicates that the shell which is started up in the window is to be what is known as a 'log-in shell', that is, it is to start by reading the file .profile or .login. The argument -display odin:0.0 tells xterm that the new window is to be shown on odin. (The redirection of input data at the end is to make sure the rsh program does not stop while waiting for input data.)

If this does not work it may be because the remote computer has not been given permission to use the display on the host computer. There is a program xhost which can be used to decide which remote computers may use the local display. If xhost is called with no parameters, it will give a list of the computers which have been given access to the local display:

```
odin$ xhost
access control enabled
(only the following hosts are allowed)
balder
freya
localhost
```

A new computer can be added to the list by keying, for example:

```
odin$ xhost +thor
```

A computer can similarly be removed from the list:

```
odin$ xhost -balder
```

To turn off the access control and allow other computers to use the local display, we can enter:

```
odin$ xhost +
```

and access control can be turned on again with the command:

```
odin$ xhost -
```

5.9 Network information using rwho and ruptime

The program rwho provides a list of users who are logged in on those computers connected to the local network.

rwho [-a]	
-a	Also list users who have been inactive for over an hour.

The list displayed on the screen is similar to the one supplied by the who program:

```
odin$ rwho
```

```
john       thor:ttyp1     Apr 18 13:58 :03
karen      odin:ttyp6     Apr 18 13:59 :20
linda      thor:ttyp0     Apr 18 13:58 :45
skanshol   odin:ttyp9     Apr 18 14:17
torbjorn   balder:ttya1   Apr 18 19:23
```

The list tells us that the user called `karen` logged in on the `odin` computer on 18th April at 13:59 and was inactive for 20 minutes.

If a remote computer has not updated its status on the host computer during the last five minutes the `rwho` program considers it to be dead. Users of a remote computer which has been inactive for over an hour will not be listed unless the option `-a` is given as an argument to the program.

```
odin$ rwho -a
david      thor:ttyp9     Apr 18 13:58 14:31
john       thor:ttyp1     Apr 18 13:58    :03
karen      odin:ttyp6     Apr 18 13:59    :20
linda      thor:ttyp0     Apr 18 13:58    :45
peter      thor:ttyp5     Apr 17 23:47 10:29
skanshol   odin:ttyp9     Apr 18 14:17
torbjorn   balder:ttya1   Apr 18 19:23
```

The program `ruptime` gives a list showing the status of the different computers on the network.

ruptime [-a] [-r] [-l] [-t]	
-r	Lists in reverse order.
-l	Lists according to greatest computing load.
-t	Lists according to which computer has been 'up' longest.

Each line in the list defines one computer. The list will be sorted into alphabetical order.

```
$ ruptime
balder up 5+22:35,  1 users,  load 1.06,  1.06,  1.11
odin   up    3:23,  2 users,  load 1.55,  0.96,  0.88
thor   up    0:54,  2 users,  load 0.62,  0.15,  0.03
```

The list shows that the `balder` computer has been 'up' for five days, 22 hours and 35 minutes (given by 5+22:35). One user has logged in and the load for the last three five-minute periods was 1.06, 1.06 and 1.11.

5.10　**Talking to other users with** `write` **and** `talk`

The simplest program to use to communicate with another user is
`write`. If you want to talk to user `karen`, for example, you simply enter:

§ **write karen**

You then key in your message and finish with `<ctrl-d>`.
Everything you write will be displayed at Karen's terminal, line for line.
If Karen wants to reply, she enters a matching command, e.g.:

§ **write hilary**

and keys in her answer. In this way, a two-way connection can be set up
in which everything one user keys in is visible on the other user's
terminal. This, of course, demands a certain amount of discipline so that
both users are not keying at the same time, producing an illegible jumble
on the screen. The `write` program will only work if both users are
running on the same computer.

A rather more advanced program giving a two-way connection is
`talk`. To talk to a user on the same computer, key:

§ **talk karen**

and to talk to a user on another computer connected to the data
network, enter, for example:

balder§ **talk karen@odin**

to talk to user `karen` on the `odin` computer. Karen's terminal will now
display the message:

```
Message from Talk_Daemon@odin at 11:16 ...
talk: connection requested by hilary@balder
talk: respond with:  talk hilary@balder
```

After Karen enters the command

odin§ **talk hilary@balder**

a two-way connection will be established between the two users `hilary`
and `karen`. Their terminal screens will be divided into two windows as
shown in figure 5.14, where they can see both what they are writing and
what is being written to them at the same time. Either of the two parties
can terminate the conversation by pressing the interrupt key, usually
`<delete>` or `<ctrl-c>`.

```
     Hilary's terminal      Karen's terminal

    ┌─────────────────┐    ┌──────────────────┐
    │ Hi Karen!       │    │ Fine thanks.     │
    │ How are you?    │    │                  │
    ├─────────────────┤    ├──────────────────┤
    │ Fine thanks.    │    │ Hi Karen!        │
    │ How are you?    │    │                  │
    └─────────────────┘    └──────────────────┘
```

Figure 5.14

Sometimes it can be a nuisance if other users start writing on your own terminal. The `mesg` program is supplied for this contingency. The command

    $ **mesg n**

(n for 'no') prevents other users from sending messages to your own terminal using the `write` or `talk` program. The command

    $ **mesg y**

(y for 'yes') re-enables the programs, allowing other users to send messages once more.

5.11   Electronic Mail

The `write` and `talk` programs described in the preceding section can only be used to communicate with other users who are logged on at the same time. A much more useful method is to send *electronic mail* (or *e-mail*). The addressee does not need to be logged on, and may also be anywhere in the world. There are two generally used programs for electronic mail, a simpler one deriving from earlier versions of System V and a more advanced one developed for BSD UNIX. In system V the simpler program is usually called `mail`, and the more advanced one (if installed) `mailx`. In the BSD system and OSF the simpler program is not available, and here the more advanced program is called `mail`.

5.11.1   Mailboxes and addresses

Both e-mail programs work on the same principle, and there are a number of identical commands. They are both used to send and to receive electronic mail. Among the files managed by the system administrator, there is a unique file for each user, in which his or her incoming mail is automatically stored. Let's call this file the user's *system mailbox*. In addition to this file, the user may have a file in his or her home directory in which to save electronic mail. This file is usually called `mbox` and we will call it the user's *local mailbox*. When reading mail from the system mailbox, the user can decide whether a message is to be thrown away or saved to the local mailbox.

As there is a degree of confusion regarding the names of the e-mail programs on different systems, you should probably check for yourself which of the two programs you are running. The simplest way is to write a message to yourself with the command:

    $ **mail** *own_log-in_ID*

If you get a message looking more or less like the following, you are using the advanced mail program:

> `Subject:`

However, if the program gives no response, but simply waits for you to key in some data, you can be reasonably sure you are running the simpler program. In this case, if you would rather run the more advanced program you can try keying `mailx` instead of `mail`.

In either case, conclude the test by keying in whatever text occurs to you, and finish the text by keying `<ctrl-d>` as *first* character of a new line.

Normally, you will not be sending e-mail to yourself, but to other users. The argument to `mail` or `mailx` will then be the intended recipient of the message. The simplest case is when the addressee has an account on the same computer as yourself: you then simply key in his or her log-in ID. Generally, you will enter the recipient's address for electronic mail. This is usually an address of the form:

> *local_address@domain*

The *local address* is often the user ID, but may also be a subscriber number. The *domain* refers to an organization, such as a company or a university. It is made up of a number of elements separated by full stops. The largest unit in the address generally comes last, and the smallest first. Often, the first element will be some kind of departmental name, followed by the name of the organization. In accordance with ISO standards, the final element of the domain is a code for the country (e.g. `us`, `uk`, `fr`, `de` or `se` for USA, UK, France, Germany and Sweden respectively). However, for historical reasons, the final element in the domain, especially in the USA, is often one of the codes `edu`, `com`, `mil` and `gov`. A few examples showing what an address may look like are:

> `steve@www.york.pq.uk`
> `anonym@jupiter.dataverket.se`
> `NN@abt2.xyzgmbh.de`
> `J.SMITH@Server.com`
> `foo@cs.univ.edu`

It should be mentioned that it is still possible to come upon old-style addresses, being used in place of the type described above. One example is an address of the form

> `system1!system2!system3!systemn!name.`

This type describes the path through the network. Another example is an address which has the name of a network at the end, such as `uucp` or `arpa`.

In the remainder of this chapter we will be describing the two different electronic mail programs separately. We will take the simpler program first.

5.11.2   The simpler e-mail program

We have already partly described how to `send` a message. The user calls the `mail` program with the recipient's address as a parameter and then keys in the message, finishing with `<ctrl-d>` (or a full stop on its own) at the start of a new line:

```
$ mail NN@dept2.xyzltd.uk
Will be in Xtown next Mon.
Can we meet?
Morning will be best.
Regards  W. White
<ctrl-d>
$
```

Any line you have not finished can be corrected using `<backspace>` or `<ctrl-u>`, but lines which have been completed cannot be corrected. If you find that this makes things difficult, you can prepare your message in advance using a text editor (see next chapter) and store it in a text file. You can then redirect the input data for the `mail` program so that it is read from the text file instead of from the terminal. Suppose, for example, that we had stored the message in a file called `mailfile`. We can now send it by means of the command:

```
$ mail someone@deptx.abcltd.uk < mailfile
```

To *read* the e-mail you have been sent, you should call the `mail` program without giving the address of a recipient. The e-mail program will then display the last message you have received:

```
$ mail
From NN@dept2.xyzltd.uk Mon Apr 29 09:11:36 1991
Meeting Monday will be fine.
How about 10 am at my office?
Regards, N. Neil
?
```

The message ends in a prompt, usually a question mark, inviting the user to key in a command to the e-mail program. The most useful commands are summarized in table 5.3.

mail **commands, simple program**	
`<return>` n +	show next message on screen
−	show previous message on screen
d	delete current message
p	show current message on screen (again)
s	save current message in `mbox` (local mailbox)
s *filename*	save current message in *filename*
r	reply to current message
m *user*	mail current message to *user*
q `<ctrl-d>`	quit, saving undeleted messages
x	quit, saving all messages
?	give list of commands

Table 5.3

Letters will be displayed in reverse order, starting with the latest. The easiest way to read your mail is therefore to key either a d or a `<return>` every time you see a question mark—the d if you want to delete the current message and `<return>` if you want to keep it.

If you want to read mail which is in some file other than the system mailbox, you can add the argument −f *filename* when you call the `mail` program. For example, if you want to read the e-mail you have stored in your local mailbox, `mbox`, and you are in your home directory, you can enter the following command:

$ **mail -f mbox**

The e-mail program will then read the messages in your local mailbox instead of those in the system mailbox. Apart from that, the program works in exactly the same way: that is, all the commands shown in table 5.3 can be used.

5.11.3 The more advanced e-mail program

As mentioned above, the more advanced e-mail program is called `mail` in a BSD or OSF system and mailx in System V. For the sake of simplicity, we will refer to it as `mail` throughout this section. System V users should therefore key `mailx` where we have keyed `mail`.

Writing messages involves the same steps as shown above:

```
$ mail karen@dept3.xyzco.uk
Subject: Order
Please supply ten cartons of
article No. 12345 no later than
week 15.
Same address as previous.
Regards / G. Green
<ctrl-d>
$
```

One difference from the simpler e-mail program is the opportunity to complete an extra Subject line before starting on the message proper.

The advanced program has a set of *tilde commands* which can be entered while a message is being written. To enter a tilde command, you must always be at the *start* of a new line. You can then key a tilde character ~ followed by a second character. A selection of the tilde commands is shown in table 5.4.

tilde commands for the advanced e-mail program	
~s *text*	change 'Subject' to *text*
~t *name*	send message also to *name*
~c *name*	send copy of message to *name*
~h	change 'Subject', recipient and who is to have copies
~v	start up a text editor to edit message
~r *filename*	read in *filename*
~w *filename*	save message in file *filename*
~p	print message on screen
<ctrl-d>	terminate, send message
~x	terminate without sending message
~q	quit: do not send message; save message in file dead.letter
~d	read in file dead.letter
~m *i*	read in text from message No. *i*
~: *mail_command*	execute specified *mail command*
?	give list of tilde commands

Table 5.4

Note that tilde commands can only be issued when a message is being *written*.

A particularly useful tilde command is ~v, which makes it possible to edit your messages using a text editor. The message can be edited like an ordinary text, and the text editor terminated in the usual way. If no particular text editor is specified, vi will be used. (See next chapter.) If you want to run a different text editor, such as emacs, this must be specified in the environment variable VISUAL.

To *read* your mail, key in the command

```
$ mail
```

without indicating a recipient. You will then get a list of all the mail you have received. It might look something like this (assuming the user is called karen):

```
Mail version SMI 4.0   Type ? for help.
"/usr/spool/mail/karen": 2 messages 2 new
>N  1 hilary    Thu May  2 09:33   12/411    book loan
 N  2 david     Thu May  2 13:14   12/401    cake
?
```

Each message is given one line in the list. Here, for example, karen has received two messages, one from hilary and one from david. As we can see, the messages are numbered—they are arranged in chronological order, so that number 1 is the oldest—and each is preceded by a letter giving the status of the message. 'N' means it is a new message which has not yet been read. The > symbol indicates the current message.

At the end of the list is a prompt character, often a question mark, indicating that the e-mail program is ready to accept a command. There are a large number of commands for the advanced e-mail program, some of which are shown in table 5.5.

A number of the commands in the table have *list* as a parameter. Lists of messages can be referred to in a number of ways. The usual one is to specify the number of an individual message, e.g. 2, or a range, e.g. 4-7. For example, the command p2 prints out message No. 2 on the screen, and the command d4-7 deletes messages 4 to 7 inclusive.

There are a number of special characters for numbered messages. A full stop means the current message, $ the latest message and * all the messages. In addition, + indicates the next message and - the previous message. For example, the command d* will delete all the messages.

A list can also specify all the messages from a particular user or all messages with a particular text in their Subject lines. The command p david, for example, will print out all the messages from david and d /new reports will delete all messages concerning new reports.

mail **commands, advanced program**	
h	display list of all message headers
=	display current message number
i	display message No. *i*
<return> n +	display next message
−	display previous message
p *list*	display messages in list
top *list*	display first lines of messages in list
d *list*	delete messages in list
u *list*	undo deletion of messages in list
hold *list* pre *list*	keep messages in list in system mailbox
s	save current message to local mailbox file mbox
s *filename*	save current message to *filename*
s *list filename*	save messages in list to *filename*
r *i*	reply to message No. *i*
R *i*	reply to message No. *i* and send reply to other users who received the message
m *user*	send a message to *user*
q <ctrl-d>	quit, keep unread messages in system mailbox and save read but undeleted mail to mbox
x	quit, keep all mail in system mailbox
? help	give list of commands

Table 5.5

When the command r, R or m is given, the mail program switches to input mode, giving the user access to all the tilde commands described earlier.

It should be mentioned here that some systems (incorrectly) have the commands r and R in table 5.5 the other way round.

Just as in the simpler e-mail program, mail can be read from a file other than the system mailbox by entering the command:

$ **mail -f** *filename*

If the argument *filename* is omitted, it is assumed that the user wishes to read from his or her local mailbox, mbox.

5.11.4 Electronic mail under X

Users of X can make use of a program called xmail, which enables them to utilize the advanced e-mail program described above more easily. The xmail program does not form part of the MIT distribution, but it is generally available free of charge. When the program is started up with the command

    $ **xmail &**

a window appears as shown in figure 5.15. The window is divided into three sections. At the top is the *index pane,* which contains a list of messages received. Clicking with the right-hand mouse button on a line in this pane causes the contents of the corresponding message to be shown in the bottom section, the *text pane.* If the user merely wishes to select a different message as the current message, without seeing its contents on the screen, a click on the appropriate line in the index pane with the left-hand mouse button will do this.

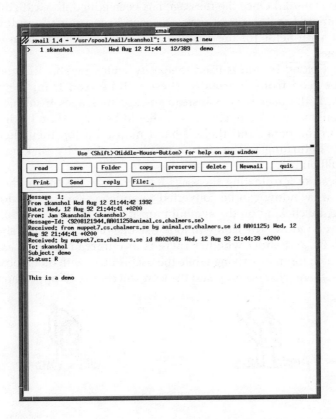

Figure 5.15

In the centre is a panel of command buttons. Each button corresponds to one or more commands in the advanced e-mail program. Placing the mouse pointer on a button and holding the right-hand mouse button pressed shows the choices under each button. To select a particular option, the mouse pointer is moved to the corresponding line and the mouse button released. The default option under a button can also be selected more simply by clicking on the button with the left-hand mouse button.

There are help texts for all buttons, as well as for the index and text panes. These are called up by placing the mouse pointer on the button or pane for which help is required, pressing the <shift> key and then pressing the middle mouse button.

When the user clicks on the [Send] button to send a new message or on [Reply] to reply to a message, a new temporary window opens in which the text of the message can be edited. This window will start up the usual text editor, vi. (If a different text editor is preferred, the name of the text editor, e.g. emacs, should be stored in the environment variable VISUAL.) Once the message has been edited, the text editor can be terminated in the usual way. A second temporary window then appears, with fields for the recipient, the subject line and who is to be sent copies.

The [Folder] button is used to specify which mailbox the messages are to be read from. Normally, these will be read from the system mailbox. If the user wishes instead to read messages from his or her local mailbox, mbox, the name mbox should be entered on the line after File: in the panel and the left-hand mouse button then clicked on [Folder]. Returning to the system mailbox is done by clicking on the [Newmail] button.

Instead of terminating the xmail program at the end of the e-mail session, its window can be converted to an icon. This can be done, for example, by clicking on the symbol immediately above the scroll bar in the index window. The icon will look like one of the examples shown in figure 5.16, and show whether there is any unread mail. xmail also keeps watch for mail arriving while the user is busy with other jobs. If this happens, there will be a beep and the icon will change its appearance.

Figure 5.16

If you are running X but not using xmail, you may find the program xbiff useful to signal whether or not any mail has come in.

The program is started up with the command

   $ **xbiff &**

A small window similar to the xmail icon will be displayed on the screen. If some mail arrives there will be a signal and the mailbox will change colour. The xbiff program cannot be used to read mail.

Another program for reading and sending mail under X is xmh. This is not based directly on the advanced e-mail program we described earlier, but on another mail program, mh. xmh can do the same things as xmail, and it is also controlled by various menus. We will not be describing xmh in detail here.

The natural e-mail program to use in OpenWindows is mailtool, which is most easily started by selecting the Programs sub-menu from the workspace menu and then selecting the Mail Tool option from this. Once mailtool is running, a window like that shown in figure 5.17 will appear.

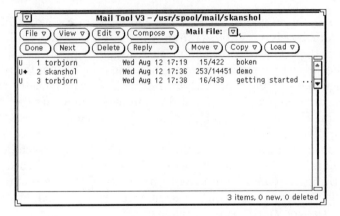

Figure 5.17

At the top is a control panel with a number of buttons, of which several have menus. Below this is a pane giving a list of all the messages received. One of these messages may be marked, as in the figure. A message can be marked by clicking on its line with the left-hand mouse button.

We shall start by describing how to *send* messages. This can be done in three ways. If we wish to write a new message we can select the default option New in the [Compose ▽] menu. If we want to send a reply to a message, we can mark the message in the list and then select the default option To Sender in the [Reply ▽] menu. If we want to send on a message we have received, we mark the message and then select the Forward option in the [Compose ▽] menu.

In all three cases the result will be a window which looks like the one in figure 5.18. On the top three lines we must fill in the name of the

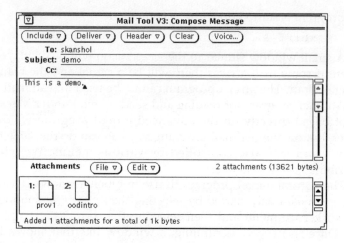

Figure 5.18

addressee, the subject of the message and the name or names of anyone who is to receive a copy. (When a message is being replied to or forwarded, part of the information is already filled in.)

The central pane is a text area where the user keys in the text of the message that is being sent. Chapter 2 describes how to delete, move and copy text, as well as how to edit the command line using the cmdtool program. The same methods and editing commands are used to enter the text of an e-mail message.

If desired, a message that has been received can be included in the text. This can be useful, for example, if we want to comment on something that has been sent to us. In this case, we can use the |Include ▽| menu. When the message is complete, a click on the menu button |Deliver ▽| will send the message off.

A handy feature of mailtool is the facility to send 'enclosures' with the message—known in mailtool as *attachments*. An attachment will always be a file, and the bottom pane of figure 5.18 shows the files available as attachments. The simplest way to specify that a particular file is to be sent as an attachment is to use the 'drag and drop' technique. Position the mouse pointer in the File Manager window on the file you wish to send as an attachment, press the left-hand button, drag the file to the bottom pane of the Mail Tool window and release the button. Another method is to select the default option Add on the |File ▽| button menu and key in the name of the directory and file in the window that pops up.

In mailtool, even sound files can be sent as attachments. A click on the |Voice...| button starts up the application Audio Tool, which can be used to record and edit sound files.

We will now describe how to *read* mail. This procedure starts from the list of messages in figure 5.17. When you double-click with the `left-hand` button on a particular message in the list, a new window will be set up, displaying the text of the message. See figure 5.19.

For a hard copy of the current message on the printer, select the `Print` option from the [File ▽] menu.

If you want to save the message, you can enter a filename against the heading **Mail File:** at the top right of figure 5.17 and then click on [Move ▽] or [Copy ▽]. Any number of messages can be saved one after the other to the same file, for example your local mailbox, `mbox`.

After reading a message you may want to delete it. In that case, click on the [Delete] button in figure 5.17.

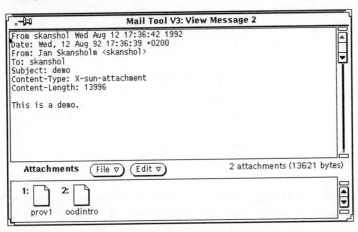

Figure 5.19

If a file has been received as an attachment to a message, you can store the file in your own file system by using the 'drag and drop' technique. Drag the file from the bottom pane of figure 5.19 to the File Manager window. Alternatively, the option `Copy Out` can be selected from the [File ▽] menu in figure 5.19.

`mailtool` will usually read the messages in the user's system mailbox. If you want to read mail in another mailbox, such as your local mailbox `mbox`, enter the name of the mailbox against the **Mail File:** heading in figure 5.17 and click on the [Load ▽] button. To return to the system mailbox, select the default alternative `Load In-Box` from the [File ▽] menu in figure 5.17.

The usual way to terminate `mailtool` is to click on the [Done] button in figure 5.17. All the changes you have made to your mailbox will then be put into effect—for example, deleted messages will disappear and the remaining messages will be renumbered. Then `mailtool` will close and its window will become an icon. It is worthwhile keeping the icon on the screen, as its appearance will tell you whether any mail has been received. This is illustrated in figures

5.20a, 5.20b and 5.20c by a letter tray indicating a mailbox with new, unread mail, one with old mail which has been read, and one which is empty.

mailtool   mailtool   mailtool

Figures 5.20a, b & c

5.12   Reading news

USENET is a worldwide system for the distribution of news, articles, contributions to discussions, programs and other material of general interest to computer users. Information on the 'network' is divided into a large number of *newsgroups*, each group dealing with a particular topic. This can be virtually anything, e.g. the C programming language, computer training, music and political discussions. The user can specify which newsgroups he or she wishes to subscribe to and which not.

Within each newsgroup, a series of *articles* are sent. Articles are numbered in chronological order within each group. Users can choose which articles they want to read within each newsgroup.

Incoming articles on the 'network' are handled by a special system program, the NNTP news server (which can be obtained from Berkeley free of charge). Articles are held centrally in the system, which makes great demands on external memory space as large amounts of data are constantly coming in.

Every user who reads the news has a special file, .newsrc, in his or her home directory. This file contains, among other things, information as to which newsgroups the user subscribes and which articles within each newsgroup the user has read. The programs we will be describing in this section do not form part of the standard distribution of UNIX and X, but they are generally available.

5.12.1 The `rn` program

To read articles, you can use the program `rn` (read news) by entering the command

> $ **rn**

This first checks that the user has a `.newsrc` file. If this is not the case, a new file is created. `rn` then displays the number of unread articles in the different newsgroups the user has subscribed to. The program will also mention any newsgroups that have been added to the service, to give the user an opportunity to include them in his or her subscription.

A large number of commands can be given to `rn`. The program works at different levels and will be in one or other of these levels at any given time.

Level 1.   At this level the user selects which newsgroups are to be handled and which are to be subscribed to.

Level 2.   At this level the user selects the articles within a specific newsgroup he or she wishes to read.

Level 3.   At this level, the user reads a specific article.

Each level has its own set of commands. Commands in `rn` do not usually end in `<return>`. A common feature of the commands at the different levels is a help command `h`. In addition, a general feature is that the 'default command' will be executed if only a `<space>` is entered. When `rn` asks for a command at level 1 or 2, it will write out a list of suggested commands. You can tell which is the 'default command', as it is always first in this list.

For reasons of space, we cannot describe all the commands here. We can only show tables of the most common ones.

We shall start at level 1, where newsgroups are handled. Every time `rn` is waiting for a command at this level it will display a line roughly like this:

> ******** 25 unread articles in com.std.c—read now? [ynq]

The name of one of the newsgroups the user has subscribed to is included in the line. The commands that may be entered are shown in table 5.6. Note that the list of suggested commands in the prompt does not cover all the possibilities.

rn **commands, level 1 (select newsgroup)**	

y
`<space>`
`<return>`
	yes, deal with this group now

n	go to next group containing unread articles
p	go to previous group containing unread articles
–	go to previous group dealt with
1	go to first group
$	go to last group
g *group_name*	go to group called *group_name*; if not subscriber, facility to subscribe is provided
/ *text*	search forwards for group with name containing string *text*
? *text*	search backwards for group with name containing string *text*
l *text*	list all unsubscribed groups with names containing string *text*
u	cancel subscription to this group
c	mark all articles in this group as read
L	display information on `.newsrc` file
q	quit program
x	quit program, but do not change `.newsrc`

Table 5.6

At level 2, when a particular newsgroup is being dealt with, rn will display a line roughly like the following every time it is waiting for a command:

```
End of article 378 (of 401)—what next? [npq]
```

The most common commands used in this situation are listed in table 5.7. An article will automatically be marked as read when its last line has been displayed.

rn **commands, level 2 (select article)**	
n <space> <return>	go to next unread article
p	go to previous unread article
–	go to previous article shown
i	go to article No. *i*
j	mark current article as read
m	mark current article as unread
k	mark all articles dealing with same subject as current article as read
/*text*	search forwards for article dealing with *text*
?*text*	search backwards for article dealing with *text*
r	send reply (via mail) to author of current message
f	send an article to the network (if user is at 'end of newsgroup' this will be an original article, otherwise a follow-up article)
F	send a follow-up article to the network, include current article, marked with >
u	cancel subscription to this group
c	mark all articles in this group as read
s *filename*	save article in *filename*
q	quit session on this group, return to level 1

Table 5.7

At level 3, where a particular article is being read, rn displays a prompt which looks like this:

—MORE—(29%)

Commands at level 3 are similar to the commands for the more program described in chapter 2.4. These are shown in table 5.8.

rn **commands, level 3 (read article)**	
<space>	go forward one page
d	go forward half a page
<return>	go forward one line
b	go back one page
g*text*	search for next page containing *text*
j	mark article as read
q	go to end of article, back to level 2

Table 5.8

5.12.2 The `xrn` program

Users running X have an alternative way of reading the news. Instead of the `rn` program, you can use `xrn`. To start `xrn`, enter the command

   $ **xrn &**

In most cases, you will then see a window like the one illustrated in figure 5.21, which is divided into four parts. From the top, these are: the upper text pane, the upper control panel, the lower text pane and the lower control panel. The two control panels contain control buttons, each of which corresponds to a command. In `xrn` it is always the left-hand mouse button that is used to click on selected buttons. When the mouse pointer is moved into one of these buttons, a help text will appear at the top of the panel, explaining what happens if the user clicks on the button.

Figure 5.21

The upper pane is used for lists of newsgroups or articles. The scroll bar at the side can be used to scroll up and down through the list. A newsgroup or an article in the upper pane can be marked by clicking with the left-hand mouse button on the corresponding line. A number of newsgroups or articles can also be marked by holding the left-hand mouse button pressed and dragging the mouse pointer across the selected lines, or by marking the first selected line using the left-hand mouse button and the last line using the right-hand button.

The xrn program may be in one of four modes.

5.12.2.1   Add

In this mode, the upper text pane gives a list of all the new newsgroups so that the user can decide whether to subscribe to any or all of the groups. When xrn is started up it automatically selects this mode if new groups have been added since the user last ran xrn. To exit from the *Add* mode, click on the Quit button. All newsgroups not selected will then be considered as not subscribed to. On leaving the *Add* mode, the program enters the *Newsgroup* mode.

5.12.2.2   Newsgroup

In this mode, the upper text pane contains a list of all the newsgroups to which the user has subscribed which contain unread articles. Here the options are the same as at level 1 in the rn program, that is, the user can choose to read articles in a particular newsgroup. If there are no new newsgroups, this mode is automatically selected when xrn is started up. In this mode, the Quit button is used to terminate xrn.

5.12.2.3   Article

This mode is entered when the user has selected a particular newsgroup to deal with. It thus corresponds to level 2 of the rn program. In the upper text pane there will be a list of headings for all the unread articles in the group. Usually, the user will want to read through the articles in order, in which case a simple click on the Next button will bring each article into the lower text pane in turn. To skip an article, the user clicks on the corresponding line in the upper pane and then on Next. After an article has been selected there are a number of operations which can be carried out on it, some of which are included in the lower control panel. To return to the *Newsgroup* mode, click on the Quit button in the upper panel.

5.12.2.4   All

This mode is selected by clicking on the All groups button in the Newsgroup mode. The lower pane will then show a list of all the newsgroups, both subscribed and unsubscribed. The scroll bar at the side can be used to move backwards and forwards through the list. For each newsgroup, it is possible to start or cancel a subscription. This is done by marking the appropriate line(s) in the lower text pane then selecting the desired operation in the lower panel. Clicking on the Quit button in the lower panel returns the user to the *Newsgroup* mode.

5.13 Summary

Communication programs	
rcp [-rp] *filename filename*	copy files between different computers
ftp [*remote_computer*]	file transfer between different computers
rsh *remote_computer command*	execute command on remote computer
rlogin *remote_computer*	log in on remote computer
telnet [*remote_computer*]	log in on remote computer
rwho [-a]	list users logged on in local network
ruptime [-a] [-r] [-l] [-t]	list status of computers in local network
write *user_ID*	communicate via terminal with other user on host computer
talk *user_ID*	communicate via two windows on terminal with other user
mesg [y] [n]	enable/disable messages on screen from other users
mail *address*	simple e-mail program in System V
mailx *address*	advanced e-mail program in System V
mail *address*	advanced e-mail program in BSD/OSF
rn	read/send USENET articles (N.B. not standard program)

Table 5.9

X programs for communication	
xmail	program for electronic mail (N.B. not standard program)
mailtool	program for electronic mail in OpenWindows
xbiff	X program signalling when e-mail has arrived
xrn	read/send USENET articles (N.B. not standard program)

Table 5.10

Six
Text Handling

The commonest type of file in a computer system is a *text file*—that is, a file containing readable text. So it is not surprising that the program most often used in a UNIX system (after the shell) is a *text editor*. A text editor allows the user to create new text files and amend existing ones, as well as (usually) copying sections of existing text files into other files.

In a UNIX system it is not uncommon for more than one text editor to be available. Which one is used is mostly a matter of taste or habit. Every user tends to have a 'favourite' text editor which he or she uses most of the time. Some users prefer a straightforward and easy-to-use text editor with relatively few commands which are not difficult to remember, while others demand a more sophisticated program with a wider range of facilities, but also with a long list of awkward commands to entrust to memory.

A text editor is an indispensable tool in a UNIX system, so a book on UNIX must describe at least some of the more commonly encountered programs. In this chapter, we have chosen to describe three different text editors: `xedit`, which is a simple, windows-oriented text editor operating under X; `textedit`, which is a rather more sophisticated windows-oriented text editor and which forms part of OpenWindows; and `vi`, which is the standard editor in UNIX, and which is intended for use on an ordinary screen.

155

The reason we have decided to describe these three in particular is that they are the most 'standardized' text editors. `vi` is one of the standard programs for UNIX and is available, generally speaking, on all UNIX installations. If you can manage `vi`, you can get by on all UNIX systems. `textedit` is part of OpenWindows and is the text editor users will normally have recourse to when running this system. `xedit` comes with the MIT distribution of X Windows and is also available on most UNIX systems where X is run. One feature of `xedit` is of particular interest: there is an advanced text editor called `emacs` which is not part of the standard UNIX system, but which is in wide use. Many of the commands found in `emacs` are also used in `xedit`; so the description of `xedit` can be treated as an introduction to `emacs` for users who may come into contact with it later.

This chapter also includes a short section on *document editing*, an activity in which the aim is not simply to produce a text file, but a neatly laid-out document.

6.1 The `xedit` program

 We will begin by describing `xedit`, as this is easy to learn and therefore useful for those who want to get to work quickly. To start up `xedit` we enter the command

    $ **xedit &**

in a terminal window. (It makes sense to run `xedit` as a background process, as you can then continue entering UNIX commands in the terminal window whilst `xedit` is in use.) Once `xedit` is running a new window will be created like the one shown in figure 6.1. The large area at the bottom is the *editing area*: this area will contain the text you are busy editing. The other large area (above the wording 'no file yet') is the *message area*: this is where `xedit` will display errors and other messages.

In the following pages we will be using the expression 'click on a button'. By this we mean that the mouse pointer is placed on a button and the `left-hand` mouse button is pressed once and immediately released. To terminate `xedit`, for example, we click on Quit.

6.1.1 Loading and saving files

`xedit` uses an internal *editing buffer*, in which it temporarily stores the text which is being edited. At the start of an editing session, the user may wish to create an entirely new text, or to fetch an existing text file and place it in the editing buffer. To create a completely new text, all we do is position the mouse pointer in the editing area and begin entering the text. Loading an existing file requires the name of the file to be

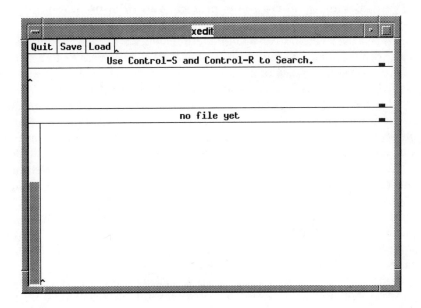

Figure 6.1

specified. This is done in the *filename area*, which is immediately to the right of the Load button. (Often it is not necessary to actually key in the filename. If the filename is already shown in one of the X windows, the filename can be marked by double-clicking on it, and then clicking the middle mouse button after the pointer has been moved to the filename area.) Once the filename has been entered, a click on Load will result in the file being loaded and the first part of it being displayed in the text area.

An alternative way of specifying which file is to be loaded to the editing buffer is to include the filename in the start command to the xedit program:

§ **xedit** *filename* **&**

When the editing of the file is complete, the user must enter the filename under which the edited text is to be saved. This again uses the filename area to the right of the Load button. (If xedit is being run to make changes to an existing file, the name will already be there, as it was entered to load the file.) It is then saved by a click on Save, which copies the contents of the editing buffer to the named file. The filename given for this need not be the same as for the file from which the text was loaded. It is worth mentioning that it does no harm to save the contents of the editing buffer from time to time while working on the text by clicking on ⟨Save⟩. This protects you from the possibility of having do all the work again, if some system failure should occur.

When the user clicks on ⟨Quit⟩ to terminate xedit, a warning is given if any changes made to the editing buffer have not been saved to file. The user then has the choice of saving the changes or not bothering to save them. In the latter case, the mouse is simply clicked on ⟨Quit⟩ again.

After saving the edited file, we may wish to start editing another file, without terminating xedit. All we need to do is enter a new filename and click on ⟨Load⟩ again. The previous contents of the editing area will then disappear and be replaced by the contents of the new file.

xedit also allows text from a file to be read in and inserted at a chosen point in a file which is being edited. This is useful if we are editing a file into which we wish to insert some text from another file. To do this, we position the editing cursor at the point where we wish the text to be inserted. We then press <meta-i> (the meta key and i at the same time). The meta key, which is included on most keyboards, is roughly the same as the ctrl key. It may be marked left, right, compose or <>. When <meta-i> is keyed in xedit, a new pop-up window will appear: see figure 6.2. This window also has a field for the filename, in which the name of the file to be inserted in the text can be entered. The mouse is then clicked on ⟨Insert File⟩ (or on ⟨Cancel⟩ if you change your mind).

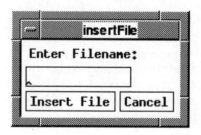

Figure 6.2

6.1.2 Entering text and moving around

The principles on which the text editor works are very straightforward. There is a special pointer in the editing area, the *editing cursor*, or simply *cursor*. This will always be between two characters. Every time a normal character is entered at the keyboard it will appear at the location of the cursor. The cursor can be moved either by using the mouse, or by means of special keyboard commands. Using the mouse is simpler. All this takes is moving the mouse pointer to the place the cursor is to be moved to and clicking the left-hand mouse button.

The keyboard commands can be useful once you are more used to the system, especially if only small movements of the cursor are required. This avoids taking your hands from the keyboard. (The keyboard commands are taken from the advanced text editor, emacs.) Table 6.1 shows the available keyboard commands to move the editing cursor.

Moving the cursor in xedit	
ctrl-f →	move forward one character
ctrl-b ←	move back one character
ctrl-p ↑	move up one line
ctrl-n ↓	move down one line
meta-f	move forward one word
meta-b	move back one word
ctrl-a	move to start of line
ctrl-e	move to end of line
ctrl-v	move forward one page
meta-v	move back one page
meta-<	move to start of file
meta->	move to end of file

Table 6.1

6.1.3 Deleting text

To remove text, keyboard commands must be used. This cannot be done simply with the mouse. There are two ways text can be removed: *deleting* and *cutting*. Text which is *deleted* is gone for good. The commands for this are shown in table 6.2.

Deleting text in xedit	
delete backspace	delete character to left of cursor
meta-delete meta-backspace	delete word to left of cursor
ctrl-d	delete character to right of cursor
meta-d	delete word to right of cursor

Table 6.2

Text which is *cut* is also lost from its location in the editing area. The difference is that the deleted text is saved in a *cut-and-paste buffer*. The text in the buffer can be 'pasted' back into the text if desired, at one or more points (see next section). The cutting commands are listed in table 6.3.

Cutting text in `xedit`	
`shift-meta-delete`	cut word to left of cursor
`shift-meta-backspace`	
`shift-meta-d`	cut word to right of cursor
`ctrl-k`	cut remainder of line
`meta-k`	cut remainder of paragraph (to next blank like)
`ctrl-w`	cut section marked by mouse

Table 6.3

The last command in table 6.3 <`ctrl-w`>, is a simple way of cutting large sections of text. The mouse is used to mark the section of text, which is then cut with <`ctrl-w`>. Marking text by using the mouse is done as described in section 2.5.1 in the context of `xterm`. There is one addition to this in `xedit`: an entire paragraph can be marked at one go by clicking four times in rapid succession with the `left-hand` mouse button. A 'paragraph' here means a section enclosed between blank lines.

6.1.4 Moving and copying text

The text which has been cut and which is stored in the cut-and-paste buffer can easily be *pasted* back into the text at the current location of the editing cursor. This is carried out by the command <`ctrl-y`>. It is also possible to use the mouse to copy text. The following methods can be used:

- *Move text.* Cut the text using an appropriate command from table 6.3. Move the cursor to the point the text is to be moved to. Press <`ctrl-y`>.

- *Copy text, alternative 1.* Cut the text using an appropriate command from table 6.3. Immediately restore the text by keying <`ctrl-y`>. Move the cursor to the point the text is to be moved to. Press <`ctrl-y`> again.

- *Copy text, alternative 2.* Mark the text to be copied using the mouse (the technique is described in section 2.5.1). Move the cursor to the point the text is to be moved to. Press the `middle` mouse button

The second method of copying has the advantage that text can also be copied from another X window using this method.

6.1.5 Searching for and replacing text strings

Before searching for a text string, make sure the mouse pointer is in the editing area. Then key<ctrl-s> or <ctrl-r>, depending whether you want to search forwards or backwards through the text. A *search window* like the one shown in figure 6.3 will then appear. Searches always start from the editing cursor. The squares marked Backward and Forward will show which direction you have selected for the search: the direction can easily be changed by clicking on these squares. The empty box ☐, the entry box, shows where text entered to the window will appear.

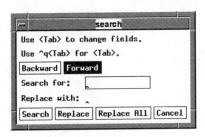

Figure 6.3

To *search for a specified text string,* proceed as follows. Make sure the entry box is on the same line as **Search for:**—if it not, press the <tab> key once. Then enter the text string you want to search for and click on Search . The editing cursor will then move to the first point where the search string occurs. If the string cannot be found, an error message will be issued. The search can be continued by repeated clicking on Search . When entering the text string to be searched for, all the usual xedit editing commands can be used, and text can also be pasted in using the mouse.

When the text you are looking for has been found, you can click on Cancel to remove the search window. It is a good idea not to remove the search window, however, as you may want to carry out a number of searches later. It is better to drag the search window outside the xedit window so that it is not in the way, and leave it on the screen.

To *search-and-replace* a specified text, the **Replace with:** line must also be filled in. The entry box can be moved to this line by pressing <tab>. At this point, the editing cursor will also move to the first occurrence of the search string. Once you have entered the new text, the old text can be replaced by it by clicking on Replace . It is also possible to leave it unchanged at the current position in the text, and instead continue the search for the next occurrence of the search string. This is done by clicking on Search . If you want to replace one string by the other everywhere it occurs, click on ⎡Replace All⎤. The changes will not necessarily be made throughout the entire text, but will always start from the position of the editing cursor and be carried out in the direction indicated, i.e. either forwards or backwards in the text. If you want the change to be made throughout the text, always make sure the editing cursor is at the very beginning or end of the text before making the change.

Unfortunately, xedit does not have an 'undo' command to allow you to change your mind afterwards, which can make large-scale changes a little dangerous. However, if things go completely wrong it is always possible to press ⎡Load⎤ to re-load the last version saved of the file you are working on.

6.2 The textedit program

The natural text editor to use in OpenWindows is textedit, which forms part of the system. It is an easy-to-use, but versatile, mouse-operated text editor. When textedit is run the screen is likely to look like figure 6.4.

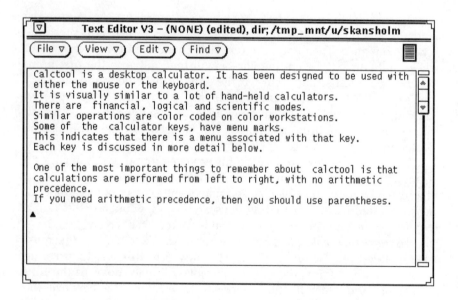

Figure 6.4

`textedit` can be started up by selecting the `Programs` sub-menu from the workspace menu, then the `Text Edit` option from this sub-menu; but it is equally possible, of course, to start the program by keying

§ **`textedit &`**

in a terminal window.

6.2.1 Loading and saving files

`textedit` uses an internal *editing buffer*, in which it temporarily stores the text which is being edited. At the start of an editing session, the user may wish to create an entirely new text, or to fetch an existing text file and place it in the editing buffer. To create a completely new text, we use the $\boxed{\text{File } \nabla}$ menu (see figure 6.5).

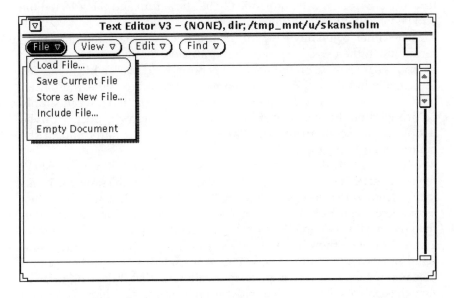

Figure 6.5

Select the first option, `Load File`, and the window shown in figure 6.6 will appear. The first line on the window must hold the name of the directory containing the file. (This line will already be filled in with the name of the directory `textedit` was started from, so often it will not be necessary to enter anything at all here.) On the second line, key the name of the file to be loaded. Once all the necessary data has been entered, click with the `left-hand` mouse key on the $\boxed{\text{Load File}}$ button, and the first lines of the text file will be displayed in the editing area.

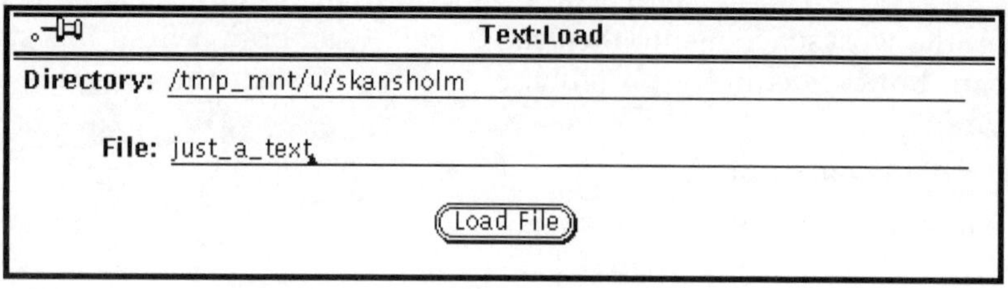

```
 ┌─────────────────────────────────────────────────────────────┐
 │ ◦─▭◖                          Text:Load                      │
 ├─────────────────────────────────────────────────────────────┤
 │ Directory: /tmp_mnt/u/skansholm _____ │
 │                                                              │
 │       File: just_a_text, _____│
 │                                                              │
 │                        ( Load File )                         │
 └─────────────────────────────────────────────────────────────┘
```

Figure 6.6

There are a few other, more convenient, ways to load files to the text editor. One has already been discussed in the context of the file manager. In the File Manager window there is a symbol for each file. If we double-click with the left-hand mouse button on the symbol for a text file, textedit will automatically be started up and the selected file will be loaded into the editing buffer.

The other convenient way to load a file uses the 'drag and drop' technique. If the textedit program is already running and its window or icon is somewhere on the screen, it is possible to mark a file in the File Manager window and drag the file to the text editor with the button held down. If textedit is on the screen as an icon, the file can simply be dropped on the icon; and if the textedit window is open it can be dropped on the small rectangular box at the right-hand end of the control panel at the top.

To save a text that has been edited as a file, again call up the File ▽ menu in figure 6.5. If you want to store the text back in the same file it was loaded from, select the option Save Current File. If you have written a completely new text or you want to save the text to a different file rather than the one it was loaded from, select instead the option Store as New File. You will then be given a 'save' window similar to the 'load' window shown in figure 6.6, where you can fill in the directory and filename for the new file. It is worth mentioning that it does no harm to save the contents of the editing buffer from time to time while working on the text. This protects you from the possibility of having do all the work again, if some system failure should occur. When the edited text is stored in an existing file, textedit will automatically produce a 'back-up' (security copy) of the old version of the file. This copy will be given the same name as the file, but with a percent sign added.

After saving the edited file, we may wish to start editing another file, without terminating textedit. All we need to do is load a new file. The previous contents of the editing area will then disappear and be replaced by the contents of the new file. To clear the editing area to start writing a new text, select the option Empty Document from the File ▽ menu shown in figure 6.5.

textedit also allows text from any file to be read in and inserted at a chosen point in a file which is being edited. To do this, we position the editing cursor at the point where we wish the text from the file to be inserted. We then select the option Include File from the File ▽ menu. A window will then appear in which we can enter the directory and filename for the file to be inserted in the text.

6.2.2 Entering text and moving around

The principles on which the text editor works are very straightforward. There is a special pointer in the editing area called the *editing cursor*, or simply the *cursor*. This will always be between two characters. Every time a normal character is entered at the keyboard it will appear at the location of the cursor. The cursor can be moved either by using the mouse, or by means of special keyboard commands. Using the mouse is simpler. All this takes is moving the mouse pointer to the place the cursor is to be moved to and clicking the left-hand mouse button.

The keyboard commands can be useful once you are more used to the system, especially if only small movements of the cursor are required. This avoids taking your hands from the keyboard. Table 6.4 shows the available keyboard commands to move the editing cursor.

Moving the cursor in textedit	
ctrl-f →	move forward one character
ctrl-b ←	move back one character
ctrl-p ↑	move up one line
ctrl-n ↓	move down one line
ctrl-shift-b	move forward one word
ctrl-,	move back one word
ctrl-.	move to end of current word
ctrl-a	move to start of line
ctrl-e	move to end of line
ctrl-shift-return Home (R7)	move to start of text
ctrl-return End (R13)	move to end of text

Table 6.4

6.2.3 Deleting text

To delete text, the text can be marked using the mouse and the Cut key pressed, as described in section 2.4.5. If you prefer not to use the keyboard, the [Edit ▽] menu button can be used (see figure 6.7).

Figure 6.7

This method of deleting text is most useful when larger sections of text need to be removed. For local changes, e.g. correcting mis-keyed characters, it is easier to use the keyboard commands. Table 6.5 shows the keyboard commands for deleting text.

Deleting text in textedit	
backspace	delete character to left of cursor
shift-backspace	delete character to right of cursor
ctrl-w	delete word to left of cursor
ctrl-shift-w	delete word to right of cursor
ctrl-u	delete to start of line
ctrl-shift—u	delete to end of line

Table 6.5

6.2.4 Moving and copying text

Moving and copying text is done exactly as described in section 2.4.5. This uses the mouse and the Cut, Paste and Copy keys. If you prefer not to use the keyboard, there are equivalent options in the [Edit ▽] menu.

6.2.5 Searching for and replacing text

Once a section of text has been marked, it is very easy to search for the next occurrence of the text. A simple press of the Find key (L9) on the keyboard takes care of it.

To carry out more general searches and to be able to replace text, there is a `Find and Replace` option available under the menu button Find ▼. When this option is selected, the window shown in figure 6.8 will appear. This window has a 'push-pin', and it can be fixed it somewhere convenient on the screen so that it does not disappear when the search is completed.

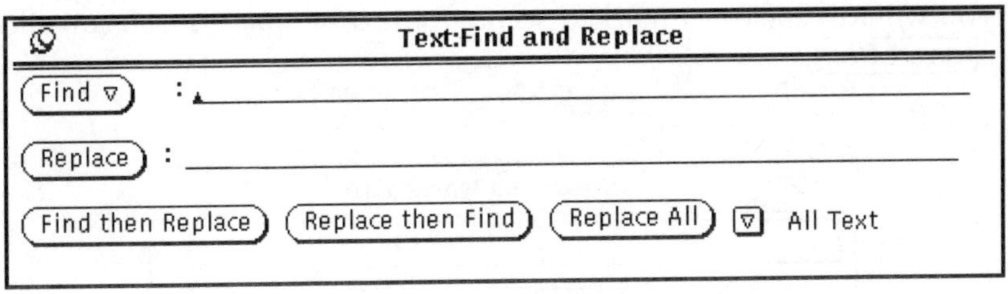

```
┌─────────────────────────────────────────────────────────────┐
│ ⍉                       Text:Find and Replace                │
│ ═══════════════════════════════════════════════════════════ │
│ ( Find ▽ )  : ▲─────────────────────────────────────────    │
│                                                              │
│ ( Replace ) : ───────────────────────────────────────────   │
│                                                              │
│ ( Find then Replace )  ( Replace then Find )  ( Replace All ) ▼ All Text │
└─────────────────────────────────────────────────────────────┘
```

Figure 6.8

On the top line, to the right of the Find ▼ button, you enter the text for which you wish to search. (If a section of text was marked when the window was called up, this will automatically be entered here.) If you only want to search for the text, you can then click on the Find ▼ button with the `left-hand` mouse button. The search will normally be carried out in a forwards direction, but a backward search can be started by selecting the `Backward` option under the Find ▼ menu button. The abbreviated menu button ▼ at bottom right can be used to determine whether the search is to be carried out on the entire text or only from the current cursor position to the end of the file (or the start, if the search is being done backwards). In the first case, select the `All Text` option (see figure 6.8), and in the second, `To End`. If the text required is found, it will be marked in the editing area after the search.

If you want to replace the 'find' text with a new text string, the new one should be entered on the second line, to the right of the Replace button. One way to replace text (the most cautious approach) is to click first on the Find ▼ button to locate the string and then, once you have confirmed it is the right place, to click on Replace to carry out the actual replacement. If the text needs replacing in several places, another click on Find ▼ will then show you the next occurrence of the search string. Alternatively, both of the last two operations can be combined by clicking on Replace then Find.

If you are certain in advance that the first occurrence of the search text will need replacing, you can click straight away on Find then Replace; and if you are sure that all occurrences need to be replaced, you can click on Replace All.

There are special functions in `textedit` to search and replace text enclosed in different types of brackets. Instead of selecting the `Find and Replace` option from the Text Editor window's $\boxed{\text{Find}\ \nabla}$ menu, select `Find Marked Text`. The window this produces is shown in figure 6.9. The top line lets you choose the type of brackets you are interested in; then, after you click on $\boxed{\text{Find Pair}}$, `textedit` will search for the next section of text enclosed in that type of brackets. If you want to remove the brackets round a text you can click on $\boxed{\text{Remove Pair}}$ and if you want to enclose a marked section of text in brackets you can click on $\boxed{\text{Insert Pair}}$.

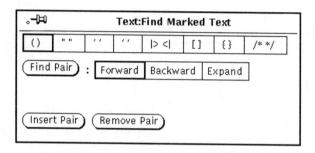

Figure 6.9

6.2.6 Changing your mind (Undo)

Many users insist that the most important command in a text editor is the command allowing you to change your mind—that is, to 'undo' a change. Earlier, in chapter 2, we saw that it is possible to reverse a deletion, move or copy in a text by using the `Undo` key (L4) on the keyboard. The key will also undo most (but not all) changes made in `textedit`. Alternatively, if you select the `Text Pane` pop-up menu from the edit window, it provides a sub-menu called `Edit`. By selecting the `Undo` option from this, you can reverse either the last change made or all the changes you have made to the current file. All types of changes can be undone by this method.

6.2.7 Some finer points

Finally, we will mention very briefly some other functions available in `textedit`.

The menu button $\boxed{\text{View}\ \nabla}$ provides facilities to search out a line with a specified line number and to find out the line number at which a marked text begins. This menu also allows you to specify what is to happen to lines that turn out too long. You can choose whether the new line occurs in the middle of a word or between words, and overlength lines can also be automatically chopped.

In the pop-up menu in the edit window there is a sub-menu called Extras. Among the options there is one which adjusts a text so that none of the lines exceeds 72 characters, there are also utilities to switch between capitals and small letters in various ways, help with inserting and removing tabs at the start of the line, and automatic tidying up of text files containing C programs.

6.3 The vi text editor

The commonest text editor used with UNIX is vi (visual). It forms part of the standard issue of UNIX and is available on all UNIX installations. vi is designed to be run on a standard screen terminal (and will of course run excellently in a terminal window under X). The whole of the terminal screen is used and the section of the file being edited is visible all the time. All the changes that are made are displayed immediately on the screen.

vi is quite a sophisticated text editor. There is a wide range of commands and facilities, and the scope of this book will not allow us to describe them all. Nor do we need to, as you can usually get by if you know a reasonable number of the commands in vi. No one can learn how to use a text editor such as vi by reading about it in a book; to be able to use a text editor well, you need to practise and get used to it. What will help you more is a guide you can use to look things up in and read up on a command you are unsure about. For this reason, all the commands we discuss are also shown in the form of a table. Some of the commands appear in the table only.

First, here is a quick introduction to vi. We will then have a more careful look at the various facilities in vi.

6.3.1 vi in five minutes

This section provides a brief introduction to the commonest editor commands. These will allow all the vital text editing work to be done.

vi is started up with the following command. The argument to the command is the file to be edited.

§ **vi** *filename*

When a file is created for the first time, this is reported on the bottom line of the screen, the *status line*. The ~ character is used by vi to indicate a blank line—see figure 6.9. If the file already exists, it will be copied into the vi editing buffer.

```
            ~
            ~
            ~
            ~
            ~
     "filename"  [New file]
```

Figure 6.9

The sequence of steps after this is illustrated in figure 6.10. While the file is being edited, vi will always be in either the *command mode* or the *input mode*. At the very beginning, it will go into command mode. It is then possible to enter commands, for example, to move the cursor, delete or insert text, replace the old text with a new one, and search for and replace text strings.

To be able to enter text to the editing buffer, vi must be switched from the command mode to input mode. The commonest commands to make space in the editing buffer to insert text are i, a, o and O. The i and a commands allow text to be added to the left and to the right of the cursor, whilst the o and O commands create a new (blank) line under and above the cursor respectively.

If the wrong character is typed when entering text, the cursor can be moved back with the <backspace> key. Entry of text will continue until the <esc> key is pressed, when vi will return to its command mode.

The editing process can be terminated in two ways: ZZ (note the capital letters!) to save the text file before terminating, and :q! ('quit') to terminate without saving the text. 'Saving' means that the contents of the editing buffer will be copied to the actual file; whereas terminating without saving means that the changes that have been made will have no effect on the text held on file. The :q! command should be used with caution, as it can ruin hours of editing work.

The screen can be moved through the editing buffer by keying <ctrl-u> ('up') or <ctrl-d> ('down'). ctrl-u results in the screen being moved half a page upwards; <ctrl-d> moves it half a page down. The cursor can be moved forward and back in the editing buffer by means of the arrow keys. If these are not provided, the h, l, j and k keys can be used instead.

A character in the editing buffer can be deleted by positioning the cursor on the character in question and pressing the x key. To delete the line indicated by the cursor, key dd.

The last editor command entered can be 'undone' by pressing the 'undo key', u.

The <ctrl-l> command re-draws the screen. Re-drawing the screen can sometimes be necessary, as communication between the terminal and the computer can be subject to interference.

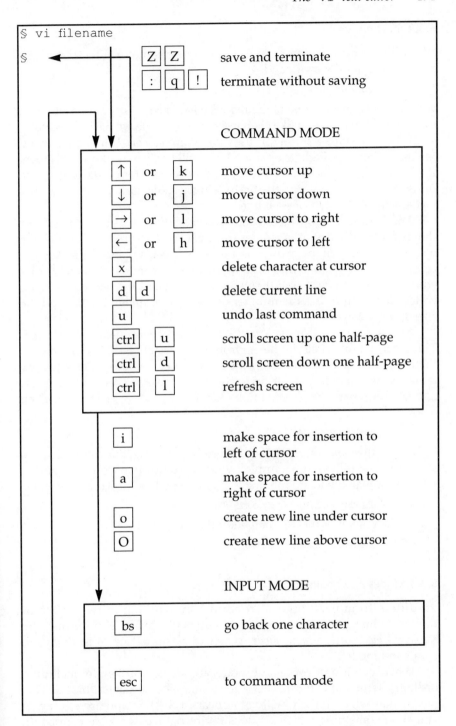

Figure 6.10

6.3.2 Starting `vi`

We will now turn to a more complete examination of `vi`. To start `vi`, as above, we enter the command

$ **vi** *filename*

where *filename* is the name of the file we wish to edit. This can be either an existing file we wish to make changes to, or a new file we wish to create.

When `vi` starts running, it uses the entire screen. If it is an existing file that is being edited, its opening lines will be displayed on the screen. If there are fewer lines in the file than there is room for on the screen, the unused lines will not be left totally empty, but marked by `vi` with a ~ character at the start of each line.

The bottom line on the screen, the *status line*, is used among other things for the display of messages from `vi`. At start-up, for example, the name of the file will be shown on this line. It is also possible to key the command `<ctrl-g>` at any time when `vi` is in command mode during editing. The status line will then show the name of the file that is being edited. It also indicates the number of the current line in the file and the size of the file itself.

For `vi` to work, it must know what type of terminal is being used. This information is held in the environment variable TERM, which means that this must be correctly set. If the screen does not look right when `vi` is started up, therefore, your first action should be to check that TERM is correct. Terminate the `vi` session by keying `<esc>:q!<return>`. Then enter

$ **echo $TERM**

to find out the value of TERM. If TERM needs correcting, this can be done as shown in the following example, which assumes that you are using a VT100 terminal. If you are running the Bourne shell or the Korn shell, enter

$ **TERM=vt100; export TERM**

and in the C shell or the TC shell enter the command

% **setenv term vt100**

6.3.3 Modes and commands

`vi` differs from most other text editors by working in two different modes. When you are running `vi`, you will always be in either the *command mode* or the *input mode*. When `vi` is started up, it is always in command mode.

When you are in command mode, *everything* you key in, including ordinary letters and figures, is interpreted as a *command* for `vi`. This means that what you key will *not* appear in the text you are editing. If you enter something which `vi` does not recognize as a legal command, it will usually react by generating a beep.

In the input mode, on the other hand, *nothing* will be interpreted as a command. *Everything* you key in will appear in the text you are editing—even character combinations which would be acceptable commands in the command mode. An example could be the command ZZ, which is the usual command to terminate vi. If you happen to be in the input mode when you give this command, vi will not be terminated, but the letters ZZ will appear in the text you are editing.

When working with vi, it is important to keep track all the time of the mode you are in. The most common mistake made by users who are not familiar with vi (and even those who are) is to try to enter commands in the input mode or text in the command mode.

It is simple to switch between the two modes. Switching from input mode to command mode is easiest—this is always done by pressing the <esc> key. There is never any danger in pressing the <esc> key: if you are already in the command mode, nothing will happen (except a beep). If you are not sure which mode you are in, therefore, you can always press the <esc> key, and you will know that, either way, you will then be in command mode.

There are a number of different commands to switch from command mode to input mode. These will be described below, some of them in the section on 'Entering text'.

In the command mode, vi will accept two types of command. The first type comprises commands consisting of one or more characters, most of which do not need a <return>. We call these commands *ordinary command*. Ordinary commands are executed immediately, and the effects are shown directly on the screen. An example of an ordinary command is x, which deletes the character at the cursor.

The second type of command starts with a colon. Let's call these commands *colon command*. All colon commands end in <return>. We have aleady seen one example of a colon command—:q! Colon commands are displayed on the status line (at the bottom of the screen) when they are entered.

6.3.4 Loading and saving files

There are two ways of specifying the file to be edited in vi. The most common way has already been demonstrated: this is to include the filename as the argument to the start-up command. However, vi can also be started up without specifying a filename:

§ **vi**

Once you are in vi, you can then enter the command

:e *filename*

The usual way to terminate vi is the command ZZ. The changes you have made will then be saved to the file before vi is terminated.

Sometimes it happens that major, incorrect changes have been made (by mistake). Instead of changing everything back, you can then use the 'emergency exit'. Key in

    :q!

and vi will then terminate without the changes being saved to file. The file you were editing will remain unchanged.

You can finish the editing of a file and start editing work on a second file without exiting from vi. First, enter the command

    :w

which saves the first file. Then key the command

    :e *new_filename*

to start editing the new file.

If you only enter :w and not :e, you will still be editing the old file. This procedure can be used to save the changes you have made from time to time.

Sometimes you will want to read in text from another file and insert it in the file you are editing. This can be done with the command

    :r *filename*

The text in the specified file will then be read into vi and inserted after the line at the cursor. The file you have read the text from will not be changed.

Finally, it can be mentioned that if the UNIX system should crash while you are editing a file in vi, you can still recover the editing you have done. When the system starts up again, you will be given a message telling you to use the following command:

    $ **vi -r** *filename*

where *filename* is the name of the file you were editing when the system crashed, and which you want to recover.

The commands for loading and saving files are summarized in table 6.6.

Loading and saving files in vi	
vi *filename*	Start vi, edit *filename*
vi	Start vi without specifying filename
:e *filename*	edit *filename*
ZZ	terminate vi, save edited file
:q!	terminate vi, leave file unchanged
:w	save edited file, stay in vi
:r *filename*	read in text in *filename*
vi -r *filename*	start vi after system crash

Table 6.6

6.3.5 Moving around in the text

In `vi` you will always have a *cursor* showing you where you are in the text at any time. There are a large number of commands that can be used to move the cursor. (Common to all of them, of course, is that you must be in command mode before keying them.) The most useful commands for moving around are listed in table 6.7. By 'words' we mean groups of characters separated by spaces or ends of lines, and by 'English words' we mean groups of characters consisting only of the letters 'a' to 'z'.

Moving around in `vi`	

`<space>`
 $\rightarrow$
 `l`
	right one character

$\leftarrow$	left one character
`h`	
`w`	right one English word
`W`	right one word
`b`	back one English word
`B`	back one word
`e`	to end of current English word
`E`	to end of current word
$\downarrow$ `j`	down one line
$\uparrow$ `k`	up one line
`^` `0`	to start of line
`$`	to end of line
`<return>` `+`	to first character not a space on next line
`-`	to first character not a space on previous line
`<ctrl-u>`	move screen one half-page up in text
`<ctrl-d>`	move screen one half-page down in text
`<ctrl-b>`	move screen one page up in text
`<ctrl-f>`	move screen one page down in text
`` ` ` ``	return to previous position
`m`x	set marker x
`` ` ``x	to mark x
`:'`x `'`X	Go to start of line with marker x

Table 6.7

A few comments on table 6.7 may help. The four commands `ctrl-u`, `ctrl-d`, `ctrl-b` and `ctrl-f` are useful when you want to move through the text in fairly large jumps, for example, when reading through it.

The three lines at the end of the table need some further explanation. You can get `vi` to remember the current position of the cursor any time you are in command mode by setting a *marker*. Simply key m*x*, where *x* is any character selected to stand for the marker. Later, you can return to the marked position by keying ` *x*. If, instead, you key :'*x*, this will take you to the start of the line containing the marker *x*.

Sometimes it can be useful to work in whole lines, for example when moving or copying large sections of text. We may also want to move the cursor to a particular line. One possibility here is the use of the line number. To move to line 25, for example, we can key 25G or :25.

There are a few special characters for line numbers which can be used in colon commands. A dollar sign stands for 'last line of file' and a full stop for 'the current line', that is, the one at the cursor. The cursor can be moved to the last line of the file, for example, by the command :$ and it can be moved ten lines forward by means of the command :.+10.

Normally, `vi` does not display line numbers, but if you want line numbers in the margin against each line you can enter the command :set nu. In a similar way, the display of line numbers can be cancelled with the command :set nonu. If you only want to know what line you are on at the moment, use the command <ctrl-g> or :.=.

Often it is simpler to use the marker technique than to keep track of line numbers. The marker is often used in a colon command, when copying, for example. It can also be used in commands to move the cursor: for example, to move to the line before the marker z we can key in :'z-1. A summary of the commands concerned with line numbers is given in table 6.8.

Line numbers in `vi`	
*n*G :*n*	move to line number *n*
G :$	move to last line of text
ctrl-g :.=	show current line number
:set nu	show line numbers for all lines
:set nonu	show no line numbers

Table 6.8

6.3.6 Keying in text

To key in text, as we have already mentioned, you must switch from the command mode to the input mode. There are a number of commands to achieve this. To key in fresh text, the commands shown in table 6.9 are used. For example, to insert fresh text after the cursor we can key an a and then key in the text we want to insert. If we wish to input text on a new line before the line where the cursor is, we can key first an O and then enter the new text. Text entry is always completed by keying <esc>, which takes us back to the command mode.

Adding text in vi	
i	insert text before cursor
a	insert text after cursor
I	insert text at start of line
A	insert text at end of line
O	insert text on a new line before the current line
o	insert text on a new line after the current line
<esc>	return to command mode

Table 6.9

When entering text, new lines can be created by pressing <return>. If a line runs on longer than the width of the screen, vi shows the remainder of the line on the next line of the screen. Usually this does not mean that the long line has been divided into several lines—vi will still see the long line as a single line even if it appears as several lines on the screen.

When you are keying in text in input mode, you can make local corrections to the text in the same way as for UNIX commands. Usually, <backspace> is used to delete the last character keyed, and <ctrl-u> to delete all the fresh text keyed in so far.

6.3.7 Deleting text

There are a number of different commands for deleting text. The most useful of these are summarized in table 6.10. All these commands can be entered only from command mode.

A special command in table 6.10 is J (join). This is used when we want to join two lines together into one line. To use the command, position the cursor on the first of the two lines and key the command J.

As can be seen, several lines can be deleted at a time by using a colon command and giving the line numbers. However, it is often simpler to set markers (see section 6.2.4) on the first and last line to be deleted. The last command in table 6.10 can then be used to avoid having to keep track of line numbers or count between lines.

Deleting text in `vi`	
x	delete character at cursor
dw	delete to end of current English word
dW	delete to end of current word
D	delete to end of line
dd	delete current line
*n*dd	delete *n* lines starting with current line
J	delete line-end character from current line (join up lines)
.	repeat previous delete or amend command
:*i*,*j*d	delete from line *i* to line *j* inclusive
:'*x*,'*y*d	delete from marker *x* to marker *y* inclusive

Table 6.10

The special characters dollar (last line of text) and full stop (current line) can also be used in colon commands. For example, we can delete all the text in the file starting from the current line with the command `: . , $d`.

6.3.8 Changing your mind

When editing text, it is perfectly normal to make mistakes now and then—for instance, to delete something which should not have been deleted or change something which should not have been changed. The chance to change your mind and 'undo' a command is therefore a very valuable facility. In `vi` there are two commands to undo mistakes: u and U. The u command undoes the last change. Only the last change can be undone with u; and if u is pressed a second time, the change will be put back. If you have made a number of changes on a particular line and wish to have the line back in the state it was before you started making changes, you can key the command U. This command restores the line to its previous state. The 'undo' commands are shown in table 6.11.

Changing your mind in `vi`	
u	undo the last change made
U	restore current line to previous state

Table 6.11

6.3.9 Searching for a specified text string

In `vi`, there is a powerful mechanism for searching for a particular text. In its simplest form, we enter a / character followed by the text string to be searched for, ending the command with <return>. For example, to search for the next point where the text string `editor` occurs we can enter /editor<return>. The search will be carried out in a forwards direction, starting from the position of the cursor. If the search string is not found by the time the end of the file is reached, the search will usually re-start automatically from the beginning of the file. If the search string is not found anywhere in the file, the message Pattern not found will appear on the status line. To search backwards through the file, we can enter a question mark instead of the / character—for example, to look for previous occurrences of the text file, we can key ?file<return>. To repeat a search for the same text string as before, a / or ? by itself is enough: the search string does not need to be re-entered.

When searching for a text string, vi normally distinguishes between capitals and small letters (upper and lower case). This means that, in our first example above, we would not find the places where Editor occurs. vi can be instructed not to differentiate between capitals and small letters by keying the command :set ic (ignore case). If we now enter the search command /editor we will find occurrences of Editor as well. To return to the normal situation, where upper and lower case are treated separately, we enter :set noic.

As we have seen, the characters / and ? have special meanings. If we want to search for a text string containing either of these characters we have to key a backslash \ before it to indicate that it is to be treated as an ordinary character. For example, to search for the text string karen/bin we would enter /karen\/bin<return>.

The search commands are summarized in table 6.12.

Searching for text strings in vi	
/*xxx*	search forwards for text string *xxx*
?*xxx*	search backwards for text string *xxx*
/	repeat search forwards
?	repeat search backwards
n	repeat search in same direction
N	repeat search in other direction
:set ic	ignore case—treat capital and small letters as identical
:set noic	treat capital and small letters as different

Table 6.12

The search string specified is in fact a *regular expression*. This means that it can contain special characters to produce a *pattern* to be matched, in roughly the same way as filename patterns in chapter 3. If you do not want to make use of this facility, you should enter the command :set nomagic. All the characters in the search string will then be treated as normal characters and you will avoid awkward surprises (except as far as $ and ^ are concerned).

Sometimes, however, regular expressions can be very useful in search strings. In table 6.13, therefore, we have shown those most often used.

Special characters for search strings in `vi`	
^	at start of string, matches start of line
$	at end of string, matches end of line
[x–y]	matches any character between x and y

Table 6.13

A couple of examples will help make this clear. The command /table$ searches for the first line ending in the string table and the command /^<space> searches for the next line starting with a space.

6.3.10 Changing the text

The simplest change to the text involves changing the character at the cursor. To do this, simply key an r followed by the new character. The command rz, for example, will replace the character at the cursor with a z. The character at the cursor can also be replaced with two or more characters: in this case, the command that is used is s. Various versions of the command c are used to replace parts of words or lines with new text.

The s and c commands both result in a switch from command mode to input mode. Everything that is keyed in after the 's' or the 'c' will thus be interpreted as new text intended to replace the old text. To finish entry of the new text and return to command mode, it is always <esc> that should be keyed.

Various commands for replacing text with new text are listed in table 6.14.

The last few commands in table 6.14 are useful when you want to carry out extensive global changes. For example, you can change all occurrences of the name 'Barry' in the file to 'Garry' by entering the command

    `:1,$s/Barry/Garry/g`

(The dollar sign in this command means 'the last line of the file'.)

As another example, suppose we have marked a section of the text that we want to be indented by beginning every line with three spaces. We have set marker a on the first line of this section of text and marker b on the last line. We can now enter the change command

    `:'a,'bs/^/   /`

(The ^ character matches the start of each line.)

Commands for changing the text in vi	
r	change character to new character
s	change character to a text string
cw	change remainder of English word
cW	change remainder of word
C	change remainder of line
.	repeat previous change or delete command
cc	change whole line
:i,js/*old text*/*new text*/	change first occurrence of *old text* between lines numbered i to j (inclusive) to *new text*
:i,js/*old text*/*new text*/g	change all occurrences of *old text* in lines numbered i to j (inclusive) to *new text*
:'x,'ys/*old text*/*new text*/	change first occurrence of *old text* between line at marker x and line at marker y (inclusive) to *new text*
:'x,'ys/*old text*/*new text*/g	change all occurrences of *old text* between line at marker x and line at marker y (inclusive) to *new text*

Table 6.14

6.3.11 Copying and moving text

There are two methods of copying and moving text in vi. In the first method, the standard commands are used, and in the second the colon commands. The first method ('cut and paste') is the more obvious one to use when copying or moving single characters, words or lines, whilst the other is preferable when it comes to dealing with a number of lines.

We will start by describing the first method. Internal to vi, there is a *cut-and-paste buffer*. (In fact, there are several buffers, but we will only be describing the ordinary buffer.) Every time a section of text is deleted with a standard command, e.g. dw or dd, the deleted section of text is placed in the buffer.

A section of text held in the buffer can be pasted back into the file by placing the cursor at the desired position and keying the command P or p. If the buffer contains characters or words, the command P or p will paste in the text from the buffer *before* or *after* the cursor respectively. If, on the other hand, the buffer is holding complete lines, the command P or p will paste in the lines from the buffer respectively *before* or *after* the line at the cursor.

As an example, let us suppose we wish to move a full line. In that case, we place the cursor on the line we want to move and enter the command dd. The line is deleted, but will be available in the cut-and-paste buffer. We can then place the cursor on the line before the point to which we want to move the deleted line. Finally, we enter the command p, which pastes in the deleted line at its new position.

Text can be copied using the cut-and-paste buffer as well as moved. For this, instead of the delete commands, we use 'yank commands'. Unlike the d commands, y commands do not delete text from the file. All they do is place a copy of the selected text in the buffer. There is a y command to match every d command—for example, there is a yW command which places a word in the buffer and a yy command which places a copy of the current line in the buffer.

As an example, suppose we want to copy a line. We start by placing the cursor on the line to be copied and keying the command yy. We then move the cursor to the position the line is to be copied to and press p.

The second method of moving and copying text uses colon commands. To move lines 25-30 to a new position after line 50, for example, we can enter

    :25,30m50

Copying is done in the same way: we simply key co instead of m:

    :25,30co50

It is also possible to use markers and the special characters dollar and full stop. The following command, for example, moves the lines between markers a and b to the end of the file.

    :'a,'bm$

A summary of the commands for moving and copying a specified section of text is given in table 6.15.

Copying and moving text in vi	
all d commands	delete and place deleted text in cut-and-paste buffer
yw	place current English word in buffer
yW	place current word in buffer
yy Y nY	place current line in buffer place n lines in buffer
P	paste cut text before cursor
p	paste cut text after cursor
:i,jmk	move lines numbered i-j to after line ik
:'x,'ym'z	move text from marker x to marker y to after marker z
:i,jcok	copy lines numbered i-j to after line k
:'x,'$y$co'z	copy text from marker x to marker y to after marker z

Table 6.15

6.4 Formatting documents

The term *word processing* is often used to describe the activity of creating different types of readable document. Often this document is required to be tidily presented and may for example include headings, paragraphing, page numbering, columns and different text sizes and styles. There are two sorts of program that can be used to create documents. We can call them *text formatting programs* and *word processing programs*.

A *text formatter* is a program which reads a plain file and uses it to generate a document on one or other type of printer. Before using a text formatter, a plain file must first be created using a text editor. This file will, of course, contain the text to be presented in the document, but it will also include formatting commands for the text formatter. Examples of these are commands to start a new page, start a new paragraph or change text size or style. Formatting commands usually have a special appearance to enable the text formatter to tell them apart from the text itself. The disadvantage of this way of working is that the user cannot see exactly how the finished document will look without running the text file through the text formatter and producing hard copy on the printer. It may be necessary to go through several print runs before the document looks exactly the way the user wants it. Another disadvantage is that the formatting commands are often quite complicated and it can take a long time to learn to use them properly. An advantage, however, is that it gives the user good control over the finer details of the finished presentation.

Examples of text formatters are `nroff`, `troff` and `TeX`. The first two of these form part of standard UNIX. `nroff` is the oldest, and is designed for printing documents on older, simpler, typewriter-style printers. `troff` is a more up-to-date version of `nroff`, and can generate hard copy on laser printers, so that a variety of type styles and sizes can be used. With the aid of a few utilities (`eqn` and `tbl`), mathematical formulae and tables can also be generated. The text formatter `TeX` is specially designed to be able to produce advanced mathematical text; it is not one of the standard programs in UNIX.

By *word processing programs* we mean for present purposes a program which shows on the screen exactly what the finished document will look like. You will sometimes see the acronym WYSIWYG (What You See Is What You Get) used in connection with this sort of program. This means that a precondition for running a word processor is that the user must have a monitor which will display the different type styles included in the document. Word processors are often controlled using the mouse and various menus. The advantage as compared with a text formatter is that it is often much easier to learn to use a word processor. Examples of word processors which can be run under X Windows are `FrameMaker`, `InterLeaf` and `Avalon`.

Seven
Shell Scripts

Up to now, we have only used the command shell interactively. In this chapter, we will be going a step further by describing how to input commands using *shell scripts*.

Shell scripts are files consisting of a sequence of commands, and can be regarded as *program* executed by the shell. Shell scripts are often used to avoid having to key in long sequences of commands over and over again.

In much the same way as statements in a standard programming language, the commands in a shell script have to follow special rules of *syntax* controlling their order and content. All shell languages include mechanisms for assigning variables, handling input and output, repeating commands etc. However, the two shell families Bourne/Korn and C/TC differ where the syntax is concerned. This means that we must make sure which language we are using in our shell scripts.

In this chapter, we will first be describing the things that are the same (or nearly the same) for all the shells. To make it easier for the reader, the constructions particular to the Bourne/Korn shell and the C/TC shell will then be described in their own separate sections. (This means that anyone interested in both shell families will find some information presented twice.)

7.1 Executing shell script files

Shell scripts consist of commands which have been placed in a text file. Suppose, for example, that we have used a text editor to create a file called howmany containing just the one line

```
who | wc -1
```

We can confirm that the file does contain the line it is supposed to by keying a cat command:

```
$ cat howmany
who | wc -1
$
```

There are three different ways to execute a shell script file, that is, to execute the commands it contains. We can enter the name of the file, we can call a shell to execute the file, and we can have the commands in the file executed directly by the current shell. We shall describe each of these in turn.

7.1.1 Entering the name of the shell script file

The simplest and most usual way of executing a shell script file is to enter its name. For a file to be successfully executed this way, it must be *executable*. A file can be made executable with the help of the program chmod, which was described in chapter 3. To change the access permissions for the file howmany so that it can be executed, we enter the command

```
$ chmod ugo+x howmany
```

The file howmany will then be executable in exactly the same way as any other program. This means that every time we want to find out how many users are logged in to the system we only need to enter the command

```
$ howmany
15
```

Before we examine a few examples of shell scripts, we must point out that if a shell script file is called by entering its name, it is assumed to contain Bourne shell commands. Unless there is some specific indication on the first line of the shell script, therefore, the Bourne shell will be used to execute the statements in the file. This even applies if the shell script file is called from within the Korn shell or the C or TC shell. If you want the shell script to be executed, instead, by the C shell, the file must start with a hash # in the first character position of the first line. It is also possible to indicate explicitly which shell is to be used: in this case, the first line should start with the two characters #! followed by the full pathname of the shell. To avoid any misunderstandings arising, we have decided to use this method. We will be starting all shell scripts written in the Bourne shell with

```
#!/bin/sh
```

those written in the Korn shell with

```
#!/usr/bin/ksh
```

and those in the C shell with

```
#!/bin/csh
```

7.1.2 Calling a shell

The second way of executing a shell script file is to call a shell with the shell script as the argument. We can thus key in

    $ **sh** *script_file*

if we want the shell script file to be executed by the Bourne shell,

    $ **ksh** *script_file*

if we want it to be executed by the Korn shell, and

    $ **csh** *script_file*

if we want it to be executed by the C shell. If we go about it in this way, there is no need to make the file executable using chmod.

    This way of executing shell script files can be useful, for example, when doing test runs of new shell scripts and de-bugging them (that is, tracking down any errors in them). It can be easier to trace bugs if the execution of the shell script can be followed through. This can be achieved by use of the shell options -v and -x, which are summarized in table 7.1. Other useful options in the shell program are given in the manual.

sh	[-v]	[-x]	[*script_file*]
ksh	[-v]	[-x]	[*script_file*]
csh	[-vV]	[-xX]	[*script_file*]
tcsh	[-vV]	[-xX]	[*script_file*]
-v	(verbose) commands are displayed while being read in to shell		
-x	each command is displayed before it is executed		
-V	As -v but takes effect before .cshrc is executed		
-X	As -x but takes effect before .cshrc is executed		

Table 7.1

For example, if we wish to test-run the shell script file my_file using the Bourne shell and see a display of each command before it is executed, we enter

    $ **sh -x my_file**

7.1.3 Execution of shell script file by current shell

When a shell script file is executed by entering its name or by calling a shell program with the file as the argument, a *new* UNIX process is created, and a *new* shell program is started up in this process. It is this new shell which executes the commands in the script file. Sometimes we do not want a new process to be created, but prefer the current shell program to directly execute the commands in the script file.

Suppose, for example, that we want to write a command procedure, terminit, which, when it is called, changes the shell variable giving the terminal type to the value vt100 and changes the prompt so that it contains the text ?>

In the Bourne shell and the Korn shell we set up the following lines in the terminit file:

```
#!/bin/sh
TERM=vt100
PS1="?> "
```

and in the Korn shell we change the first line in the file from #!/bin/sh to #!/usr/bin/ksh. We then execute the shell script file by entering the command:

```
$ terminit
$
```

Notice that the prompt has not changed. This is because the the shell variable PS1 has not been changed in the current shell, but in a different process. The solution to the problem is to use the *dot operator*:

```
$ . terminit
?>
```

The shell script file is now executed in the same process, and the shell variables TERM and PS1 are changed as intended.

In the C shell and the TC shell, the terminit file looks like this:

```
#!/bin/csh
set term=vt100
set prompt="?> "
```

After the call

```
% terminit
%
```

we can see that the prompt has not changed. This is because the the shell variable prompt has not been changed in the same process, but in a different one. To make sure that the commands in the shell script file are run in the same process, so that the correct shell variable is affected, we use the C shell or TC shell command source:

```
$ source terminit
?>
```

Now the shell variables `prompt` and `term` will be changed in the current versions of the C shell and the TC shell.

7.2 Commands

For the sake of completeness, this section provides a summary of the rules governing how commands are given to the shell. In part, this repeats what has been said in earlier chapters.

A *simple command* consists of a sequence of *words* separated by one or more spaces or tab characters. The shell interprets the first word as the name of the program to be run and the remainder as arguments for the program.

$$program\ arg_1\ arg_2\ ...\ arg_n$$

When the program terminates, it sends a *return code*, which can be used to determine whether the program terminated correctly or whether there was an error.

A program will normally read input data from the *standard input* file and write output data to the *standard output*. If a command contains no redirection operators, the standard input will automatically be connected to the keyboard and the standard output to the screen. The redirecton of input and output data from and to files specified by the user is carried out by means of the command operators >, >>, < and <<:

$$program\ arg_1\ arg_2\ ...\ arg_n\ >\ \textit{file}$$
$$program\ arg_1\ arg_2\ ...\ arg_n\ >>\ \textit{file}$$
$$program\ arg_1\ arg_2\ ...\ arg_n\ <\ \textit{file}$$
$$program\ arg_1\ arg_2\ ...\ arg_n\ <<\ \textit{text\_string}$$

The first three of the examples above were discussed in chapter 4.1, so they need no further comment here. The fourth redirection command << is used to supply data to a program which has been called directly. How this works is best illustrated by an example. Suppose we want to sort the three names `linda`, `david` and `john` into alphabetical order. As we saw earlier, we can do this by keying

```
$ sort
linda
david
john
<ctrl-d>
david
john
linda
$
```

Normally, the end of input data is marked by a `<ctrl-d>`. However, this will only work if we are issuing the sort command from the keyboard. If we wish to include the sort in a shell script file, we cannot finish with `<ctrl-d>`, and in this case we use the operator `<<` to specify a different end marker. If we decide to use the text string END as the end marker, for example, we can enter

```
$ sort << END
linda
david
john
END
david
john
linda
$
```

We saw earlier that a succession of simple commands separated by the command operator | forms a pipeline. This operator results in output data from one program being taken as input data to the next. For example:

```
$ cal 1992 | wc -1
   40
```

We have also seen how to create new processes and execute commands in the background by means of the command operator &:

```
$ sleep &
```

If a number of commands are entered on the same line separated by the command operator &, this indicates that the commands are to be executed in parallel, that is, at the same time. We can enter, for example

```
$ cat /etc/termcap & cal 1992 & who & date
```

We also know that commands separated by a ; will be executed in sequence, from left to right:

```
$ cal 10 1992 ; who ; date
```

A number of simple commands can thus be set up at the same time by means of the command operators ; and &. This is referred to as assembling the commands in a *command list*. There are two other operators, && and | |, which we did not discuss earlier and which can also be used in constructing command lists.

If two commands are separated by the operator && the command to the right of the operator will only be executed if the command to the left terminates correctly:

```
$ cal 10 1992 && who && date
```

```
     October 1992
  S  M Tu  W Th  F  S
              1  2  3
  4  5  6  7  8  9 10
 11 12 13 14 15 16 17
 18 19 20 21 22 23 ?4
 25 26 27 28 29 30 31


 david      ttyp2     Mar 20 12:29
 john       ttyp8     Mar 20 13:21
 linda      ttypd     Mar 20 14:03


 Thu May 28 10:35:30 GMT DST 1992
 §
```

If the command to the left of the operator && does not terminate correctly, the command to the right will not be executed:

```
§ cl 10 1992 && who && date
cl: Command not found.
§
```

When two commands are separated by the operator | |, the command to the right of the operator will only be executed if the command to the left does not terminate correctly. Compare the two following examples:

```
§ cal 10 1992 || who
     October 1992
  S  M Tu  W Th  F  S
              1  2  3
  4  5  6  7  8  9 10
 11 12 13 14 15 16 17
 18 19 20 21 22 23 24
 25 26 27 28 29 30 31
 §
```

and:

```
§ cl 10 1992 || who
cl: Command not found.
 david      ttyp2     Mar 20 12:29
 john       ttyp8     Mar 20 13:21
 linda      ttypd     Mar 20 14:03
 §
```

Round brackets () can be used to convert a command list into a simple command. This mechanism can be useful, for example, where output data from several programs in a command list is to be saved to the same file:

$ (cal 1992; date; who) > temp

What in fact happens is that the command or commands between the brackets are started up in a new process and all the output data is redirected to the file `temp`. The same result could be achieved with the rather longer command:

$ cal 1992 > temp; date >> temp; who >> temp

7.3 Quotes and other symbols

There are four mechanisms which can be used to suppress the special functions of shell command operators in different ways. These are shown in table 7.2.

Quotes and other symbols	
Symbol	Result
"	Cancels the function of the following characters: `' < > # * ? | & ; ( ) [ ] ^` `<space> <newline> <tab>` ~ (in Korn shell, C shell, TC shell)
'	as above plus following characters: `$ \ "`
\	Cancels the function of the following character
`command`	Executes *command*

Table 7.2

7.3.1 Double quotation marks (")

If we want to display the character > using the `echo` program, it is easy to make the mistake of attempting this as follows:

$ echo >

This will result in an error message, as the > symbol is a command operator and will be processed by the shell program instead of being passed to `echo` as an argument. For the > symbol to be displayed, the shell must be persuaded to treat it as an ordinary character: the special function of the > must be suppressed. One way of doing this is to enclose the symbol in double quotation marks:

$ echo ">"
>

The following symbols lose their special function and are treated as ordinary characters if they are enclosed in double quotation marks:

```
 '    <    >    #    *    ?    |
 &    ;    (    )    [    ]    ^
<space> <newline> <tab>
 ~ (in Korn shell, C shell, TC shell)
```

Symbols which are not suppressed are:

```
 $  `  "  \
```

These retain their special function.

Spaces included between the double quotes will be kept as spaces. An example of this is the following command, which searches for the text string `Peter Johnson` in the file `/etc/passwd`:

```
$ grep "Peter Johnson" /etc/passwd
```

7.3.2 Single quotation marks (')

Suppose we have set up a shell variable, `message`, by means of the command

```
$ message="hello there"
```

if we are running the Bourne shell or the Korn shell, or

```
% set message="hello there"
```

if we are running the C shell or the TC shell. Now study the following example:

```
$ echo $message
hello there
$ echo "$message"
hello there
```

To display the text string `$message` we must enclose it, as shown in chapter 4, in *single* quotation marks:

```
$ echo '$message'
$message
```

The following symbols lose their special function and are treated as ordinary characters if they are enclosed in single quotation marks:

```
 '    <    >    #    *    ?    |
 &    ;    (    )    [    ]    ^
 $    `    "    \
<space> <newline> <tab>
 ~ (in Korn shell, C shell, TC shell)
```

7.3.3 Backslash (\)

The backslash symbol \ suppresses the special function of the following character, as can be demonstrated with the commands below:

```
$ echo \$message
$message
$ echo \<  \>  \"  \'  \`  \$  \|
<  >  "  '  `  $  |
$ echo \\
\
$
```

7.3.4 Back-apostrophe (`)

If a command is enclosed in back-apostrophes (`) the command will be executed and the standard output from the program will be entered at that position. This is best explained using examples:

```
$ echo "The present date is `date`"
The present date is Thu May 28 10:40:00 GMT DST 1992
```

Commands enclosed in back-apostrophes may also have command operators:

```
$ echo "There are `who | wc -1` users logged on"
There are 5 users logged on
$
```

To save output data from a command in a variable, we can use the following commands in the Bourne shell and the Korn shell:

```
$ today=`date`
$ echo "Today's date is $today"
Today's date is Thu May 28 10:40:00 GMT DST 1992
```

In the C shell or the TC shell the above commands become:

```
$ set today=`date`
$ echo "Today's date is $today"
Today's date is Thu May 28 10:40:00 GMT DST 1992
```

7.4 Comments

Most programming languages allow *comments* to be included in programs. In shell script languages, this is done by starting the text with a hash # character (followed by a space). The remainder of the line will then be treated as a comment.

```
#!/bin/sh
# This is an example of how comments
# can be included in shell scripts
date           # display date and time
cal 10 1992 # display calendar for 1992
```

When the above program is run, only the current date and time, followed by a calendar, will be displayed on the screen.

7.5 Text output

As we saw earlier, the output of text strings to the 'standard output' file (usually the screen) is by means of the echo program:

```
$ echo Hello there
Hello there
$
```

If the argument to echo contains command operators, the effect of the operators must be suppressed by enclosing them in single or double quotation marks, for example:

```
$ echo "****** Hello there ******"
****** Hello there ******
$
```

echo automatically advances one line after the argument to a program has been written to the standard output.

In BSD and OSF, the line advance can be prevented by adding the option -n:

```
$ echo -n Hello there
Hello there$
```

In System V the formatting code \c (continuous) is used to switch off the line advance:

```
$ echo "Enter terminal type: \c"
Enter terminal type: $
```

Also in System V, the formatting code \t (tab) can be used to produce output in columns at the predefined tab positions (every 8th column):

```
$ echo "1\t2\t3\t4\t5\t6\t7"
1       2       3       4       5       6       7
$
```

New lines can be generated with the System V formatting code \n. e.g.:

```
$ echo "Adam\nPeter\nSimon"
Adam
Peter
Simon
$
```

In the Korn Shell there is, as well as echo, a text output command print. This command is used in exactly the same way as echo, but it accepts all the arguments available in the System V and BSD/OSF versions of UNIX. Either -n or \c can be used to suppress the line advance, for example. The print command also accepts the argument \t for output in columns and \n to generate a new line. (See the examples above.)

7.6 Return codes and exit

It will often happen that errors result when a program is run. Errors occur when the user of a program does not follow the correct rules and conventions for the program in question. The user may enter a wrong number of arguments, the wrong sort of argument etc. As a programmer of shell scripts, the user can both locate and generate errors in his or her program.

Every time a program terminates, a *return code* will be sent back as part of the standard procedure. By convention, when a program terminates correctly the value 0 will be returned and, if some error has occured, the return code will be ≠0.

Return codes	
Value	Meaning
0	Program has terminated correctly.
≠0	Program has not terminated correctly (the meaning of this return code is specific to each program).

Table 7.3

The operation exit can be used in a shell script file to terminate the file program and send back a return code. In the Bourne shell and the Korn shell, we write:

        exit *return_code*

and in the C shell and the TC shell:

        exit (*return_code*)

The following shell script, stored in a file called true, gives the return code 0. In the Bourne shell, the content of the file is:

```
#!/bin/sh
exit 0
```

and in the C shell:

```
#!/bin/csh
exit (0)
```

To check that a program has returned a zero code on terminating, we can display the contents of the predefined shell variable holding the return code generated by the last command. This variable is called ? in the Bourne and Korn shells and `status` in the C/TC shell:

```
$ true; echo $?
0
% true; echo $status
0
```

The program `true` and a corresponding program `false` are included as standard programs and are documented in the UNIX manual. (However, for reasons of efficiency the standard programs are not implemented in any shell language.)

7.7 Specific to the Bourne and Korn shells

In this section, we will be dealing with constructions specific to the Bourne and Korn shells.

7.7.1 Interactive input

The input command `read` is used when we want the value of one or more shell variables to be read from the standard input.

```
$ read a b c
one 12345     fifteen
$ echo $c $a $b
fifteen one 12345
$ read fulline
Once upon a time
$ echo $fulline
Once upon a time
$
```

In chapter 7.1.3 we wrote a shell script file called `terminit` to set up the shell variables holding the terminal type and the prompt. We will now alter this script so that the operator can enter the values directly:

```
#!/bin/sh
echo "Enter terminal type and prompt"
read TERM
read PS1
```

A test run of the shell script gives:

```
$ . terminit
Enter terminal type and prompt
vt100
?>
?>
```

Note that, as in chapter 7.1.3, we had to use the dot operator when calling the shell script file.

7.7.2 Arithmetical operations

As the Bourne shell has no built-in mechanism to calculate arithmetical expressions (the Korn shell has—see next section) we have to use the program `expr` (for example) to do this. We can key

```
$ expr 15 + 25
40
$ expr 8 "*" 5
40
$ variable=15
$ expr $variable + 25
40
$
```

The arithmetical operators in table 7.4 can be used for calculations using the `expr` program.

Arithmetical operators for `expr`	
+	addition
–	subtraction
*	multiplication
/	division (integer part of result)
%	modulus (remainder)

Table 7.4

Note that where a symbol has a particular meaning for the shell program, this function must be suppressed. Otherwise an error will result:

```
$ expr 2 * 2
expr: syntax error
$ expr 2 \* 2
4
```

Operands and operators must be separated by at least one space:

```
$ expr 2+2
2+2
$ expr 2 + 2
4
$
$ res1=`expr 5 / 2`
$ res2=`expr 5 % 2`
$ echo $res1 $res2
2 1
$
```

It is also possible to form logical expressions using the operators in table 7.5. Logical calculations using the `expr` program will give as the result either the value 1, which is regarded as 'true', or the value 0, which is regarded as 'false'.

Relational operators for `expr`	
Example	Returns 'true' if
x = y	x is equal to y
x != y	x and y are not equal
x < y	x is less than y
x > y	x is greater than y
x <= y	x is less than or equal to y
x >= y	x is greater than or equal to y

Table 7.5

Note that the characters < and > have a special meaning for the shell. We must therefore make sure that their special function is always suppressed. The following examples illustrate the use of the relational operators:

```
$ expr 7 = 19
0
$ expr 7 \< 19
1
$ x=123
$ y=1234
$ z1=`expr $x <= $y`
$ z2=`expr $x > $y`
$ echo $z1 $z2
1 0
```

7.7.3 Arithmetical expressions in the Korn shell

In the Korn shell, arithmetical calculations can be carried out by using the built-in command `let`. (This corresponds to the operator @ in the C shell and the TC shell.)

```
$ let variable=15
$ let variable=$variable+25
$ let variable="$variable + 25"
$ let variable=variable+25
$ echo $variable
90
```

Note that the expression following the `let` does not require a dollar sign before the name of a variable to obtain the value of the variable. See the fourth line in the example above.

If we attempt to assign a non-numeric value using `let`, an error message will be displayed:

```
$ name=mike
$ let variable=name
ksh: mike: bad number
```

It is also possible to use all the integer operators in the C programming language (with a few exceptions) in a `let` command. The commonest arithmetical operators are shown in table 7.6.

Arithmetical operators in the Korn shell	
+	addition
–	subtraction
*	multiplication
/	division (integer part of result)
%	modulus (remainder)

Table 7.6

Some examples in illustration:

```
$ let res1="5 / 2"
$ let res2="5 % 2"
$ echo $res1 $res2
2 1
```

Arithmetic expressions may also include comparisons. These are carried out using the operators in table 7.7 and result in a value of either 1 ('true') or 0 ('false').

Arithmetical comparisons in the Korn shell	
Example	Returns 'true' if
x == y	x is equal to y
x != y	x and y are not equal
x < y	x is less than y
x > y	x is greater than y
x <= y	x is less than or equal to y
x >= y	x is greater than or equal to y

Table 7.7

Here are some examples illustrating the use of relational operators

```
$ let x=123
$ let y=1234
$ let z1="x <= y"
$ let z2="x > y"
$ echo $z1 $z2
1 0
$
```

Note that the expression to the right of the assignment operator must be enclosed in double quotation marks if it contains the symbol < or >. To simplify things for the user, therefore, there is an alternative way of writing arithmetical expressions. Instead of keying `let`, the arithmetical expression can be enclosed in double brackets.

```
$ (( z1 = x <= y ))
$ (( z2 = x > y ))
$ echo $z1 $z2
1 0
$
```

One-dimensional arrays can be set up in the Korn shell. The assignment of an array is made as follows:

```
$ set -A computers thor odin balder
```

It is also possible to specify lists of numerical values, e.g.:

```
$ set -A numlist 15 25 8 32 99
$ echo ${numlist[*]}
15 25 8 32 99
```

If a list contains numerical values, we can use the command `let` with the position of the element in the list (its index) to process the list, for example:

```
$ let numlist[2]=50
$ let numlist[4]=numlist[2]*3
$ (( numlist[0]=1 ))
$ (( numlist[1]=numlist[0] + 2 ))
$ echo ${numlist[*]}
1 3 50 32 150
```

Note that the lowest index for the array is 0:

```
$ echo ${numlist[0]}
1
```

Alternatively, the first element in the list can be extracted as follows:

```
$ echo $numlist
1
```

Array variables do not need to be dimensioned before they can be used: space will be created automatically as required. The following example shows how an array of five random numbers can be generated and displayed:

```
#!/usr/bin/ksh
for i in 0 1 2 3 4
do
        (( vector[i]=RANDOM ))
done
print ${vector[*]}
```

The program generates five random numbers which are stored in the array variable `vector`. The random numbers are generated using the Korn shell's built-in random number generator. Every time the shell variable RANDOM is read a new randomly-generated whole number is obtained.

7.7.4 The `if` command

Traditional programming languages always include a condition statement, generally known as an `if` command. A construction permitting certain commands to be executed under particular conditions also exists in the Bourne shell and the Korn shell. At its simplest, it takes the form:

```
if logical_expression
then
        command
        command
        . . .
fi
```

If the logical expression is 'true', the commands between `then` and `fi` are carried out; if not, no command is executed.

The `if` command can be balanced by an `else` section:

```
if logical_expression
then
        command
        command
        . . .
else
        command
        command
        . . .
fi
```

The sequence of commands between `else` and `fi` will be executed if the logical expression is 'false'.

An `if` command may also contain any number of `elif` sections:

```
if logical_expression
then
        command
        command
        . . .
elif logical_expression
then
        command
        command
        . . .
else
        command
        command
        . . .
fi
```

The sequence of commands in each `elif` section will be executed if all previous logical expressions in the `if` command are 'false' and the logical expression at the start of the `elif` section is 'true'.

7.7.5 Logical expressions

For the *logical expressions* included in `if` commands in the Bourne shell and the Korn shell, the value 0 is regarded as 'true' and all other values as 'false'. C programmers should note this particularly, as it differs from what applies in the C programming language. It is also different from what happens in the `expr` program.

In the Bourne shell there are two methods for stating a logical expression, using respectively a *command* and a *test expression*. (Both these methods for stating a logical expression also apply, of course, for the Korn shell. However, as we shall be describing below, there are two additional ways of stating a logical expression in the Korn shell, using *conditional expressions* and *arithmetical expressions*, where arithmetical expressions largely follow the same rules as test expressions.) If the logical expression is to be included in an `if` command in the Bourne shell, we can write either

```
if command
then
        . . .
```

or

```
if [ test_expression ]
then
        . . .
```

Note that the *test expression* has to be within spaces and enclosed in square brackets.

Using the first method, a *command* is entered where the logical expression is to be. The command will then be executed and the return code from the command will give the value of the logical expression. A command which executes normally and gives the return code 0 will thus give the value 'true'. As an example, here is an if command which first attempts to list the content of a directory dir1. If this is successful, the command then switches to that directory.

```
if ls dir1
then
      cd dir1
fi
```

In the second method, a *test expression* is set up using the operators and rules defined for the program test (for a full description see the UNIX manual test(1)). There are three classes of operator: *relational operators*, *logical operators* and *file operators*.

Using the relational operators, which are listed in table 7.8, text strings or integers can be compared with each other. (These relational operators also apply for *conditional expressions* in the Korn shell.)

Relational operators for *test expressions* in the Bourne and Korn shells and *conditional expression* in the Korn shell		
Operator	Returns the value 'true' if	Example
=	two strings are equal	$str = simon
!=	two strings are not equal	$str != peter
-n	a string is not empty	-n $str
-z	a string is empty	-z $str
-eq	two integers are equal	$num -eq 15
-ne	two integers are not equal	$num -ne 10
-lt	one integer is less than another	$num -lt 50
-le	one integer is less than or equal to another	$num -le 5
-gt	one integer is greater than another	$num -gt 10
-ge	one integer is greater than or equal to another	$num -ge 5

Table 7.8

The following command tests whether the user ID is mike. If it is, the text string Hello Mike is written to the screen:

```
if [ $LOGNAME = mike ]
then
      echo "Hello Mike"
fi
```

Using the logical operators shown in table 7.9, more complicated *test expressions* can be formed, including 'not', 'and' and 'or'.

Logical operators in *test expressions* in the Bourne and Korn shells		
Operator	Returns 'true' if	Example
!	an expression is 'false'	`! -z $var`
-a	both expressions are 'true' (AND)	`$i -gt 1 -a $j -le 9`
-o	either of the expressions is 'true' (OR)	`$e = SV -o $t -le 50`

Table 7.9

The command

```
if [ $LOGNAME = david -a $TERM = vt100 ]
then
        echo "Hello there"
fi
```

will write the text string `Hello there` to the screen if the user ID is david and the content of the environment variable `TERM` is `vt100`.

The third class of operator in the *test expressions* comprises file operators, which are shown in table 7.10. These can be used to examine various characteristics of files. (The operators shown in the table also exist in the Korn shell *conditional expressions*.)

File operators for *test expressions* in the Bourne and Korn shells and *conditional expressions* in the Korn shell		
Operator	Returns 'true' if a file	Example
-r	exists and can be read	`-r` *<filename>*
-w	exists and can be written to	`-w` *<filename>*
-x	exists and can be executed	`-x` *<filename>*
-f	exists and is a plain file	`-f` *<filename>*
-d	exists and is a directory file	`-d` *<filename>*
-s	exists and is not empty	`-s` *<filename>*

Table 7.10

The following command checks to see whether the file /etc/passwd can be read. If so, it displays the text File /etc/passwd can be read.

```
if [ -r /etc/passwd ]
then
        echo "File /etc/passwd can be read"
fi
```

The next command checks to see whether the file /etc is a directory file. If so, the text string /etc is a directory file will be written to the screen.

```
if [ -d /etc ]
then
    echo "/etc is a directory file"
fi
```

In the following example, we illustrate a shell script file which can be used to start up a suitable window manager (the program only makes sense if X is being run). When the program is run, the following question is displayed on the screen:

```
Which window manager (twm, mwm) ?
```

The user then keys in twm or mwm and the window manager will be started up as a background process.

```
#!/bin/sh
echo "Which window manager (twm, mwm) ?"
read reply
if [ $reply = twm ]
then
    twm &
elif [ $reply = mwm ]
then
    mwm &
else
    echo "Illegal option"
fi
```

The next example demonstrates a shell script which displays different greetings depending on the time of day. If the user karen runs the shell script good, one of the following messages will be written to the screen:

```
Good morning karen
Good afternoon karen
Good evening karen
```

The shell script looks like this:

```
#!/bin/sh
hour=`date | cut -c12-13`
if [ $hour -ge 0 -a $hour -lt 12 ]
then
    echo "Good morning $LOGNAME"
elif [ $hour -ge 12 -a $hour -lt 18 ]
then
    echo "Good afternoon $LOGNAME"
else
    echo "Good evening $LOGNAME"
fi
```

On the second line of this script, the program `cut` is used to pull characters 12 and 13 out of the output produced by the `date` program. These are the two characters indicating what hour of the day it is. The `cut` program is only available in System V. In BSD or OSF we would have had to use instead the program `colrm`, which removes specified characters. The equivalent line in BSD or OSF would have called `colrm` twice, once to remove characters 1 to 11, and once to remove all characters starting from the third in the remaining string:

```
hour=`date | colrm 1 11 | colrm 3`
```

(If the second argument to `colrm` is omitted, it is assumed that characters are to be removed to the end of the text string.)

As well as the two methods described above (*command* and *test expression*), the Korn shell offers, as we mentioned, two other methods for specifying logical expressions. A *conditional expression* or an *arithmetical expression* can be used. Conditional expressions must be enclosed in double square brackets and arithmetical expressions in double round brackets. Note that in both cases there must be a space before and after the brackets. This means that a logical expression to be included, for example, in an `if` command may also take the following forms in the Korn shell:

```
if [[ conditional expression ]]
then
    . . .
```

and

```
if (( arithmetical expression ))
then
    . . .
```

Conditional expressions in the Korn shell mainly look like the *test expressions* described above. However, there are more operators and in some cases they are more general. The relational operators listed in table 7.8 above also apply for *conditional expression*: the only difference is that, in *conditional expression*, it is permissible to use a *pattern* on the right of the operators = and !=n. (A pattern is formed in the same way as a filename pattern, using the special characters *, ?, [and].)

The logical operators that can be used in *conditional expressions* are given in table 7.11.

Logical operators for *conditional expression* **in the Korn shell**		
Operator	Returns 'true' if	Example
! *e*	expression is 'false'	! -z $var
e1 && *e2*	expressions e1 and e2 are 'true'	$i -gt 1 && $j -le 9
e1 || *e2*	either of expressions e1 and e2 is 'true'	$e = SV || $t -le 50

Table 7.11

The file operators given in table 7.10 can be used in the Korn shell's *conditional expressions*, but in *conditional expressions* there are more file operators that can be used. Two of these are given in table 7.12, along with an operator to test flags.

Extra operators for *conditional expressions* in the Korn shell		
Operator	Returns 'true' if	Example
−a *file*	the file *file* exists	−a /etc/passwd
−O *file*	the file *file* exists and user is the file's owner	−O /etc/f1
−o *flag*	the flag *flag* is set	−o noglob

Table 7.12

In the following example, a check is run to see whether the environment variable $FCEDIT ends in the text emacs:

```
if [[ $FCEDIT = *emacs ]]
then
      print Editing with emacs
fi
```

The following lines test whether the flag allexport is set:

```
if [[ -o allexport ]]
then
      print All variables exported
fi
```

The last of the methods for specifying logical expressions in the Korn shell uses the built-in *arithmetical* expressions described in section 7.7.3 above. An arithmetical expression must be enclosed in double round brackets. If the value enclosed in the brackets has the value 'true' (actually ≠0), the entire expression, including the brackets, will take on the value 0, which is interpreted by the Korn shell as 'true'; and if the value within the brackets is 'false' the entire expression will take on the value 1.

This is illustrated by the following example, which checks whether the shell has been running for more than an hour:

```
#!/usr/bin/ksh
if (( SECONDS > 3600 ))
then
      print You have been logged on for $SECONDS seconds
fi
```

The next example displays the words 'HEADS' or 'TAILS' at random. (The example uses the arithmetical operator %, which calculates the remainder from integer division.)

```
#!/usr/bin/ksh
if (( RANDOM % 2 ))
then
    print HEADS
else
    print TAILS
fi
```

7.7.6 The `while` command

In the Bourne shell and the Korn shell, there are three different commands which can be used to execute a sequence of commands a number of times—the `while` command, the `until` command and the `for` command. We will take the `while` command first.

The `while` command has the following form:

> `while` *logical expression*
> `do` *command*
> *command*
>
>   . . .
>
> `done`

If the logical expression is 'true', the commands between `do` and `done` will be executed. After this, the logical expression will be re-calculated. If it is still 'true', the sequence of commands will be executed again, and so on. This will be repeated until a re-calculation results in the logical expression being 'false'. Just as with the `if` command, the logical expression can be formed using either a *command* or a *test expression*. It can thus take the form

> `while` *command*

or

> `while` [*test expression*]

This also applies in the Korn shell, where, however, logical expressions can also be formed using *conditional expressions* or *arithmetical expressions*, as we saw in the previous section. Thus, in the Korn shell the `while` can also take the forms

> `while` [[*conditional expression*]]

and

> `while` ((*arithmetical expression*))

Here are a couple of examples of the use of the `while` command. The following command produces an endless repetition:

```
$ while true
> do
>      echo "again and"
> done
again and
again and
. . .
```

The program `true` always gives the return code 0, which is regarded as 'true'.

In the next example we have set up a shell script which asks the user to enter a positive whole number. A series of whole numbers will then be produced on the screen, one per line. The first is the same as the number entered, the next is one smaller, and so on. Running the program produces the following picture:

```
Enter a positive whole number:
3
3
2
1
$
```

The shell script contains the following lines:

```
#!/bin/sh
echo "Enter a positive whole number:"
read num
while [ $num -gt 0 ]
do
     echo $num
     num=`expr $num - 1`
done
```

In the Korn shell, the last example could alternatively look like this:

```
#!/usr/bin/ksh
print "Enter a positive whole number:"
read num
while (( num > 0 ))
do
     print $num
     (( num = num - 1 ))
done
```

7.7.7 The `until` command

The next repeat command is the `until` command. This works in a similar way to the `while` command, but the other way round: the sequence of commands is executed as long as the logical condition is 'false'—that is, until it becomes 'true'. The `until` command has the form:

> `until` *logical expression*
> `do` *command*
>   *command*
>   . . .
> `done`

As for the previous commands, the logical expression in the Bourne shell is formed either by means of a *command* or by means of a *test espression*. Thus, we can use either the form

> `until` *command*

or the form

> `until` `[` *test expression* `]`

In the Korn shell, as before, we can also form the logical expression from a *conditional expression* or an *arithmetical expression*, which means we can also use the forms

> `until` `[[` *conditional expression* `]]`

or

> `until` `((` *arithmetical expression* `))`

The following example demonstrates a logical expression formed using a command:

```
$ until false
> do
>       echo "again and"
> done
again and
again and
. . .
```

7.7.8 The `for` command

The third repeat command in the Bourne shell and the Korn shell is the `for` command. This takes the form:

> `for` *variable* `in` *list*
> `do`
>   *command*
>   *command*
>   . . .
> `done`

where *variable* can be any shell variable and *list* is a list of text strings. The commands between `do` and `done` will be repeated as many times as there are elements in the list. Each text string in the *list* will be assigned to the *variable* in turn, starting from the left. An example is:

```
$ for index in john linda "Adam Smith"
> do
>       echo $index
> done
john
linda
Adam Smith
$
```

Here, the command `echo $index` is repeated three times. The first time, the value `john` is assigned to the variable `index`, the second time `linda` and the third time `Adam Smith`. Note that if there are spaces in the text string it needs to be enclosed in single or double quotation marks.

7.7.9 Arguments for shell scripts

As we have seen, the general form of a UNIX command is:

$$program\ arg_1\ arg_2\ ...\ arg_n$$

When a program is called it can be given a number of *arguments*. This applies equally if the program is a shell script. To enable the user to access the current arguments for a shell script, the Bourne shell and the Korn shell have a number of predefined variables. Variables with the names 1, 2, 3, 4, 5, 6, 7, 8 and 9 hold the first nine arguments. To access the value of the first argument then, we can write $1 in the shell script, $2 to access the value of the second argument, etc. In a similar way, the predefined variable with the name 0 holds the name of the shell script file itself, that is, the text appearing at the start of the command line when it is called. In addition, there is a variable # which holds the number of arguments and a variable * which holds a list of all the arguments. These predefined variables are summarized in table 7.13.

Arguments for the Bourne shell and the Korn shell	
Expression	Gives
$#	number of arguments for shell script
$*	all arguments for shell script
$0	name of shell script file
$1	first argument for shell script
$2	second argument for shell script
$n	nth argument for shell script

Table 7.13

For our first example, we shall take a shell script file `sh1`, which contains the following commands:

```
#!/bin/sh
echo Name of shell script file = $0
echo and number of arguments = $#
```

We can now show what happens when the shell script is called:

```
$ sh1 peter
Name of shell script file = sh1
and number of arguments = 1
$ sh1 Once upon a time
Name of shell script file = sh1
and number of arguments = 4
$
```

Next, we demonstrate a shell script which displays all its argument when it is called. Suppose the following script is stored in the file sh2:

```
#!/bin/sh
for i in $*
do
    echo $i
done
```

When the script is test run:

```
$ sh2 karen peter linda john
karen
peter
linda
john
$
```

It should be mentioned here that if the list of text strings is left out at the start of the for command, it is assumed that $* has been entered. We could therefore have written the shell script for sh2 more simply as:

```
#!/bin/sh
for i
do
    echo $i
done
```

Each of the arguments can of course be dealt with separately. We can write, for example:

```
for i in $1 $2 $3 $4 $5 $6 ...
```

Suppose the following lines had been stored in the shell script sh3:

```
#!/bin/sh
echo Argument No. 1 = $1
echo Argument No. 2 = $2
echo Argument No. 3 = $3
echo Argument No. 4 = $4
```

A test run would produce:

```
$ sh3 karen peter linda john
Argument No. 1 = karen
Argument No. 2 = peter
Argument No. 3 = linda
Argument No. 4 = john
```

If the program sh3 had been called with only two arguments, the result would have been:

```
$ sh3 karen peter
Argument No. 1 = karen
Argument No. 2 = peter
Argument No. 3 =
Argument No. 4 =
```

The shell script attention shown below is used to display a message on the screen when a particular user logs in to the system. The program is best run as a background process.

```
$ attention sarah &
```

The ID of the user to be monitored must be entered, otherwise an error message will be displayed:

```
$ attention &
Error: Program requires argument
attention user_ID
```

The shell script attention looks like this:

```
#!/bin/sh
if [ $# -ne 1 ]
then
    echo "Error: Program requires argument"
    echo "$0 user_ID"
    exit 1
fi
while true
do
    str=`who | grep $1`
    if [ -n $str ]
    then
        echo "$1 NOW LOGGED ON"
        exit 0
    else
        sleep 60
    fi
done
```

7.7.10 The `case` command

We have seen how to use the `if` command with `elif` elements to produce a command which selects from a number of alternatives. In the Bourne shell and the Korn shell, however, there is also a `case` command which is specially designed for multiple-choice sitations. This command has the form:

```
case    string_expression
in
        string_pattern)     command
                            command

                            . . .
                            command  ;;
        string_pattern)     command
                            command

                            . . .
                            command  ;;

    . . .
        string_pattern)     command
                            command

                            . . .
                            command  ;;
esac
```

The *string expression* on the first line can be compared with any number of *string pattern*. The comparison is carried out in sequence from the top downwards, and if one of the *string patterns* matches the *string expression* the commands between the matching *string_pattern* and the next `;;` are carried out in sequence.

A string pattern may include the symbol |, which allows two or more text strings to be tried on the same option. In the following example, the same option will be activated if the variable v contains an x or a y:

```
case $v
in
    x|y)  . . .
```

String patterns can be built up in the same way as described for filename patterns in chapter 3.4.3. This means that a string pattern can include one or more *wild card* characters. These are the *, which matches any string, the ?, which matches any single character, and the construction [. . .], which matches any single character included among those shown in the square brackets.

As an example of how *wild cards* can be used, we show here how a 'default' option can be set up, which is activated if the string expression matches none of the other string patterns in the `case` command. We simply include the string pattern * as the last option:

```
case ...
in
        ...
    *) ...
esac
```

We will now construct a shell script program `conv`, which converts figures to text strings. A run of the program might look like this:

```
$ conv 5
five
$ conv
Error: no argument
$ conv mike
Wrong type of argument
$
```

Here is the program:

```
#!/bin/sh
if [ $# -ne 1 ]
then
    echo "Error: no argument"
    exit 1
fi
case $1 in
    0) echo "zero";;
    1) echo "one";;
    2) echo "two";;
    3) echo "three";;
    4) echo "four";;
    5) echo "five";;
    6) echo "six";;
    7) echo "seven";;
    8) echo "eight";;
    9) echo "nine";;
    *) echo "Wrong type of argument"
esac
```

The next example shows a simple menu program. When the program is run the user sees the lines:

```
1.  List current users.
2.  Send electronic mail.
3.  Read electronic mail.
q.  Exit.

Enter choice:
```

The user can then enter an option by keying 1, 2, 3 or q. The appropriate program will then be run.

The menu program looks like this:

```
#!/bin/sh
while true
do
      echo ""
      echo "1. List current users."
      echo "2. Send electronic mail."
      echo "3. Read electronic mail."
      echo "q. Exit."
      echo ""
      echo "Enter choice:"
      read reply
      case $reply in
          1)   who ;;
          2)   echo "To what addressee? "
               read addr
               mail $addr ;;
          3)   mail ;;
          q|Q) exit;;
          *)   echo "Illegal option!!!"
      esac
done
```

7.7.11 The `select` command

The `select` command in the Korn shell is a special mechanism for use
in writing menu programs. The command has the form

```
select variable in list
do
                command
                command
                . . .
                command
done
```

where *list* is a list of text strings (the various options in the menu). When the program is run, the different menu texts will be written out one to a line together with a line number. The user will then be expected to enter one of the line numbers in reply. The line number will be converted, using *list*, to the corresponding menu text and stored in *variable*. If *variable* is empty (i.e. zero), this means that none of the alternatives in *list* matches the user's reply. Note that the user's actual answer, that is, the character actually entered by the user, is stored in the shell variable REPLY. The wording of the prompt line can be set up using the shell variable PS3, which contains the value #? if nothing else has been specified.

The use of the `select` command usually goes together with the `case` command. Here is a variant of the menu program described above:

```
#!/usr/bin/ksh
PS3="Enter number corresponding to your choice:"
select reply in \
        "List current users." \
        "Send electronic mail." \
        "Read electronic mail." \
        "Exit."
do
        case $reply in
        "List current users.")
            who ;;
        "Send electronic mail.")
            print -n "To what addressee? "
            read addr
            mail $addr ;;
        "Read electronic mail.")
            mail ;;
        "Exit.")
            exit ;;
        *)  print "Illegal option!!! No $REPLY"
        esac
done
```

The result of running the program may look like this:

```
1) List current users.
2) Send electronic mail.
3) Read electronic mail.
4) Exit.
Enter number corresponding to your choice: 1
torbjorn    console     May 12 17:01
Enter number corresponding to your choice: 45
Illegal option!!! No 45
Enter number corresponding to your choice: 4
```

7.8 Specific to the C and TC shells

In this section, we will be dealing with constructions specific to the C and TC shells.

7.8.1 Interactive input

In both shells there is a read-in mechanism ($<) with which an entire line can be read from the standard input.

```
% set fulline=($<)
Once upon a time
% echo $fulline
Once upon a time
%
```

In chapter 7.1.3 we wrote a shell script file called `terminit` to set up the shell variables holding the terminal type and the prompt. We will now alter this script so that the operator can enter the values directly:

The shell script `terminit` will now look like this:

```
#!/bin/csh
echo "Enter terminal type and prompt"
set term=($<)
set prompt=($<)
```

A test run of the shell script gives:

```
% source terminit
Enter terminal type and prompt
vt100
?>
?>
```

Note that, as in chapter 7.1.3, we have had to use the operator `source` when calling the shell script file.

7.8.2 Arithmetical expressions

In the C shell and the TC shell, arithmetical calculations can be carried out by using the symbol @. This symbol is used for arithmetical calculations in exactly the same way as `set` is used in connection with ordinary shell variables:

```
% @ variable=15
% @ variable = $variable + 25
% echo $variable
40
```

If we attempt to assign a non-numeric value using the @ symbol, an error message will be displayed:

```
% @ variable = mike
@: Expression syntax
%
```

The arithmetical operators in table 7.14 can be used with the @ symbol.

Arithmetical operators in the C and TC shells	
+	addition
-	subtraction
*	multiplication
/	division (integer part of result)
%	modulus (remainder)

Table 7.14

Let us inspect some examples:

```
% @ res1 = 5 / 2
% @ res2 = 5 % 2
% echo $res1 $res2
2 1
```

The operators ++ and -- respectively increase and decrease the content of a numerical variable by 1:

```
% @ res = 99
% echo $res
99
% @ res++
% echo $res
100
% @ res--
% echo $res
99
```

Logical calculations can be carried out using the operators in table 7.15. and will give as the result either the value 1, ('true') or 0 ('false').

Arithmetical comparisons in the C and TC shells	
Example	Returns 'true' if
x == y	x is equal to y
x != y	x and y are not equal
x < y	x is less than y
x > y	x is greater than y
x <= y	x is less than or equal to y
x >= y	x is greater than or equal to y

Table 7.15

The following examples illustrate the use of the relational operators. Note that any expression including the character < or > must be enclosed in brackets.

```
% @ x = 123
% @ y = 1234
% @ z1 = ( $x <= $y )
% @ z2 = ( $x > $y )
% echo $z1 $z2
1 0
%
```

In chapter 4.4.3 we explained that the value of an ordinary shell variable could be a *list* consisting of any number of *elements*. The value was indicated as a list by enclosing it in round brackets:

```
% set computers = (thor odin balder)
```

It is also possible to specify lists of numerical values, e.g.:

```
% set numlist (15 25 8 32 99)
% echo $numlist
%15 25 8 32 99
```

If a list contains numerical values, we can use the @ symbol to process individual elements in the list. Different elements in a list can be selected in the same way as described in chapter 4.4.3. E.g.:

```
% @ numlist[3] = 50
% @ numlist[5] = $numlist[3] * 3
% echo $numlist
15 25 50 32 150
% echo $numlist[2-4]
25 50 32
```

7.8.3 The `if` command

The C shell and the TC shell have an `if` command which corresponds to the `if` statement in ordinary traditional programming languages. The simplest variant of the `if` command takes the form:

> `if` (*logical_expression*) *command*

If the logical expression enclosed in the brackets is 'true', the commands will be carried out; if not, nothing will happen. If we want a number of commands to be executed under certain conditions, we can use the following variant of the `if` command:

```
if ( logical_expression )
then
        command
        command
        . . .
endif
```

If the logical expression is 'true', all the commands betwen `then` and `endif` will be carried out; if not, no command is executed. We can add an `else` section:

```
if ( logical_expression )
then
        command
        command
        . . .
else
        command
        command
        . . .
endif
```

If the logical expression is 'false', the commands between `else` and `endif` will be executed.

An `if` command may also contain any number of `else if` sections:

```
if ( logical_expression ) then
        command
        command
        . . .
else if ( logical_expression ) then
        command
        command
        . . .
else if ( logical_expression ) then
        command
        command
        . . .
else
        command
        command
        . . .
end if
```

The commands in any `else if` section will be executed if all the logical expressions before the `else if` section in question are 'false' and the condition at the start of that `else if` section is 'true'.

7.8.4 Logical expressions

Logical expressions in the C shell and the TC shell are formed in a way which is not unlike logical expressions in the C programming language. If a logical expression has the value 0 it is regarded as 'false' and if it has any other value it is regarded as 'true'. (Note that this is the exact opposite of the rule in the Bourne shell and the Korn shell.)

There are three classes of operator which can be used to form logical expressions: *relational operators, logical operators* and *file operators*. The relational operators are listed in table 7.16. Note that it is important to leave a space either side of the equality and inequality operators.

Relational operators in the C shell and the TC shell		
Operator	Returns the value 'true' if	Example
==	two strings are equal	$str == karen
!=	two strings are not equal	$str != mike
=~	the string on the left matches the string pattern on the right	$str =~ k*n
!~	the string on the left does not match the string pattern on the right	$str !~ m???e
==	two integers are equal	$num == 15
!=	two integers are not equal	$num != 10
<	one integer is less than another	$num < 50
<=	one integer is less than or equal to another	$num <= 5
>	one integer is greater than another	$num > 10
>=	one integer is greater than or equal to another	$num >= 5

Table 7.16

The following `if` command tests whether the user ID is `mike`. If it is, the text string `Hello Mike` is written to the screen:

```
if ( $LOGNAME == mike ) echo "Hello Mike"
```

The operators `=~` and `!~` in table 7.16 are the same as `==` and `!=` respectively, except that they allow the expression on the right to be a pattern, in the same way as for filename patterns (see chapter 3.4.3). This means that the expression may include the special characters `*`, `?`, `[` and `]`.

The logical operators 'not', 'and' and 'or' are shown in table 7.17.

Logical operators in the C and TC shells		
Operator	Returns 'true' if	Example
!	an expression is 'false'	!($term == xterm)
&&	both expressions are 'true'	$i > 1 && $j <= 9
||	either of the expressions is 'true'	$e == SV || $t <= 50

Table 7.17

The command

```
if ( $LOGNAME == david && $TERM == vt100 ) then
    echo "Hello there"
    date
endif
```

will write the text string `Hello there` and the current date to the screen if the user ID is `david` and the content of the environment variable `TERM` is `vt100`.

The third class of operator comprises file operators. These can be used to examine various characteristics of files, and are shown in table 7.18.

File operators in the C and TC shells		
Operator	Returns 'true' if a file	Example
-r	exists and can be read	-r *<filename>*
-w	exists and can be written to	-w *<filename>*
-f	is a plain file	-f *<filename>*
-d	is a directory file	-d *<filename>*
-z	contains no information	-z *<filename>*

Table 7.18

The following command checks to see whether the file `/etc/passwd` can be read. If so, it displays the text `File /etc/passwd:` and the contents of `/etc/passwd`. Otherwise, it displays the text `File /etc/passwd cannot be read`.

```
if ( -r /etc/passwd ) then
    echo "File /etc/passwd:"
    cat /etc/passwd
else
    echo "File /etc/passwd cannot be read"
endif
```

The next command checks to see whether the file `/etc` is a directory file. If so, the user will be moved to that directory.

```
% if ( -d /etc ) cd /etc
```

In the following example we illustrate a shell script file which can be used to start up a suitable window manager (the program only makes sense if X is being run). When the program is run, the following question is displayed on the screen:

```
Which window manager (twm, mwm) ?
```

The user then keys in `twm` or `mwm` and the window manager will be started up as a background process.

```
#!/bin/csh
echo "Which window manager (twm, mwm) ?"
set reply=($<)
echo "reply : $reply"
if ( $reply == twm ) then
    twm &
else if ( $reply == mwm ) then
    mwm &
else
    echo "Illegal option"
endif
```

The next example demonstrates a shell script which displays different greetings depending on the time of day. If the user karen runs the shell script good, one of the following messages will be written to the screen:

```
Good morning karen
Good afternoon karen
Good evening karen
```

The shell script looks like this:

```
#!/bin/csh
set hour=`date | cut -c12-13`
if ( $hour >= 0 && $hour < 12 ) then
    echo "Good morning $LOGNAME"
else if ( $hour >= 12 && $hour < 18 ) then
    echo "Good afternoon $LOGNAME"
else
    echo "Good evening $LOGNAME"
endif
```

On the second line of this script, the program cut is used to pull characters 12 and 13 out of the output produced by the date program. These are the two characters indicating what hour of the day it is. The cut program is only available in System V. In BSD or OSF we would have had to use instead the program colrm, which removes specified characters. The equivalent line in BSD or OSF would have called colrm twice:

```
set hour=`date | colrm 1 11 | colrm 3`
```

(If the second argument to colrm is omitted, it is assumed that characters are to be removed to the end of the text string.)

7.8.5 The while command

In the C shell and the TC shell, there are two different commands which can be used to execute a sequence of commands a number of times—the `while` command and the `foreach` command. We will take the while command first.

The while command has the following form:

```
while ( logical expression )
        command
        command

        . . .
end
```

If the logical expression is 'true', the sequence of commands will be executed until `end` is reached. After this, the logical expression will be re-calculated. If it is still 'true', these commands will be executed again, and so on. This will be repeated until a re-calculation results in the logical expression being 'false'. The logical expression is calculated in the same way as described for the `if` command.

The following command produces an endless repetition:

```
% while ( 1 )
?       echo "again and"
? end
again and
again and
    . . .
```

where the logical expression 1 has the meaning 'true'.

In the next example we have set up a shell script which asks the user to enter a positive whole number. A series of whole numbers will then be produced on the screen, one per line. The first is the same as the number entered, the next is one smaller, and so on. Running the program produces the following picture:

```
% Enter a positive whole number:
3
3
2
1
%
```

The shell script contains the following lines:

```
#!/bin/csh
echo "Enter a positive whole number:"
set num=($<)
while ( $num > 0 )
      echo $num
      @ num = $num - 1
end
```

7.8.6 The `foreach` command

The other command in the C shell and the TC shell which can be used to produce a repetition is the `foreach` command. This takes the following form:

```
foreach variable ( list )
    command
    command
    . . .
end
```

Any number of commands may be included between `foreach` and `end`. These will be executed once for each element in the *list*. The first time, *variable* will be given the value of the first element in the list, the second time that of the second element, and so on. To take an example:

```
% foreach colour ( yellow white "pitch black" )
%       echo $colour
% end
yellow
white
pitch black
%
```

The command `echo $colour` is repeated three times as shown. Note that the text string must be enclosed in single or double quotation marks if it contains spaces.

As we saw earlier, the shell variable `path` holds a list of directory names. As a further example, here is a way of displaying all the directory names in this variable:

```
foreach dir ( $path )
    echo dir
end
```

7.8.7 Arguments for shell scripts

As we have seen, the general form of a UNIX command is:

program arg_1 arg_2 ... arg_n

When a program is called it can be given a number of *arguments*. This applies equally if the program is a shell script. To enable the user to access the current arguments for a shell script, the C shell and the TC shell have a number of predefined variables. The variable `argv` is a list containing the arguments for the shell script. Thus, if we write `$argv` we will get a list of all the arguments. The first argument can be accessed in `argv[1]`, the second in `argv[2]` and so on; so to get the value of the second argument, for example, we can write `$argv[2]`. (Alternatively, we can use the variables called 1, 2, 3, 4, 5, 6, 7, 8 and 9, which hold the first nine arguments. To access the value of the first argument, for example, we can write $1, and the expression $* will produce a list of all the arguments.

The predefined variable with the name 0 holds the name of the shell script file itself, that is, the text appearing at the start of the command line when it is called.

The number of arguments can be found by examining the length of argv, that is, by keying $#argv. These predefined variables are summarized in table 7.13.

Arguments for the C shell and the TC shell	
Expression	Gives
$#argv	number of arguments for shell script
$argv $*	all arguments for shell script
$0	name of shell script file
$argv[1] $1	first argument for shell script
$argv[2] $2	second argument for shell script
$argv[*n*] $*n*	*n*th argument for shell script

Table 7.19

For our first example, we shall take a shell script file csh1, which contains the following commands:

```
#!/bin/csh
echo Name of shell script file = $0
echo and number of arguments = $#argv
```

We can now show what happens when the shell script is called:

```
% csh1 peter
Name of shell script file = csh1
and number of arguments = 1
% csh1 Once upon a time
Name of shell script file = csh1
and number of arguments = 4
%
```

In the next example, we have written a shell script which displays all its arguments.

```
#!/bin/csh
foreach i ( $argv )
    echo $i
end
```

(Instead of `$argv`, we could have written `$*`.) We now call `csh2`:

```
% csh2 karen peter linda john
karen
peter
linda
john
%
```

The next example shows how each of the arguments can be dealt with separately. Suppose the following lines are stored in the shell script file `csh3`:

```
#!/bin/csh
echo Argument No. 1 = $argv[1]
echo Argument No. 2 = $argv[2]
echo Argument No. 3 = $argv[3]
echo Argument No. 4 = $argv[4]
```

A test run would produce:

```
% csh3 karen peter linda john
Argument No. 1 = karen
Argument No. 2 = peter
Argument No. 3 = linda
Argument No. 4 = john
%
```

If we call the program `csh3` with less than four arguments, we will get the error message `Subscript out of range`, since the script has attempted to access the value of an argument which does not exist. This error check does not take place if the alternative writing `$1` is used instead of `$argv[1]` etc.

The shell script `attention` shown below is used to display a message on the screen when a particular user logs in to the system. The program is best run as a background process.

```
% attention sarah &
```

The ID of the user to be monitored must be entered, otherwise an error message will be displayed:

```
% attention &
Error: Program requires argument
attention user_ID
```

The shell script `attention` looks like this:

```csh
#!/bin/csh
if ( $#argv != 1 ) then
    echo "Error: Program requires argument"
    echo "$0 user_ID"
    exit (1)
endif
while ( 1 )
    set str=`who | grep $argv[1]`
    if ( "$str" != "" ) then
    echo "$argv[1] NOW LOGGED ON"
        exit (0)
    else
     sleep 60
    endif
end
```

7.8.8 The `switch` command

We have seen how to use the `if` command with `else if` elements to produce a command which selects from a number of alternatives. In the C shell and the TC shell there is also a `switch` command which is specially designed for multiple-choice situations. This command has the form:

```
switch ( string_expression )
        case string_pattern:
                                command
                                command
                                . . .
                                command
                                breaksw
        case string_pattern:
                                command
                                command
                                . . .
                                command
                                breaksw
        . . .
        case string_pattern:
                                command
                                command
                                . . .
                                command
                                breaksw
```

```
default:
```
> *command*
> *command*
> . . .
> *command*

```
endsw
```

Note that there should not be any command at the ends of the lines starting with `case`. The *string expression* on the first line can be compared with any number of *string patterns*. The comparison is carried out in sequence from the top downwards, and if one of the *string patterns* matches the *string expression* the commands between the matching *string_pattern* and the next `breaksw` are carried out in sequence. The `default` sequence at the end is executed if the *string expression* does not match any of the *string patterns*.

String patterns can be built up in the same way as described for filename patterns in chapter 3.4.3. This means that a string pattern can include one or more *wild card* characters. These are the *, which matches any string, the ?, which matches any single character, and the construction [. . .], which matches any single character included among those shown inside the square brackets.

We will now construct a shell script program `conv`, which converts figures to text strings. A run of the program might look like this:

```
% conv 5
five
% conv
Error: no argument
% conv mike
Wrong type of argument
%
```

Here is the program:

```
#!/bin/csh
if ( $#argv != 1 ) then
    echo "Error: no argument"
    exit (1)
endif
switch ( $argv[1] )
    case 0:
            echo "zero"
            breaksw
    case 1:
            echo "one"
            breaksw
    case 2:
            echo "two"
              breaksw
```

```
case 3:
        echo "three"
        breaksw
case 4:
        echo "four"
        breaksw
case 5:
        echo "five"
        breaksw
case 6:
        echo "six"
        breaksw
case 7:
        echo "seven"
        breaksw
case 8:
        echo "eight"
        breaksw
case 9:
        echo "nine"
        breaksw
default:
        echo "Wrong type of argument"
endsw
```

The next example shows a simple menu program. When the program is run the user sees the lines:

```
1. List current users.
2. Send electronic mail.
3. Read electronic mail.
q. Exit.
Enter choice:
```

The user can then enter an option by keying 1, 2, 3 or q. The appropriate program will then be run.

The menu program looks like this:

```
#!/bin/csh
while ( 1 )
    echo ""
    echo "1. List current users."
    echo "2. Send electronic mail."
    echo "3. Read electronic mail."
    echo "q. Exit."
    echo ""
    echo "Enter choice:"
    set reply=($<)
```

```
        switch ( "$reply" )
            case 1:
                    who
                    breaksw
            case 2:
                    echo "To what addressee? "
                    read addr
                    mail $addr
                    breaksw
            case 3:
                    mail
                    breaksw
            case q:
            case Q:
                    exit
                    breaksw
            default:
                    echo "Illegal option!!!"
                    breaksw
        endsw
    end
```

7.9 Signals

Via the operating system, *signals* can be sent to UNIX programs which are being executed. There are various different types of signal, each with its own unique number. When the interrupt key on the terminal is pressed, for example, a signal of type 2 (SIGINT) is sent to the program reading from the terminal. The user can determine which key is to serve as the interrupt key by means of the stty program, but it will generally be <ctrl-c> or <delete>.

Using the program kill, a signal of any type can be sent to a particular process. The format is:

$ **kill** *-signal_type   process_number*

If the first argument, specifying the signal type, is omitted, a type 15 signal (SIGTERM) will be sent. What usually happens is that a UNIX program will abort when it receives a signal, but the program can define for itself what should happen when various signals are received. An exception to this is signal type 9 (SIGKILL). This signal always aborts the receiving program, and there is no way to 'protect' a program against signal type 9. This means that the command

$ kill -9 *process_number*

can kill off many processes which otherwise refuse to die.

The commonest signals which a shell script programmer needs to be aware of are shown in table 7.20.

Some signal types		
1	SIGHUP	generated when user logs off
2	SIGINT	generated when interrupt key is pressed
9	SIGKILL	generated e.g. by kill -9
15	SIGTERM	generated e.g. by kill

Table 7.20

In the Bourne shell and the Korn shell, the trap command is used to define what is to happen when a signal is received. The command has the following form:

    trap *list_of_commands list_of_signals*

At the end of the command line is a list of the signal types to be dealt with. The first argument is the command or a list of commands to be executed when a signal of one of the types listed is received. The following shell script, shint, displays the time and date every five seconds. When the user presses the interrupt key it displays the message No more then terminates using exit.

```
#!/bin/sh
trap 'echo "No more"; exit' 2 15
while true
do
        date
        sleep 5
done
```

If the user does not wish the shell script to terminate when one of the defined signals is received, the call to exit should not be included:

```
#!/bin/sh
trap 'echo "Interrupted but continuing"' 2 15
while true
do
        echo "again and"
        sleep 30
done
```

If the program shnoint above is run in the background and an attempt is made to kill it with the kill program without specifying a signal number, this will fail, as a type 15 signal will be sent:

```
$ shnoint &
1234
$ again and
again and
again and
kill 1234
$ Interrupted but continuing
again and
again and
...
```

The `shnoint` program cannot be killed by signals of type 2 or 15. However, the program has not protected itself against other ways of being killed:

```
again and
again and
kill -1 1234
1234 Hangup
$
```

It is possible, as in the following example, to define various things to be done for various types of signal.

```
#!/bin/sh
trap 'echo "No more"; exit' 1
trap 'echo "Interrupted but continuing"' 2 15
while true
do
            echo "again and"
            sleep 30
done
```

In the C shell and the TC shell, the command `onintr` is used to define what is to be done when the user presses the interrupt key, that is, when the program receives a type 2 signal. The command is

```
onintr location_name
```

or

```
onintr -
```

If a location name is given as an argument to `onintr` the program will jump to the location given and continue from there when the user presses the interrupt key. If a minus sign is entered as the argument instead, it will not be possible to abort the program by pressing the interrupt key.

The following shell script, `cshint`, displays the time and date every five seconds. When the user presses the interrupt key it terminates and displays the message `No more`.

```
#!/bin/csh
onintr finish
while ( 1 )
      date
      sleep 5
end
finish:
echo "No more"
```

If the user does not wish the shell script to terminate when one of the defined signals is received, the second line should be changed to

```
onintr -
```

and the last two lines omitted.

7.10 Summary

Bourne shell and Korn shell	C shell and TC shell
Startup files	
`.profile`	`.login` `.cshrc`
Default prompts	
`$` `>`	`%` `?`
Redirection	
`<   <<   >   >>   |`	same
Command lists	
`&   &&   ;   ||`	same
Quotes and other symbols	
`" ' \ `` `	same
Return codes	
`exit` *return_code*	`exit` (*return_code*)
Filename patterns (wild cards)	
`?   *   []`	same
Assignment of shell variables	

variable=*string*
variable=`` `command` ``
variable=`` `expr $variable + 1` ``
	`set` *variable*=`string`
	`set` *variable*=`` `command` ``
	`@` *variable*=`$variable + 1`

Bourne shell and Korn shell	C shell and TC shell

Specific to Korn shell
`let` *variable*`="`$*variable* `+ 1"`
`((`*variable*`=`$*variable* `+ 1))`	

Assignment of environment variables	
variable`=`*string* `export` *variable*	`setenv` *variable* *string*
Interactive read-in	
`read` *variable*	`set` *variable*`=($<)`
Comments	
`#` *comment*	same
Read in new environment	
`.` *filename*	`source` *filename*
Arguments for shell scripts	

`$#`
`$*`
`$0`
`$`*n*
	`$#argv`
	`$*, $argv`
	`$0`
	`$`*n*`, $argv[`*n*`]`

`if` **command**	

`if [` *expression* `]`
`then`
　. . . . .
`fi`
	`if (` *expression* `) then`
	　. . . . .
	`endif`

`if [` *expression* `]`
`then`
　. . . . .
`else`
　. . . . .
`fi`
	`if (` *expression* `) then`
	　. . . . .
	`else`
	　. . . . .
	`endif`

`if [` *expression* `]`
`then`
　. . . . .
`elif [` *expression* `]`
`then`
　. . . . .
`else`
　. . . . .
`fi`
	`if (` *expression* `) then`
	　. . . . .
	`else if (` *expression* `) then`
	　. . . . .
	`else`
	　. . . . .
	`endif`

Bourne shell and Korn shell	C shell and TC shell
for command	

for *variable* in *string_list*
do
  . . . . .
done
	foreach *variable* (*string_list*)
	
	  . . . . .
	end

while command	

while [*expression*]
do
  . . . . .
done
	while (*expression*)
	
	  . . . . .
	end

Multiple choice	

case *expression* in
    pattern1)
    . . . . . .
    ;;
    pattern2)
    . . . . . .
    ;;
    *)
    . . . . . .
    ;;
esac
	switch (*expression*)
	    case *pattern1*:
	      . . . . . .
	      breaksw
	    case *pattern2*:
	      . . . . . .
	      breaksw
	    default:
	      . . . . . .
	      breaksw
	endsw

Expressions in if and while commands	
-f *file* -d *file* -s *file* -z *string* -n *string* *string1* = *string2* *string1* != *string2* *num1* -eq *num2* *num1* -ne *num2* *num1* -lt *num2* *num1* -le *num2* *num1* -gt *num2* *num1* -ge *num2* *expression1* -a *expression2* *expression1* -o *expression2*	-f *file* -d *file* ! -z *file* *string* == " " *string* != " " *string1* == *string2* *string1* != *string2* *num1* == *num2* *num1* != *num2* *num1* < *num2* *num1* <= *num2* *num1* > *num2* *num1* >= *num2* *expression1* && *expression2* *expression1* || *expression2*

Eight
Program Development

In the previous chapter we explained how to write programs in the form of shell scripts. Up to now, however, we have not discussed how to write 'real' programs in a *programming language*. The UNIX operating system is in very large part designed to be used when writing programs, and was developed for just this purpose. All commonly used languages (and a good many others) can generally be installed under UNIX, and there are often a number of different programming languages available in any UNIX system. As well as programming languages, there are also utilities to help with 'debugging' programs (that is, tracking down errors in them) and organizing the user's files.

This chapter provides a brief description of the program development process and how to compile and 'link' a program. There is also an introduction to the popular UNIX program make, which can be used to keep things in order when a large program built up from several parts is being developed.

8.1 Compiling and link editing

A computer program is actually nothing other than a text written in one or other programming language. Here, as an example, is a very trivial

239

program written in the 'C' programming language. We are using C as a demonstration language here because we can be sure that this language will be available in any UNIX system. C and UNIX are historically related, since it was C that was used to write UNIX itself. The principles involved in program development are much the same for the commoner programming languages, however, so C will serve very well as a demonstration language. This is our C program:

```
#include <stdio.h>
main()
{
        printf("Hello!\n");
}
```

We will not go into any details of the language here. The function of the program is quite simply to display at the terminal, on a separate line, the text:

```
Hello!
```

As the program is a text, it can be created using a text editor, such as vi or xedit, and saved in a text file. Suppose we have saved the program in a text file called hello.c. (It is conventional to use the extension .c for all files containing C programs.) Sometimes the program text itself is called the *source code* and the file in which it is stored the *source code file*.

The next step in the programming work is usually to *compile* the program. A special program, a *compiler*, reads the program and checks that it conforms to the rules of the language. There must, of course, be (at least) one compiler for each programming language which is going to be used on any UNIX system. To compile our demonstration program, we use the program cc (C compiler):

$ **cc -c hello.c**

If the program is found to include any syntactical errors (that is, errors in the use of the language), the compiler will produce error messages, either on the standard output (which is what cc will normally do) or to a special error message file. In this case a text editor can be used to correct the errors in the program text, after which a fresh attempt at compilation can be run.

If the program is free of syntactical errors, the compiler translates the program into what is known as *machine code*. Machine code is a version of the program in code which can be interpreted and executed by the computer hardware. (For humans, on the other hand, machine code can sometimes be very difficult to interpret.) The compiler places the machine code in an *object file*. We can also say that the object file contains the *object code*. Object files normally have names ending in the extension .o. In our example, the C compiler will produce a file called hello.o.

In most programs, ready-written standard routines are used for such tasks as reading in input data to the program or producing text output. All the common languages have a range of standard routines. Our program, for instance, calls the standard function printf to write to the terminal ('function' is the word used in C). Standard functions, of course, are compiled in advance, and their object files are located in a special directory. Before our program can be loaded and run on the computer, the machine code for the standard functions it will be using must be added to it. This step is known as *link editing*, and the program which links the different object files into a complete, executable program is called the *link editor*. In UNIX, the link editing program is called ld. Many compilers, including cc, are constructed so that they automatically call the link editor themselves when the compilation stage is finished. In this case, no special link editing command needs to be given by the user. If, in place of the compilation command above, we simply enter

> $ **cc hello.c**

the C compiler will call the ld program itself. (The argument -c indicates that the link editor call is not to be made). The result of this command is that we end up with an *executable file* holding a complete program which can be directly run. (If we allow the compiler to call the link editor for itself, as this command does, the object file will not be saved. It can therefore be regarded as a temporary intermediate result.) As we have given no other instructions in the command, the executable file will be given the default name a.out. If we want the executable file to have a different name, for example hlo, we can change the command to

> $ **cc -o hlo hello.c**

Running, *executing* the program is now very simple. It is simply a matter of entering the name of the program, which is the same as that of the executable file:

> $ **a.out**

or

> $ **hlo**

depending on which compile command was eventually entered.

A program may well consist of a number of separate program texts which have been compiled separately and linked to form an executable file. As an example, we will construct a C program consisting of two separate functions, one of which is sayhello, stored in the text file sayhello.c. (It is assumed that the C compiler conforms to the ANSI standard.)

```
#include <stdio.h>
void sayhello(char *s)
{
        printf("Hello %s!\n",s);
}
```

the other being `main`, in the text file `hello2.c`:

```
extern void sayhello(char *s);
main()
{
        sayhello("Mike");
}
```

(As in the first example, the details of the language do not need to be understood in this example either.) Every C program must contain a function called `main`. This is where the execution of the program begins when it is run. The function `sayhello` can be compiled separately using the command

$ **cc -c sayhello.c**

We will then have an object file called `sayhello.o`. The argument `-c` is vital in this case, as the program cannot yet be linked. To compile the function `main` and produce the object file `hello2.o`, we enter the corresponding command

$ **cc -c hello2.c**

To link the entire program, we key:

$ **cc sayhello.o hello2.o**

As both the files entered as arguments are object files, `cc` will skip the compilation stage and simply call the link editor `ld`, which links the two object files `sayhello.o` and `hello2.o` along with the standard functions to produce the executable file `a.out`. This is what you will see when you execute the program:

$ **a.out**
Hello Mike!

This way of going about things can be generalized, so that a program can be made up of any number of separately compiled sections. This is naturally an advantage, as it means the separate parts can be made small enough to handle easily. As well as this, it allows a number of people to work on the program development, each producing a different part of the program. It is also possible to expand the directory of ready-compiled functions with specially written functions.

 Application programs running under X have a very special structure. Each program consists of a main routine, which carries out a number of set-up tasks, and a number of functions, each of which takes care of a specific event. The main routine will make contact with the X

server, and all the different objects required (windows, menus, scroll bars etc.) will be described and set up. For every event we wish to know about (for example, when the user presses a mouse button or a key) we must define an *event handler*—that is, a function to take care of the event. For some of the objects specified there will also need to be special functions, known as *callback functions*, which will be called if the user does something special with the object, e.g. selects a particular option from a menu.

When the main routine has completed all its set-up tasks, it passes control to a wait function, which waits for an event to happen. When one occurs, a call will automatically be made to the function designed to attend to that particular event.

As mentioned in chapter 1, it is no trivial task writing an application to run under X. The basic utilities, *Xlib*, are at a very low level and are difficult to use. It is true that there are collections of 'toolkit' utilities at a rather higher level (such as *Xt Intrinsics* and *Widgets* or *XView*), but it is still difficult to know which utilities should be called and what the (fairly complicated) arguments should be.

A very great help to the applications programmer is offered by the applications development utilities which are now becoming available, for example the `guide` program in OpenWindows. A user of one of these utilities simply draws on the screen the different objects he or she wants in the application program—for example various menus and buttons. When everything is ready, the utility automatically generates a 'program skeleton' (usually in C). This skeleton contains the parts of the resulting application which will be communicating with the X system. All that is left for the programmer to do is to fill in the sections which do the application-related calculations.

8.2 Interpreting

There is an alternative way of running your own programs. Instead of compiling and linking programs, you can use an *interpreter*. The way an interpreter works is reminiscent of a compiler, with the decisive difference that an interpreter does not translate the program into machine code. Instead, it interprets the program and carries out for itself the operations which would have been done if the program had been run 'for real'. It looks as if the program is being executed, but in fact it is the interpreter that is being run throughout.

There are many programming languages for which interpreting is the normal way of working. Examples of these are LISP and Smalltalk. (It is simpler to write an interpreter than a compiler, and it may be that for some languages there is simply no way of compiling them.) However, interpreting can also be useful for 'ordinary' languages too, such as Pascal, if the user wishes to write and test a relatively short program quickly. One advantage of interpreting is that it is often quicker to interpret a program than to go through a complete compilation and linking process.

The disadvantage of interpreting is that the actual execution of the program is slower, as the program is not translated into machine code. The interpreter is kept busy interpreting the program and executing the different steps. Another problem is that it can take a long time to run larger programs, as the entire text of the program has to be interpreted every time the program is run. The program cannot be built up from ready-compiled sections, as with the compilation method.

8.3 Error-tracing

A compiler or interpreter will discover syntactical errors in a program. These may be, for example, the wrong use of brackets or a mis-spelled variable name. However, logical errors in a program cannot be discovered by compilation (although the compiler will sometimes warn about things it thinks look 'suspicious'). Logical errors will only make themselves felt when a program is run. Many of these errors are easy to find, and with a little experience you soon get to know which are the most common mistakes to look for. Sometimes, however, programming errors can be difficult to track down. This is where a debugging program can come in useful. A *debugger* is a utility which can be used to test-run a program under controlled conditions. The program can be run step by step, allowing a check of the current values of the program's variables etc. after every step. It is also usually possible to set break points, that is, to make the program halt from time to time at specified points or whenever the value of certain variables changes. It is not always an easy thing to learn to use a debugger. There are usually a lot of facilities and the number of commands for a debugger tends to be large. In a 'symbolic debugger' it is possible to refer to the variables by the names they have in the program, which is a basic condition if the debugger is to be at all easy to use.

In most professional compilers, there is also a debugger which is specially designed for the programming language and compiler in question. Examples of debuggers supplied as standard in UNIX systems are the programs adb and dbx. adb is a debugger working at machine code level, which is not particularly easy to use; whilst dbx is a debugger which works at program text level and is principally designed for use with programs written in C. Further details are given in the manual.

8.4 The make **program**

If we have a really large program made up of many separate program text files which may include other files themselves, it can be difficult to keep track of all the files during program development. For example, if a small change is made in one file, some other files, but not all of them, may need to be re-compiled. One way of doing this, of course, is to re-compile all the parts of the program and link it together again after every little change; but this would be very time-consuming. If, on the other hand, we only re-compile certain sections, we can never be really sure we have re-compiled everything we needed to.

To resolve these problems, we can use the make program. Before the program can be used, we have to write ourselves a special text file, known as the makefile. In this, we save instructions describing how the program is made up, and how the different files relate to and depend on each other. The example below shows a makefile describing the construction of the demonstration program in section 8.1, which displayed the text 'Hello Mike!' (Note that lines two, four and six must start with a tab character.)

```
hlo2: hello2.o sayhello.o
        cc hello2.o sayhello.o -o hlo2
hello2.o: hello2.c
        cc -c hello2.c
sayhello.o: sayhello.c
        cc -c sayhello.c
```

We are calling the executable file hlo2. The first line says that hlo2 is dependent on the files hello2.o and sayhello.o. The second line shows the UNIX command to be run to create hlo2, starting from the files it is dependent on. The third and fourth lines specify that the file hello2.o is dependent on the file hello2.c and that hello2.o is the result of compiling hello2.c using the cc program. (In fact, make could have worked this out for itself, but we have included the line for demonstration purposes.) The last two lines correspondingly show how sayhello.o is dependent on sayhello.c.

The point of all this is that, by reference to the information in the makefile, make can construct the program hlo2 without error and in the simplest possible way at any time. This is possible because details of when a file was last altered are stored for every file in the file system. Let's say that we have written the two program text files sayhello.c and hello2.c but we have not yet done any compilations. We now enter the simple command

```
$ make
```

The `make` program automatically looks at the `makefile` file in the current directory and executes all the UNIX commands necessary to construct the program. We thus see a display of the commands which have been executed:

```
cc -c hello2.c
cc hello2.o sayhello.o -o hlo2
```

If we were now to enter the command `make` a second time, this is what would happen:

```
$ make
`hlo2' is up to date
```

No compilations were necessary. Suppose we now make an alteration to the file `sayhello.c` and then wish to recreate the program:

```
$ make
cc -c sayhello.c
cc hello2.o sayhello.o -o hlo2
```

This is exactly what is required, as there was no need to re-compile `hello2.c`.

The `make` program is very easy to use. What is difficult is setting up the `makefile` file. (There are many other facilities which we have not shown here.) However, for a program which is built up from a large number of source code files, a program like `make` is virtually indispensable. Larger programs supplied to a UNIX system are often supplied in source code form together with a `makefile` describing how the program is constructed.

Nine

A Little about System Administration

As UNIX is a multi-user system involving programs at various levels of complication, there is often a person or group of people responsible for the administration of the UNIX system itself. In earlier chapters we discussed UNIX from the user's angle. In this chapter we will be presenting some of the system administrator's tasks.

The system administrator need not have a lot to do in a well-configured UNIX system. The commonest jobs are:

- adding and removing users;

- copying from and to tape;

- installing new application programs;

- supporting ordinary users with advice and tips.

System V has a menu-driven program `sysadm`, which helps the system administrator to carry out the most frequent tasks. Its counterpart under IBM's AIX is the `smit` program, and the corresponding program in Hewlett Packard's HP/UX is `sam`. In Sun's

Solaris 2.0 system it is possible to handle most of the system administrator's work from the graphical and window-oriented program `admintool`.

9.1 Superuser privileges

Most of the tasks falling to the system administrator cannot be done by an ordinary user. They require special privileges allowing the user, among other things, to read and write to all files without any problems involving access permissions. These will be referred to from now on as *superuser privileges.*

Superuser powers can be called up either by logging on with the user ID `root`:

```
login: root
Password: password
#
```

or the program `su` can be run with the same ID:

```
$ su root
Password: password
#
```

It is also possible to leave out the user ID `root`:

```
$ su
Password: password
#
```

The shell prompt will change to a # to draw attention to the fact that full rights are available.

9.2 Starting up and shutting down the system

A system administrator needs to know how a UNIX system is started up ('booted') and shut down.

UNIX computers are often started up simply by being switched on. It will then take a minute or two before the operating system is loaded, the file system checked and repaired if necessary, the printer system is started up, the communication system set going and so on.

A UNIX system is shut down by running the `shutdown` program. Only after this, the power can be safely switched off. The reason the system cannot simply be switched off is that this would damage the file system. In most cases, the file system will be automatically repaired when the system is started up again, but a good deal of the information an ordinary user is processing when the current is switched off will very probably be lost. Another reason for running `shutdown` before switching off is that a warning message will automatically be shown on all user terminals before the system halts.

If the `shutdown` command is given in System V without any argument, a number of questions will need to be answered manually. The option `-y` indicates that all the questions are to be answered automatically with a default value.

> # **shutdown -y**

The option `-gseconds` is used to enter the time in seconds from the moment the command is given to the time the system is to halt (the default being 60 seconds). The command

> # **shutdown -g300**

for example, means that the system will halt after 300 seconds. The option `-icondition` can be used to control whether the system simply shuts down or whether it shuts down and then re-boots. If this option is not used or the option `-is` is entered instead, the system will only shut down. If the system is to re-boot, the option `-i6` can be entered, e.g.:

> # **shutdown -i6**

A number of options can be combined, e.g.:

> # **shutdown -y -g0 -i6**

Table 9.1 provides a summary of the most common options and arguments for the `shutdown` program in System V.

Shutdown of system (System V)	
`shutdown [-y] [-gseconds] [-icondition]`	
`-y`	all questions automatically answered with a default value.
`-gn`	system to be shut down after *n* seconds.
`-i0`	system to be shut down and current can then be safely switched off.
`-i1`	system to be shut down in such a way that only the system administrator has access to it via the console terminal
`-is`	as 1 but system will only 'install' the most primitive file systems concerned with the system—i.e. the users' file systems cannot be assumed to be included.
`-i2`	system to be re-booted to usual multi-user condition.
`-i6`	system to be re-booted to usual system condition (usually condition 2, multi-user working).

Table 9.1

In BSD and OSF, the time when the system is to halt using the shutdown program can be given in three ways. If the system is to shut down without any delay, the command to be entered is:

shutdown -h now

where the -h indicates that the system will be shut down in such a way that the power to the computer can be switched off. The argument now means that the system is to shut down immediately. The system can be shut down at a specific time by entering the time in the format *hours:minutes* (N.B. 24-hour clock!), e.g.:

shutdown -h 17:30

If, instead, the system is required to shut down after *n* minutes, the format +*n* can be used:

shutdown -h +10

Sometimes it is desired that the system should shut down and then automatically re-boot. For this, the option -r is used, e.g.:

shutdown -r now

In Table 9.2 we give a list of the commonest options and arguments for the shutdown program in BSD and OSF.

Shutdown of system (OSF/BSD)	
shutdown [-rhf] *time* [*message*]	
-r	system to re-boot automatically.
-h	system halts and power can then be switched off safely.
-f	system to be shut down in such a way that when it boots no lengthy check of file system is carried out.
time	time when system is to shut down.
message	warning message to appear at ordinary users' terminals.

Table 9.2

9.3 Adding and removing users

When a new user needs to be added to the system or a current user is to be removed, the /etc/passwd file has to be updated with an extra line. In System V, the file /etc/shadow will also need modifying. The update can be carried out either manually using a text editor, or by means of an appropriate utility.

9.3.1 The `/etc/passwd` file

Every line in the `/etc/passwd` file consists of seven fields, separated by colons:

<id> : *<passwd>* : *<uid>* : *<gid>* : *<user_info>* : *<home_directory>* : *<shell>*

The first term, *<id>*, is the user ID, which must be unique (i.e. no other user can have the same ID).

The second term, *<passwd>*, is the password entered by the user, which is stored in encrypted form. It should be mentioned that the *<passwd>* field must be empty when a new user is installed. In System V the encrypted password is not stored in this file; it is held instead in the file `/etc/shadow`.

The third field, *<uid>*, will be a unique user number (a whole number).

The fourth field, *<gid>*, is the number of the group to which the user will belong. The group number *<gid>* is defined in the `/etc/group` file, which is constructed on the same principle as the `/etc/passwd` file.

The fifth field, *<user_info>*, has no special significance but is generally used to store information such as the user's name, telephone number, etc.

The sixth field, *<home_directory>*, holds the name of the user's home directory, the directory he or she will be sent to after logging in.

The seventh and last field, *<shell>*, is the name of the program to be run when the user logs in. This program is most commonly a shell. Table 9.3 summarizes the contents of the `/etc/passwd` file.

Contents of `/etc/passwd` file	
Field	Contents
<id>	user ID
<passwd>	Encrypted password. In System V this field is not used. The password is held instead in the `/etc/shadow` file.
<uid>	unique user number
<gid>	group number, see `/etc/group` file
<user_info>	comments
<home_directory>	user's home directory
<shell>	any program, usually a shell

Table 9.3

SV ### 9.3.2 The `/etc/shadow` file

In System V, the `/etc/shadow` file also needs updating with a new line. Each line in the file consists of nine fields, separated by colons:

<id> : *<passwd>* : *<lastchange>* : *<minimum>* : *<maximum>* : *<warn>* :
<inactive> : *<expire>* : *<flag>*

The first field, *<id>*, holds the user ID and will match the corresponding field in `/etc/passwd`.

The second field, *<passwd>*, is the password entered by the user, which is stored in encrypted form.

The third field, *<lastchange>*, defines the number of days between 1.1.1970 and the date when the password was last changed.

The fourth field, *<minimum>*, defines (in days) the shortest permissible period between two changes of password, as users are not permitted to change their passwords as often as they like.

The fifth field, *<maximum>*, defines the greatest number of days for which a password is valid, that is, a password must be changed within a specified number of days.

The sixth field, *<warn>*, defines the number of days for which a warning message will be displayed at log-in before a password becomes invalid.

The seventh field, *<inactive>*, defines the maximum number of inactive days, as users are not permitted to remain inactive for an indefinite period.

The eighth field, *<expire>*, defines the latest permissible log-in date. After this date the user will no longer be allowed to log in on the system.

The ninth field, *<flag>*, is not currently used, but reserved for future requirements.

Table 9.4 summarizes the contents of the `/etc/shadow` file.

Contents of `/etc/shadow` **file**	
Field	Contents
<id>	user ID
<passwd>	encrypted password
<lastchange>	number of days between 1.1.1970 and the date when the password was last changed
<minimum>	minimum number of days between password changes
<maximum>	maximum number of days between password changes
<warn>	number of days for which warning displayed before password loses validity
<inactive>	number of permitted inactive days
<expire>	date after which log-in no longer permitted
<flag>	reserved for future use

Table 9.4

9.3.3 Adding and removing users in BSD and OSF

When a new user is to be added to the system, the following must be done:

1. Create a new entry in the /etc/passwd file.
2. Create home directory for user.
3. Create start-up files in user's home directory.

The /etc/passwd file is updated using the program vipw, a variant of vi which locks the file being edited. A new line is added, holding the new user ID, group status, home directory etc.

Let us look at an example. Suppose that a new user linda is to be added to the system. The first thing to be done is to check that the user ID is not already in use on the system. This can be done by searching through the /etc/passwd file using a text editor or the program grep:

```
# grep linda /etc/passwd
```

It is then a matter of finding a unique user number, e.g. 114. We then elect to assign linda to group number 16. (The groupname is defined in the /etc/group file.) We then set linda's home directory to /home/linda. Finally, Linda has indicated that she wishes to use the Korn shell (i.e. /usr/bin/ksh). The new line in /etc/passwd will therefore be:

```
linda::114:16::/home/linda:/usr/bin/ksh
```

Note that the <*passwd*> field is empty. If anything had been entered it would effectively have made it impossible for linda to log in. The password should be set as quickly as possible to prevent any unauthorized person getting into the system:

```
# passwd linda
New password: password
Re-enter new password: password
#
```

The next job is to create the home directory /home/linda:

```
# mkdir /home/linda
```

After this, the owner and group for the directory must be changed to linda and 16 respectively. This is done by means of chown and chgrp:

```
# chown linda /home/linda
# chgrp 16 /home/linda
#
```

The final step in the installation procedure is to create start-up files in the user's home directory. The system administrator will copy, as appropriate, an already working .profile file for the Bourne shell and the Korn shell or the .login, .cshrc and .logout files for the C and TC shells. Note that these files must also be given linda as owner and 16 as the group:

```
# cp <existing .profile> /home/linda/.profile
# chown linda /home/linda/.profile
# chgrp 16 /home/linda.profile
```

When the system administrator working under BSD or OSF needs to remove a user from the system, the following tasks need to be carried out:

1. Remove entry in /etc/passwd file.

2. Remove user's home directory.

9.3.4 Adding and removing users in System V

SV In System V it is considerably more difficult than in BSD and OSF to edit for yourself the central files defining the users, that is, /etc/passwd and /etc/shadow. The installation of a new user is therefore generally done using a utility program. Most UNIX suppliers can provide a menu-driven program of this type.

The standard program useradd can be used in System V to create a new user. Suppose that the user linda is to be added to the system. This is done by means of the command

```
# useradd -m linda
```

where the option -m indicates that a home directory is to be created automatically. After this, the new user must be allocated a password using the passwd program:

```
# passwd linda
New password: password
Re-enter new password: password
#
```

Table 9.5 summarizes the arguments to the useradd program, which is used to control details of the new user's 'user attributes':

Options for useradd	
-g *group*	defines group allocation by means of an integer or a text string (taken from the /etc/group file)
-d *directory*	defines the pathname of the user's home directory
-s *shell*	defines the pathname of the desired shell
-c *comments*	defines the comments in the comment field of the /etc/passwd file
-m	creates home directory
-e *date*	defines the date after which log-in no longer possible, e.g. 1/1/95
-f *number*	defines the maximum number of permitted inactive days.

Table 9.5

The following command

useradd -m -g guest -d /home/john -s /usr/bin/ksh john

creates a new user `john` with a home directory `/home/john` and assigns him to the group `guest`. The new user will be using the `/usr/bin/ksh` shell when he logs in on the system.

A user can be removed from System V using the `userdel` program.

userdel -r john

where the option `-r` means that the user's entire home directory will also be removed, that is, all plain files and sub-directories.

In Solaris, the window-oriented program `admintool` can be used to add and remove users. The program is started in the usual way, either from a terminal window or from a purpose-designed menu. When `admintool` is run, the user is given a window and invited to select either `Database Manager` or `Host Manager`. The system administrator should mark the line `Database Manager` and click on the Open button. A new window will then appear with a list of different databases. In this new window, mark the line `Passwd Database` and click on the Open button. The window used for adding and removing users will then open, as shown in figure 9.1. In the list of users, mark the user you wish to amend. A user can be removed from the system by means of the Delete button. The Modify... button is used to amend the details for an existing user. If, instead, the Add... button is selected, the system administrator is provided with a 'form' to be completed with the information described earlier in this section.

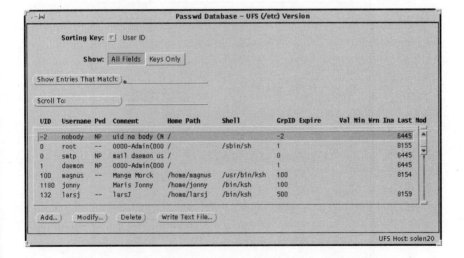

Figure 9.1

9.4 Creating a user group

It is often useful to divide users among *user groups*. The advantage of this is that members of a group can create files with access permissions preventing other users from reading, writing to or executing the group's files. The /etc/group file is constructed on the same principles as the /etc/passwd file. Each line defines a group and consists of four fields:

<groupname> : *<passwd>* : *<gid>* : *<user_list>*

The *<groupname>* field is the symbolic name of the group (must be unique). The *<passwd>* field may contain an encrypted group password. The *<gid>* field is a unique group number (derived from /etc/passwd). The last field is a list of users belonging to other groups but who may still have facilities to operate on the group's files. The content of the /etc/group file is summarized in table 9.6.

Contents of /etc/group file	
File	Contents
<groupname>	symbolic name of group
<passwd>	encrypted group password
<gid>	group number, derived from /etc/passwd
<user_list>	users belonging to other groups but still allowed to use the group's files

Table 9.6

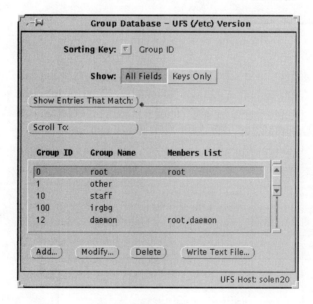

Figure 9.2

In Solaris, the `admintool` program can also be used to create user groups. `admintool` is started up as usual, and the `Database Manager` option is selected from the first pop-up window. In the new pop-up window, the `Group Database` is selected from the list of various databases. This will result in the window shown in figure 9.2, which is used to add or remove user groups in the system. After marking the group to be dealt with, the system administrator can remove the group in question using the [Delete] button or make any necessary changes using the [Modify...] button. If the [Add...] button is selected instead, a 'form' will appear, which must be completed with information on the new group.

9.5 Copying using `tar`

Using the program `tar` (tape archive), entire directories or single files can be copied to and from an 'archive file'. The archive file is normally kept on magnetic tape, but can also be another file. The `tar` program is used among other things for making backups (security copies). `tar` is also used to distribute data and software from various program suppliers. A call to `tar` takes the form

§ **tar** *code file ...*

First we enter a number of codes describing what `tar` is meant to do. After this we list the directories or single files to be copied to and from the archive file. If nothing particular is specified it is assumed that the archive file will be one of the system's tape drives. The meaning of the codes is given in table 9.7.

Codes for `tar`	
c	create a new archive file and copy listed files to it
x	reload listed files from archive file
v	(verbose) program will display what is being done
f *filename*	use *filename* as archive file in place of default file
t	write out table of archive file contents

Table 9.7

We will now describe a number of typical ways of using the `tar` program.

9.5.1 Copying the entire file system

The following command creates an archive file containing all the files in the system. The archive file will be stored on magnetic tape.

§ **tar cv /**

Alternatively, we can enter

```
$ cd /
$ tar cv .
```

The code c denotes that a new archive file is to be created and that the directory specified (i.e. /) is to be copied to it. The code v indicates that the program will list the files copied.

If we wish instead to store the archive file on some unit other than the system's default unit we can use the f code followed by the unit's name. For example, if we want to copy to the unit /dev/tape we would key

```
$ tar cvf /dev/tape /
```

9.5.2 Copying specific files

If only certain specific files are to be copied, this will be given in the argument to tar. Filename patterns can be used, but they must then be enclosed, for example, in single quotes so that the shell does not expand them.

```
$ tar cv /home/linda '/home/john/*.c'
```

This command copies to the archive file the directory /home/linda and all files ending in .c in the directory /home/john.

9.5.3 Reloading the entire tape

Including the code x results in all the files being reloaded from the archive file:

```
$ tar xv
```

9.5.4 Loading back particular files from the tape

If only some specific files are to be reloaded from the archive file, these can be specified in the argument. Filename patterns can be used, but here too they must be enclosed in single quotes:

```
$ tar xv /home/linda '/home/john/*.c'
```

This command command reads back into the system the directory /home/linda and all files ending in .c in the directory /home/john.

9.5.5 Absolute or relative filenames

The file or files to be copied using tar can be given after the codes for the program, as we have seen. Files can be specified in two different ways, *absolute* or *relative*:

```
$ tar cv /home/linda/spool
a /home/linda/spool 1 blocks
$
```

or

```
$ cd /home/linda
$ tar cv spool
a spool 1 blocka
$
```

The difference between these two different options may appear insignificant but is very important. Both commands copy the specified files to the archive file. In addition, both save the specified filenames in the archive file. This means that the first command saves the filename /home/linda/spool and the second the filename spool.

Files whose filenames are stored in the form of pathnames wll always be reloaded back in their original position:

```
$ tar xv
x /home/linda/spool, 143 bytes, 1 tape blocks
$
```

whilst files whose filenames are stored as simple filenames will always be loaded into the file system relative to the current directory. If, for example, we want to read the file with the filename spool back into the directory /home/linda, we must make sure we are there first:

```
$ cd /home/linda
$ tar xv
x spool, 143 bytes, 1 tape blocks
$
```

The advantage of relatively referenced files is that they can be reloaded into any directory, whilst abolutely referenced files will always load back to the same position.

9.5.6 Listing the content of a tape

Using the code t gives a list of the contents of a tape, that is, the filenames held on it. This key is useful when you are unsure whether the names of files are stored relatively or absolutely. The command is:

```
$ tar t
```

Note that no copying of the files themselves results from this command.

9.6 Copying using cpio

By means of the program cpio (copy in and out) files can be copied into the file system from tape, out from the file system to tape and from one directory to another.

```
cpio -o[Bv]              copy out
cpio -i[Bvdmtu]          copy in
cpio -p[vdmu]            copy in and out
```

The effect of the options is shown in table 9.8.

Options for `cpio`	
o	copy out
i	copy in
p	copy in and out
B	input and output by blocks (5120 bytes)
v	(verbose) program displays what is being done
d	create/retain hierarchical directory structure
m	retain modification date (otherwise copies will be given current date)
t	write table of contents of backup medium
u	unconditional copy (normally files older than existing files are not copied)

Table 9.8

9.6.1 Copying out

To copy out to tape, we give the `cpio` program the option o. The program will then produce, on the standard output, a file which contains the copied files in archive format. `cpio` reads the standard input expecting to find there the names of the files to be copied. Every filename must have its own line on the standard input. This means that when copying out we do *not* enter the filenames as arguments to `cpio`. We can of course create a file containing filenames in advance using a text editor, but often the programs find or ls can be used to generate lists of filenames, as in the following example:

$ **find . -print | cpio -o > /dev/tape**
$ **ls | cpio -o > /dev/tape**

If we want to copy the entire file system, therefore, we can key in the following:

$ **find / -print | cpio -ov > /dev/tape**

The option v means that the program will list the files as they are copied.

In the next example we show how to copy all the files which have been changed during the last seven days. (This is specified with the argument -mtime -7 given to find.)

$ **find / -mtime -7 -print | cpio -ov > /dev/tape**

There are a number of arguments for find which can be useful. The following command, for example, copies all the files owned by the user linda:

> $ **find** / **-user linda -print** | cpio **-ov** > /dev/tape

And here is how to copy all linda's files which have been changed during the last seven days:

> $ **find** / **-mtime -7 -user linda -print** | cpio **-ov** > /dev/tape

9.6.2 Copying in

To copy in, the cpio program expects the previously stored archive file to be specified as standard input. If all the files on a tape are to be read into the file system, for example, the following command would be used:

> $ **cpio -ivdm < /dev/tape**

Note that it is necessary to include the option d for the directory structure to be re-loaded.

When we do not want to copy in all the files from the archive file, we can give as the argument to cpio a list of the files to be copied in. Filename patterns may be used, but they must be enclosed in single quotes. To read back the file /home/linda plus all the files of C programs in the directory /home/john, for example, we can key the command:

> $ **cpio -ivdm /home/linda ' /home/john/*.c' < /dev/tape**

9.6.3 Listing the contents of a tape

Using the option t will produce a list of names of the files stored on the tape:

> $ **cpio -it < /dev/tape**

This command does not copy the files themselves.

9.6.4 Internal copying

By means of the option p, we can copy from one sub-directory to another:

> $ **find** . **-print** |cpio **-pd** ../spool

This command produces a list of filenames in the current directory. The list is sent as input data to cpio, which stores copies in the directory ../spool.

9.7 Summary

Programs for the system administrator	
su root	replace current user by root
shutdown	halt system
chown *<name> <filename>*	set up *name* as user of *filename*
chgrp *<group> <filename>*	set group for *filename* as *group*
useradd	System V. Add a new user
userdel	System V. Delete a user
sysadm	System V. Menu-driven utility
admintool	Window-oriented utility under X in Sun's Solaris
smit	Menu-driven utility in IBM's AIX
sam	Menu-driven utility in HP's HP/UX

Table 9.9

Copying	
tar c /	Copy entire file system
tar c /home/linda '/home/john/*.c'	Copy specified files
tar x	Reload entire tape
tar x /home/linda '/home/john/*.c'	Load specified files from tape
tar t	Show list of tape contents
find / -print | cpio -o > /dev/tape	Copy entire file system
find / -mtime -7 -print | cpio -o > /dev/tape	Copy specified files
cpio -idm < /dev/tape	Reload entire tape
cpio -idv /home/linda '/home/john/*.c' < /dev/tape	Load specified files from tape
cpio -it < /dev/tape	Show list of tape contents

Table 9.10

Index